PRAISE FOR

GREEN SWANS

"John Elkington has once again proven his status as one of the great thinkers of our time."

—**Paul Polman,** from his foreword

"Once again, John has found the right words at the right time to help us make sense of what's going on. The insight, analysis, and reflection in *Green Swans* is golden. So much of the storytelling and synthesizing resonates with my own experience imagining the enterprises that I want to exist to deliver vital public goods, and then building them with the help of others. Pioneers can see patterns early and have the courage, or naïveté, to just try to add to the design. They can be too early. They can find arrows in their back, too. On surviving and, if lucky enough to succeed, they know the impossible happens and that purpose helps. To those that thought renewables would always be small and expensive, for example, watch that beautiful Green Swan move! It's time to make friends with the exponential."

—**James Cameron,** Chairman of the Overseas Development Institute, Founder of Climate Change Capital, and a former member of the UK Prime Minister's Business Advisory Board

"The best leaders are willing to give up what is no longer working and commit to what is needed to succeed in a new, completely changed operating environment. When John Elkington issued a 'product recall' for his groundbreaking concept of the 'triple bottom line,' it was because he is that type of leader. If you want to be a leader that meets the demands of the 21st century, read *Green Swans*, and then become one."

—**Jay Coen Gilbert,** Co-Founder of B Lab, the organization behind the B Corporation movement

"John Elkington is one of the true pioneers in the sustainability movement and has made a real contribution to the way business thinks about its role in the world. With this new book, John uses his exceptional creativity and insight to give us further food for thought on the challenges we face, and alternative and original ways of thinking about them."

—**Dame Polly Courtice,** Director of the University of Cambridge Institute for Sustainability Leadership (CISL). Also Founder Director of The Prince of Wales's Business and Sustainability Programme, and Academic Director of the University's Master of Studies in Sustainability Leadership

"*Green Swans* is a brilliant, challenging, and enchanting book. Its brilliance lies in the way John has synthesized and built on the thinking of so many others to put forward yet one more 'Big Idea'—which he has done many times before. It challenges executives and investors to think and act at the system level. It is enchanting in the way John weaves autobiography into a compelling narrative to make all of us 'qualified optimists.' It is also brave. John puts his e-mail address in this book and invites all readers to engage in a conversation with him. I hope you do. It is always worth talking to John."

—**Professor Robert G. Eccles,** Visiting Professor of Management Practice, Saïd Business School University of Oxford, Founding Chairman of the Sustainability Accounting Standards Board (SASB) and one of the founders of the International Integrated Reporting Council (IIRC)

"Sustainable business legend John Elkington rightly declares that we have painted ourselves into 'the mother of all corners.' In *Green Swans*, his most important book yet, one can feel John's clever mind and earnest soul wrestling with the ultimate Rubik's Cube puzzle of all human history: How to transform capitalism to an economic system that is actually regenerative, like all other living systems on this planet. An essential guide for business leaders and a profound yet realistic dose of hope for the challenging 'Exponential Twenties' that lie ahead."

—**John Fullerton,** Founder of Capital Institute, author of *Regenerative Capitalism: How Universal Principles and Patterns Will Shape the New Economy*, and former Managing Director of JPMorgan

"*Green Swans* is a delightful, disturbing, and hopeful read. As we enter what John refers to as the 'Exponential Decade' of the 2020s, the stakes couldn't be higher for humanity and planet earth. During these turbulent and promising times, I for one am extremely grateful for the steady guidance, wisdom, brutal honesty, and insights John shares here. Drawing on his decades of thought leadership on the role of business in creating a better world, John at once validates the vital role that business will have in innovating and scaling new solutions, but also gives a clarion call—indeed an imperative challenge—to shift from stakeholder value to system value. *Green Swans* offers a blueprint for the future-fit businesses of tomorrow."

—**Nicholas Haan,** Faculty Chair, Global Grand Challenges, Singularity University

"Capitalism is entering a new phase, as companies and investors acknowledge the need to address the interests of a fuller range of stakeholders. John Elkington, one of the pioneers of the sustainability movement, is a great guide to the changes under way. His critique is clear-eyed, but his underlying optimism about Green Swan solutions is inspiring."

—**Adi Ignatius,** Editor-in-Chief, *Harvard Business Review*

"Welcome to the new renaissance. John Elkington does not fall into the trap of painting a dystopian nightmare scenario that leaves us without hope. Instead, *Green Swans* makes us believe in miracles. Not metaphysical miracles, but those that seem impossible today because we look at their feasibility from a business-as-usual perspective, defined by the status quo. Like John, I am realistically optimistic. Like him, too, I also say 'neutrality be damned.' I hope this brilliant book kickstarts new and honest conversations in boardrooms around the world. Conversations about what side of history we are on, and what steps we will now take to become 'future fit leaders'. Read on to get a sense of where breakthrough mindsets and innovation will take us as we work to deliver the Global Goals. It always seems impossible until it's done."

—**Lise Kingo,** CEO & Executive Director, United Nations Global Compact, the world's biggest sustainable business platform

"Our economy urgently needs re-orienting in a green direction, with governments, businesses and civil society taking on—together—ambitious green missions. John Elkington's *Green Swans*, paradigm-shifting innovation breakthroughs, point the way to this brighter future."

—**Mariana Mazzucato,** Professor in Economics of Innovation and Public Value at University College London and Founder/Director of the UCL Institute for Innovation and Public Purpose. Author of *The Entrepreneurial State* and *The Value of Everything*

"Japan is one of the most unsustainable advanced nations, with demographic, economic, and environmental challenges. John Elkington explains that all such countries now need to create new generations of Green Swan solutions, driving transformation and regeneration. This book is a perfect guide for a Japan that rose from the ashes and must now learn how to play a significant role in the regeneration of our planet."

—**Hiro Motoki,** President, E-Square, Japan

"When I produced my book *2052: A Global Forecast for the Next Forty Years* as a report to the Club of Rome in 2012, I invited John to contribute an essay on the future role of the military in sustainability. Typically, he is more optimistic than I, although in this new book he balances that out with a clear-eyed view of the 'Black Swan' challenges we face in the coming decades. But then his 'Green Swans' fly in and we are back on track for rapid progress! I hope he is right, in spite of the fact that my mood in 2052 was more somber—and still is."

—**Professor Jørgen Randers,** Professor Emeritus of Climate Strategy at the BI Norwegian Business School, and science-based activist since co-authoring *The Limits to Growth* in 1972

"In *Green Swans*, John Elkington gifts us his wisdom, vision and experience to guide us through the business, social and environmental transformations we need en route to a regenerative future. An urgently necessary book."

—**Cathy Runciman,** Co-Founder, Atlas of the Future, and former Managing Director of Time Out International

"All his life, John has been a pioneer in the environment movement and in his acute understanding of how capitalism has a central part to play in it. His insights have always been ahead of the curve and phrases of his coinage are the currency of our age—the 'triple bottom line' being just one of them. This book captures the passion of a man at the peak of his powers, drawing together a lifetime of observations into a manifesto for muscular humanism and capitalism with conscience. What shines through it all is a belief that now the time is at hand for proving that the future remains ours to make. No hollow intellectualism, just unfettered urging that we should bring out the best in ourselves . . . now. A hugely important book."

—**Sir Tim Smit,** Founder and Executive Vice Chair of The Eden Project and Co-Founder of the Lost Gardens of Heligan

"We need John Elkington's optimism, and his insight, more than ever, and here he sets out a bracing and inspiring vision of the path we must take if we are to transform ourselves and secure the future for our planet. *Green Swans* is a welcome and well-researched manifesto and should be compulsory reading in every boardroom."

—**Tanya Steele,** CEO, WWF UK

GREEN SWANS

THE COMING BOOM IN
REGENERATIVE CAPITALISM

GREEN
SWANS

JOHN ELKINGTON

**FAST
COMPANY**
Press

Fast Company Press
New York, New York
www.fastcompanypress.com

This work is being published under the Fast Company Press imprint by an exclusive arrangement with Fast Company. Fast Company and the Fast Company logo are registered trademarks of Mansueto Ventures, LLC. The Fast Company Press logo is a wholly owned trademark of Mansueto Ventures, LLC.

Distributed by Greenleaf Book Group

For ordering information or special discounts for bulk purchases, please contact Greenleaf Book Group at PO Box 91869, Austin, TX 78709, 512.891.6100.

Design and composition by Greenleaf Book Group
Cover design by Greenleaf Book Group

For permission to reproduce copyrighted material, grateful acknowledgment is made to the following:
For excerpt from "The Best-Performing CEOs in the World" by Harvard Business Review staff from Harvard Business Review. November 2015 issue. Copyright © 2015. Reproduced by permission of Harvard Business Review.
From "Novo Nordisk CEO Lars Sorensen on What Propelled Him to the Top" by Adi Ignatius and Daniel McGinn from Harvard Business Review. November 2015 issue. Copyright © 2015. Reproduced by permission of Harvard Business Review.
From "The History of Antibiotics" from the Microbiology Society website. Accessed October 2, 2019 at https://microbiologysociety.org/members-outreach-resources/outreach-resources/antibiotics-unearthed/antibiotics-and-antibiotic-resistance/the-history-of-antibiotics.html. Copyright © 2019. Reproduced by permission of the Microbiology Society. All rights reserved.

Publisher's Cataloging-in-Publication data is available.

Print ISBN: 978-1-7324391-2-2

eBook ISBN: 978-1-7324391-3-9

Part of the Tree Neutral® program, which offsets the number of trees consumed in the production and printing of this book by taking proactive steps, such as planting trees in direct proportion to the number of trees used: www.treeneutral.com

TreeNeutral®

Printed in the United States of America on acid-free paper

19 20 21 22 23 24   10 9 8 7 6 5 4 3 2 1

First Edition

Dedicated to my father, Tim Elkington (1920–2019),
A pilot who helped me love flight and things with wings.

To my mother, Pat Elkington (née Adamson, 1922–2019),
Who encouraged my love for wildlife, women, and words.

And to their great-grandson, our grandson, Gene Lushington,
Born in 2018, into this world of Black Swans and Green.

Contents

UPENDING CAPITALISM

Genesis of the Green Swan

The Green Swan is a symbol of radically better times to come. It's also a template for exponential change toward the distant goal of a sustainable future for all. Getting from here to there will be no trivial task, however. Times of disruptive change upend market and political pecking orders, creating political shock waves that can last for decades—even generations.

As a decade, meanwhile, the 2020s do not yet seem to have sticky branding like the "Noughties" or the "Teens," but they will, and that branding will likely reflect a period of exponential change. The Exponential Twenties? To paraphrase Dickens, this will be the worst of times for those clinging to the old order, yet potentially the best of times for those embracing and driving the new. Buckle your safety belt.

This book, my twentieth, has had an unusually long genesis. It has morphed and mutated considerably along the way. You can expect an often personal account of a learning journey that has taken me around the world and, at times, deep into the future. It's an investigation, an exploration, not a definitive, unified field theory. It is intended as the beginning of a conversation, not the end.

Like the fictional Forrest Gump, played by Tom Hanks in a film of the same name featuring a slow-witted man who was witness to—and sometimes unwittingly had a hand in—major cultural events, I have been involved in many initiatives that have shaped the change agenda. In citing some of those experiences, I aim not to out-Gump Gump but to demonstrate that my conclusions and recommendations are based on real-world interactions, not just desk research.

I have also been profoundly influenced by what I have read. Most obviously here, I have been inspired by the work of Lebanese-American author, risk analyst, and former options trader Nassim Nicholas Taleb. In his 2007 book, *The Black Swan*, Taleb provides a series of timely lessons about the "impact of the highly improbable," as his subtitle put it.[1] His timing was impeccable, as the global economy descended that same year into a financial meltdown few had seen coming.

Early on in his book, Taleb noted that he was sticking his neck out, in claiming that "against many of our habits of thought [. . .] our world is dominated by the extreme, the unknown, and the very improbable (improbable according to our current knowledge)—and all the while we spend our time engaged in small talk, focusing on the known, and the repeated."[2] Nowhere is that more true than with the "wicked" and "super wicked" challenges we will explore later.

Rather than sticking tightly to Taleb's definitions and methodology, though, what follows riffs off his metaphor of the "Black Swan," referring to unpredicted—and generally unpredictable—events driven largely by negative exponentials, in whose wake nothing is the same. Just as the world's most populous nation vaunts "socialism with Chinese characteristics," we will explore aspects of capitalism, democracy, and sustainability with either Black or Green Swan characteristics—and sometimes a combination of both. Some working notes on how to identify Black and Green Swans can be found in the Annex (page 254). People also now talk of "Gray Swans," which are predictable and may have been predicted, but which when ignored for too long erupt in ways that can rock the world on its heels.[3] One of the most obvious is the trend of aging in modern societies. There are many benefits from our living longer lives, but it has been estimated that by 2020 the number of people over sixty-five in the world would outnumber, for the first time in history, children aged five and under. Again, there are many things to be said in favor of experience, but as Camilla Cavendish put it in her book *Extra Time*, an aging world will bring many systemic challenges that we have only just begun to think through.[4]

This growing color spectrum of Swans is where the riffing comes in. To the reasonably well-defined categories of Black and Gray Swans, I want to add two other emergent concepts: "Green Swans," which are systemic solutions to global challenges, solutions that tap into positive exponentials, and "Ugly Ducklings," defined as embryonic innovations and trajectories that can take us in various directions— good, bad, or ugly.

As this book went to press, I soft launched the Green Swan agenda at a major business summit in Copenhagen, hosted by Dansk Industri (Confederation of Danish Industry)—attended by the country's new prime minister, Mette Frederiksen; various committed royals from Denmark and Sweden; and 1,300 CEOs and business leaders. I noted that this was highly appropriate, given that one of Denmark's most famous sons had been Hans Christian Andersen, author of "The Ugly Duckling." But what truly blew me away that day was the way that the Danish government, the country's leading industry federation, and the wider business community are now working together to drive a wildly ambitious green transformation.

A Green Swan economy in the making? Certainly, their timing looks exquisite. For one thing I learned while working in Japan over the years is that successful businesses and economies invest into a downturn, aiming to emerge on the other side ahead of their competitors. My assumption in researching this book has been that the world is headed into some sort of historic U-bend, well beyond a single, normal recession, where the established macroeconomic and political order goes down the tubes, and new ones surface. As we head deeper into the bottom of the U-bend, we enter a period of maximum confusion and uncertainty. Historically, too, this is often the point at which major wars occur.

In the process, established ideologies and mind-sets are coming under intense pressure—among them capitalism, democracy, and sustainability (a concept I helped launch decades back). What follows is an investigation into the complex interplay of all three ideologies. In retrospect, I have been on a learning journey that has taken decades to date and, in some ways, feels as if it is only just beginning.

All three concepts—capitalism, democracy, and sustainability— represent fiercely contested territory. *Don't talk about capitalism*, I was advised. *It triggers visceral, uncontrollable reactions.* True, though such reactions can take people in very different directions. Talk to some climate activists and you are told that capitalism can do nothing but harm. But talk to some Americans, even those abused by that country's most exploitative forms of capitalism, and many will tolerate no criticism of "their" system—even when it does them little discernable good.

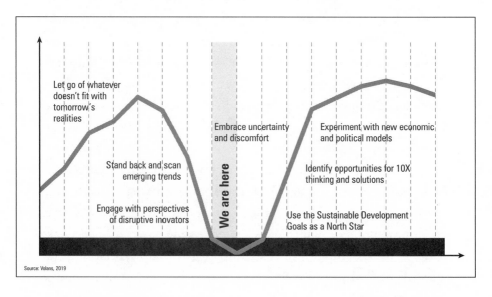

Figure 1: Into the U-bend

Such positions, quasi-religious in their reliance on faith over evidence, serve as a red-flag warning that we are stepping into a giant minefield. Still, the ways in which capitalism, democracy, and sustainability interact, for good or ill, is our subject here. The timing is particularly interesting, given that even some leading capitalists are now increasingly critical of today's capitalist system, while many democratic leaders are warning that democracies are at greater risk than at any time since the 1930s.

Capitalism is partly in the spotlight because it has embedded pernicious forms of myopia in our economies, which now threaten to crash the global biosphere. These problems were massively accentuated by neoliberalism. Yet our default setting, neoliberal or not, is to deny the very possibility of collapse, as professor Jem Bendell argues.[5] Denial, however, cannot mask the pace at which we are destabilizing the climate, unraveling the web of life, acidifying the oceans, and creating teeth-rattling wealth divides. Indeed, the evidence suggests that the next decade, the 2020s, will see flocks of those proverbial chickens coming home to roost—with the prevailing scientific and economic paradigms shifting at unprecedented speed.

American-style capitalism has opened up immense wealth divides that are spurring intense concern and criticism. As a result, newspapers like the *Financial Times* have been running full-page articles with titles like "Capitalism Keeps CEOs Awake at Night."[6] Ray Dalio, an American investor worth almost $17 billion by Bloomberg's estimates, who has embraced capitalism since he was a precocious twelve-year-old, took to warning his followers on social media: "I'm a capitalist, and even I think capitalism is broken."[7] Capitalism is in crisis, concluded the economist Irwin Stelzer in *The Sunday Times*, under a headline reading, "Save Capitalism from Capitalists."[8]

I am pessimistic in the short term, and there will be times when it shows, but I am a qualified long-term optimist. Our species may have backed itself into the mother of all evolutionary corners, but sometimes such moments are when our best work is done. The qualification of my optimism stems from the fact that we have to choose to evolve not only ourselves but also capitalism and democracy, none of them trivial tasks.

So what do I mean when I talk about capitalism? *Don't quote Wikipedia*, authors are told, but what a wonderful resource it can be, thanks to its anti-capitalist business model. Yes, it's true that I once discovered via my Wikipedia page that I had a Danish wife I knew nothing about—but more often than not I find it genuinely distills the wisdom of the crowd.

Ask Wikipedia to define capitalism and it mentions private property, capital accumulation, wage labor, voluntary exchange, a price system, and competitive markets.[9] A useful starting point, though most of us would add other things to the list. However long your list may end up being, pretty much everything on it must now evolve at warp speed if capitalism is to survive the twenty-first century and deliver on well-intentioned slogans pledging "a better world for all."

As a long-time student of economic cycles, I sense that the likeliest outcome is a future in which key elements of capitalism crash and burn, and some then rise again from the ashes—something that has happened many times before. A future of dark and bright phoenixes, you might say, rising from the smoking debris of our economies, societies, and, most tragically for the deep future, our natural environment.

Establishing this point does not make an individual either pro- or anti-capitalist, but rather an observer of what it is that capitalism actually does, how it behaves, and how it impacts the wider world. Like nature, capitalism goes through energetic cycles, what popular economists would call "booms" and "busts." In our economies, these are periods of intense excitement shading into "irrational exuberance," driven by new forms of innovation that ride up and down the hype cycle, with a rising backbeat of investment and growth. Typically booms are followed by various forms of bust, profound unravelings, triggering adaptation, and, if things go well, recovery.

Talk about capitalism, then, and you're talking about a high-octane and extremely volatile form of wealth creation and destruction. Over the decades, I have explored capitalism and its alternatives, using a wide range of lenses and metaphors, such as green capitalism, the triple bottom line, the chrysalis economy, and breakdown and breakthrough. As I look back, the aim throughout was to compare and contrast two different trajectories in our world: Black Swan dynamics that (in malign cases) led to chaos and even extinction, and the Green Swan dynamics that potentially lead, via evolution and adaptation, to a better place.

As F. Scott Fitzgerald concluded, "The test of a first-rate intelligence is the ability to hold two opposed ideas in mind at the same time and still retain the ability to function." I make no claims for my intelligence, or for my brain's ability to function under stress, but this book is evidence of a lifelong and ongoing struggle to make sense of two radically opposed ideas.

The first idea is this: We are headed into a hellish world of systemic breakdowns. Key elements of our climate, our biosphere, our economies, and our societies will come apart at an accelerating rate. Start-up entrepreneurs talk of their "burn rate," the speed at which they spend other people's money. Viewed as a start-up, the subspecies of post-industrialization *Homo sapiens* that some call *Homo economicus*[10] and others *Homo industrialis* has burned through the planet's resources at a dizzying rate—and is now entering a very different reality, what some call the "Age of Consequences,"[11] others "The Anthropocene."

This future, where a single species has a global impact akin to geological forces, is a world first. As the process continues, the world will be plagued by malign flocks of Nassim Nicholas Taleb's Black Swans, understood here to be challenges that get exponentially worse in ways that most of us struggle to understand, let alone tackle and solve.[12]

Black Swans are dramatic events that are outliers—beyond the realm of normal expectations—have a major impact, and yet are often "inappropriately rationalized after the fact with the benefit of hindsight."[13] In simple terms, that means we fail to learn from our mistakes, unwittingly heading into the jaws of the next round of disasters.

Think of the plight of oil-rich Venezuela, once described as the

Switzerland of South America. As I wrote these words, the country's central bank published statistics showing that the economy had shrunk by half since President Maduro took office. Venezuela's construction sector had shrunk by 95%, manufacturing by 75%, oil production was lower than at any time since the 1940s, and the official inflation rate was reported to be an inconceivable 130,060%.[14]

Was Venezuela's meltdown a true Black Swan event, though? With standard economics predicting such outcomes if economies are mismanaged to such a degree, some might question whether this was truly unforeseeable. They would probably use the same arguments with the 9/11 attacks and the collapse of the World Trade Center towers.[15] In the same way, they might say, the Chernobyl nuclear disaster was not a true Black Swan, because the safety systems were shut down for technical reasons, with results that should have been foreseen.

In what follows, we will take a slightly looser approach, with the Black Swan labeling signaling that an event came as an existential shock to many people, if not all of them. Hyperinflation in Germany after the First World War, for example, set the scene for the rise of Nazism—so you could argue it was part of a Black Swan unforeseen by those imposing punitive reparations on a defeated enemy. Reparations of this sort were standard practice at the time, energetically practiced by the Germans too,[16] but the longer-term consequences were surely beyond the imaginations of most of those putting pen to paper in 1919.[17]

Similarly, some would say that climate change is now merely a Gray Swan, given that we have been talking about the risks for many decades. On the other hand, the levels of climate-induced societal collapse that are likely to follow our crossing of the two degrees of warming threshold will likely be Black Swans. Our surprisingly fragile economies, societies, and natural environment could well unravel at hitherto unimaginable speeds.

The second, radically opposed idea tussling in my brain is that at least some parts of the world are now heading toward some sort of breakthrough future, and that more could soon follow in their wake. This world is one of extraordinary creativity, innovation, and enterprise. The environmental and natural resource burn rate of many key players here is shrinking, often at an accelerating pace. This could be a radically different future, and one increasingly characterized by Green Swans.

Recent discussion of the financial impact of climate chaos as a "Green Swan" is to mislabel a Black Swan.[18] Instead, here is what I mean when I say "Green Swans":

> A **Green Swan** is a profound market shift, generally catalyzed by some combination of Black or Gray Swan challenges and changing paradigms, values, mind-sets, politics, policies, technologies, business models, and other key factors. A Green Swan delivers exponential progress in the form of economic, social, and environmental wealth creation. At worst, it achieves this outcome in two dimensions while holding the third steady.[19] There may be a period of adjustment where one or more dimensions underperform, but the aim is an integrated breakthrough in all three dimensions.

Green Swans are extraordinary—in the sense of out-of-the-ordinary forms of progress—driven and shaped by positive exponentials. In a counterintuitive pairing, they often rise phoenixlike out of the ashes left by Black Swans. Think of the way the natural world can recover and flourish after a volcano erupts or after destructive fishing pressure is removed. However, generally Green Swans are less likely to take us by surprise, as we typically have to plan for and work toward them over a considerable period of time.

It will come as no surprise to hear that there are many different perspectives both on how we should rein in Black Swan problems and how we co-evolve Green Swan solutions. While developing this book, to capture and explore some of those perspectives, I worked with Atlas of the Future to create a twenty-minute video called *Green Swans: Sketching a Manifesto for Tomorrow's Capitalism*.[20]

The consensus was surprisingly upbeat. Indeed, those of us who grew up in a world where incremental change was the best we could hope for now risk being wrong-footed by a future where the potential for exponential solutions to exponential problems undergoes explosive growth. Be very clear, though: These Black and Green trajectories are not either-or scenarios. They are parallel realities, already emergent and slugging it out all around us. Some Black Swans will sport green feathers, and vice versa.

Much as we may want people to be nicer to one another, the struggle between Black and Green sectors of the economy has been, is, and will always be brutal. It is a Darwinian struggle for existence. People rarely surrender what they see as their birthright and future without a fight, even if their efforts threaten to crash the future for other people or other species. That said, we often misunderstand nature, assuming it only uses competition to spur evolution, whereas the truth is that the natural world is largely concerned with collaboration—symbioses. The following pages spotlight many examples of symbioses linking our economies, societies, and natural environment. They sit at the very heart of almost all Green Swans solutions.

Meanwhile, various forces are turning up the heat under the global pressure cooker. Some people conclude that the vessel can now only explode. Climate-induced societal collapse is inevitable, they argue, preprogrammed into our global system, and will accelerate in unimaginable ways.[21] They conclude that the science now shows that climate-induced societal collapse is imminent—and that at times it will impact rich nations as brutally as it does poorer nations.

A few years ago such warnings would have been dismissed as ill-informed scaremongering, fit only for science fiction dystopias. No longer. In recent years climate-induced societal collapse has moved sharply from the realms of sci-fi to everyday reality. Think of New Orleans, drowned by Hurricane Katrina. Or, for various reasons including climate change, of Indonesia's plan to abandon its sinking capital city, Jakarta.[22] The inconvenient truth is that we are moving into a world of what some call "wicked" and even "super wicked" problems.

Finally, to stretch our brains still further, there is a fourth key term alongside Black, Gray, and Green Swans that needs explanation before we dive in: "Ugly Ducklings." In the fairy tale of the same name, the Ugly Duckling is a baby swan dismissed by its community for looking so unlike any of the other birds around—all of them ducks. Similarly, the future often looks totally alien when we first spot it. Here is what I mean by the term:

> An **Ugly Duckling** is an early-stage concept, mind-set, technology, or venture with the potential to become either a Black Swan (often driven by "bad" exponentials) or Green Swan (driven by "good" exponentials). Its potential future evolution is very hard to detect early on, unless you know what you are looking for. Tomorrow's breakthrough solution often looks seriously weird today. The net result is that we give them significantly less attention and resources than they need—or than the future of the 2030s and beyond would want us to in hindsight.

It seems to be hardwired into most of us to view anyone who seeks to transform the future with suspicion, at least early on. In some cases, such reactions rein in bad exponentials, stalling Ugly Ducklings that are latent Black Swans. But basic statistics suggest that it is also likely to hold back—even derail—emerging Green Swan solutions.

There is nothing new about this problem; indeed, it was central to *The Power of Unreasonable People*,[23] a book I wrote with the late Pamela Hartigan. That book went into the hands of all three thousand participants at 2008's annual World Economic Forum summit in Davos.[24] One of my favorite perspectives on this theme had appeared a decade earlier, with the extraordinary 1997 Apple ad celebrating "the crazy ones, misfits, rebels, troublemakers, round pegs in square holes." These are people who "see things differently," who "push the human race forward." The punchline: "Because the people who are crazy enough to think they can change the world, are the ones who do."

But are we crazy enough to rise to the challenges now headed our way? To be truly future fit, we must completely rethink how we run our planet. In that spirit, here is one step I took as I began to think through how to respond to this new epoch: the Anthropocene. Perhaps counterintuitively, at a time when it was breaking through at long last, I withdrew a key part of my life's work from the market, or I at least signaled a desire to do so.

So how often are management concepts subjected to product recalls by the people who coined them? It is hard to think of a single case. By contrast, if an industrial product like a car fails in a well-run market, the manufacturer pulls it back, tests it, and re-equips it if necessary. In case manufacturers grow careless, governments regulate and run periodic road safety tests to ensure that public safety is being accounted for.

Management concepts, by contrast, operate in poorly regulated environments where failures are often swept under boardroom or faculty carpets. Yet poor management systems can jeopardize lives in the air, at sea, on roads, or in hospitals. They can also put entire businesses, sectors, and economies at risk.[25]

With this in mind, I announced a management concept recall via the Harvard Business Review. With 2019 marking the twenty-fifth anniversary of the "triple bottom line," a term I coined back in 1994 to mean a sustainability framework that examines a company's social, environmental, and economic impact, I announced a strategic recall in order to do some "re-engineering." That recall evolved into our Tomorrow's Capitalism Inquiry[26]—and then into *Green Swans*, distilling some of the lessons learned along the way.

My concern was that, misused, the triple bottom line could give people the idea that they were on the right path, even as the world slips toward Black or Gray Swan outcomes. The implicit question is: What would the triple bottom line look like in a future with increasingly Green Swan characteristics? Perhaps, increasingly, each dimension would be fully integrated—and all three pointed toward the regeneration of our economies, societies, and biosphere?

It turned out that I had dodged a bullet with the recall, even if that was no part of my intention. A few months later, Anand Giridharadas published his provocative book, *Winners Take All*.[27] With a reputation for skewering plutocrats, Giridharadas argues that the wealthy are using philanthropy to pretend they are changing the world, while maintaining the status quo. He gave the example of the Sackler family, whose fortune derives from the same drugs that have caused the US opioid crisis. An estimated two million Americans suffer from what is called opioid use disorder, based on addiction to these powerful painkillers.[28] Obsessed with their financial bottom lines, opioid drug makers flooded America with seventy-six billion pills between 2006 and 2012 alone.[29] Enough to supply every adult and child in the country with thirty-six opioid pills a year—when a ten-day supply can hook one in five people.

Even the fabled Johnson & Johnson, with the "secret sauce" of its ethical "credo," has been whacked with a $572 million court claim because of its role in causing the opioid crisis.[30] Another dark Gray Swan, which a former head of the US Food and Drug Administration has described as "one of the greatest mistakes of modern medicine":[31] Really, what were we thinking?

Whereas some might argue that it is better for people like the Sacklers to spend at least a modicum of their wealth on good works rather than luxuries, Giridharadas disagrees, emphatically. "If they'd bought yachts," he counters, "they would have been brought to justice by journalists and regulators and criminal investigators way faster."[32] Even such well-received interventions as BlackRock CEO Larry Fink's letters to shareholders, encouraging greater action on ethical, social, and environmental matters, can be seen as an evasive tactic as long as BlackRock continues to hold shares in climate-destabilizing companies like ExxonMobil. Nor did Giridharadas have much time for the triple bottom line, quoting my recall of the concept.

In the same spirit, our Tomorrow's Capitalism Inquiry has been driven by a growing sense that the failings of modern capitalism cannot be solved simply by individual companies working with their supply chains, or even in concert with other committed companies. Such approaches are crucial in exploring the limits of the possible, no question, and in co-evolving solutions to global challenges. But, ultimately, the challenge now facing us is *political*.

Even so, I was delighted to be quoted by *Fast Company* when the news broke that the Business Roundtable, a lobbying group composed of leading American CEOs, had announced that they would no longer put shareholders before everyone else. That shareholder primacy, in effect, would be a thing of the past. As Rick Wartzman reported: "The Business Roundtable, a lobbying group composed of the nation's leading CEOs, just announced that its members 'share a fundamental commitment to all of our stakeholders'—each of whom 'is essential'—while pledging 'to deliver value to all of them, for the future success of our companies, our communities, and our country.'"[33]

He went on to say, "With its 'Statement on the Purpose of a Corporation,' the Roundtable has affirmed the need for 'meeting or exceeding customer expectations;' 'investing in our employees,' including by 'compensating them fairly and providing important benefits,' as well as offering training and education so that they can 'develop new skills for a rapidly changing world;' 'dealing fairly and ethically with our suppliers;' 'supporting the communities in which we work;' and 'generating long-term value for shareholders.'"

Jamie Dimon, the CEO of JPMorgan Chase and the Roundtable's chairman, noted that he hoped that this declaration "will help to set a new standard for corporate leadership." Wartzman commented, "It is, without question, a huge deal." My own comment was to the effect that leading companies "would resign from all trade and industry groups which lobby to slow or stall necessary systemic changes." Then they would turn around and "forcefully and publicly lobby for a meaningful price on carbon and for the breakup of monopolies and oligopolies."

In this context, and with encouragement from colleagues and a wide range of stakeholders, I have decided to double down—or perhaps that should be triple down—on the triple bottom line. Its meaning may have been diluted over time, but here in *Green Swans* I take a crack at updating it for the 2020s. Indeed, the wider context of a world in growing turmoil suggests that such multidimensional thinking and tools are needed more urgently now than ever.

"Capitalism is under threat," concludes American economist Irwin Stelzer. But the growing calls for systemic change, he says, are too often ignored by capitalists who fail "to hear the sound of approaching tumbrils."[34] Over half of Americans aged twenty-three to thirty-eight "would prefer to live in a socialist (46%) or communist (6%) nation."

Unfortunately, many capitalists who can see this growing threat to the system upon which their wealth depends still limit themselves to what Stelzer defines as "virtue-signaling," including calls for modest increases in their own tax burdens and increased philanthropy. Without fundamental changes to such things as inheritance taxes, immigration, free trade rules, executive compensation, median pay for all employees, and the re-pricing of things like carbon—in short, real systemic change—capitalism will come off the rails.

Intriguingly, we see a number of business leaders now acknowledging this publicly, notably Salesforce Chairman and co-CEO Marc Benioff. He says, "Nationally, increasing taxes on high-income individuals like myself would help generate the trillions of dollars that we desperately need to improve education and health care and fight climate change."[35]

Such changes will take sustained, bare-knuckled politics. I believe that systemic change is possible, indeed inevitable. Over almost five decades, I have worked to understand the thinking behind capitalism and to nudge it in new, more sustainable directions. An early book of mine, published in 1987, was called *The Green Capitalists*.[36] This was a couple of years before the Berlin Wall fell, and the message was that while capitalism was our future, it was unfit for purpose—so we needed to reinvent and transform it. The beat goes on.

Along the way I have been hugely privileged to operate at the leading edge of a growing array of social movements, helping bring the relevant agendas—along with the relevant rebels, troublemakers, and apparently crazy ones—into the business world and, crucially, into boardrooms and C-suites. It is not always possible, and not always successful even when it is possible, but we have made a fair amount of progress. That said, these are not normal times. Today's capitalism cannot survive in anything like its current form, so it must be upended. All around, tomorrow's capitalisms are struggling to be born. We must help select out the best among them and give them a head start.

Consider what follows as an invitation to engage. My email address is john@volans.com. Without wanting to tempt fate, I sense that the next decade will be the most exciting, challenging, and, at times, dangerous of my working life. Either capitalism must be transformed root and branch, with new definitions of impact, value, and wealth creation—or it will be replaced. The ultimate test is whether whatever form of wealth creation we do evolve by the 2030s is capable of actively restoring and regenerating our natural environment and, in parallel, our economies and societies.

If that sounds strikingly like the sort of Green New Deals now proposed for the 2020s, that is no accident. As President Franklin D. Roosevelt, architect of the original New Deal, summed up both the opportunity and the risk: "In our seeking for economic and political progress, we all go up—or else we all go down." By extension, will we now allow Black Swans to pull us down, or will we harness Green Swan dynamics to create forms of wealth that many of today's minds would consider improbable or even impossible? For those minded to go in the second direction, what follows is more of a manifesto, not yet a detailed road map. That comes next—although if you know where to look, it is already surfacing all around. In this book's concluding section (page 248) I spotlight Stanford University's $73 trillion plan to switch 143 countries around the world to 100% renewable energy by 2050. Now that really would be a Green Swan worthy of the name.

John Elkington,
London, December 2019

FOREWORD

BY PAUL POLMAN

John Elkington has once again proven his status as one of the great thinkers of our time in *Green Swans*. Charting the course of the changing face of capitalism and its corollary to the evolving green economy, this book paints an optimistic picture of the future for people and the planet, built around clean energy and carbon-free industries.

But change will be unpredictable and disruptive, as traditional commerce and market realities are upended and the world gravitates towards new circular and regenerative models of growth—a transition that is both necessary and inevitable as we head towards a global population of ten billion people that places ever-increasing pressure on our natural capital. It's become an over-used expression, but a world full of plastic, deforestation, and pollution is quite simply "unsustainable."

Fortunately, we have the means to undo this damage. Focusing capital on the long-term; greater energy efficiency and use of renewables; more sustainable food systems; smarter infrastructure planning; changing consumption patterns; and better use of technologies can all help us to live within our planetary boundaries. And provided we fully embrace these opportunities, we can create a historic U-bend moment that exponentially transforms our global economy beyond recognition.

To reach the necessary tipping points it's clear that we need a new generation of fearless and accountable leaders who understand that capitalism is a damaged system. It's an ideology whose credibility is fatally compromised because of the perverse outcomes it has engineered: runaway climate change, the biggest inter-generational crime ever committed, and gross inequality—a scar on the conscience of humanity.

Capitalism needs to be reinvented for the 21ˢᵗ century. This means discarding the tired reflex that has driven economic development since Adam Smith first proclaimed its utility over two hundred years ago—self-interest—in favor of working for the common good. The famous "invisible hand" has reached its limitations and instead inclusive capitalism is needed to establish a new social contract that truly leaves no one behind.

It also requires supercharging inventive models of cooperation, which recognize that you can only deliver real transformational change—at speed, at scale, and with maximum impact—provided you join forces in deep and purposeful collaboration with others. Cross-sectoral, public-private partnerships—across business, government, NGOs, civil society, academia, and local organizations—that simultaneously draw on individual strengths and expertise and collectively raise ambitions. No single actor has the capacity or license to act alone.

However, as this book identifies, there is one group that can make an outsized contribution in helping to put the world back on track: the business community. Its resources and innovation make it ideally positioned to leave a lasting impression. And it's in business's best interest to do so. A world where systemic environmental and social challenges persist is not a world in which business can thrive and prosper over the long-term. Business cannot succeed in failed societies, nor can it afford to be a bystander in a system that gives it life in the first place.

Indeed, in the face of deteriorating global governance and increases in populism and nationalism, responsible business needs to step up and de-risk the political process. Without this engagement, politicians will lack the confidence and mandate needed to completely redesign our social and economic structures, which have plainly become outdated and are holding us back.

John Elkington's prescription for a new way of doing business—one that nurtures the "Green Swans" of the future—could not come at a more crucial time. As we race towards a doomsday scenario where we do irreversible damage to our planet, we have to urgently hit the reset button.

It's time to embark on a "decade of delivery" that ensures we fully realize the 2030 development agenda. And while the moral case is overwhelming, the economic argument is equally compelling, as the cost of inaction already significantly exceeds the cost of action. The UN's Sustainable Development Goals are quite simply the world's greatest business plan—the growth story of the century.

We still have a small window of opportunity to act, but it's a window that's closing. For anyone interested in playing a positive and constructive role in support of this crucial movement for change this book is compulsory reading.

Paul Polman is a former CEO of Unilever and now the Co-Founder and Chair of IMAGINE, and Chair of the International Chamber of Commerce, The B Team, and the Saïd Business School.

DIVING INTO TOMORROW

Black, Gray, and Green

S wans have long been symbols of beauty, elegance, and effortlessness. But this extraordinary bird also symbolizes the potential for change and, in particular, for transformation. That is highly relevant here given that the coming decade, the Exponential Twenties, will see the pressures for both transformational change and regeneration heading off the scale.

In the work of Nassim Nicholas Taleb, particularly as outlined in his highly influential book *The Black Swan*, the focus was frequently on transformations that were *degenerative*. For him, a Black Swan—both words capitalized—is a rare event characterized by its extreme impact and its retrospective (though not prospective) predictability. A typical question after a Black Swan event would be the following: "How did we/they fail to spot that one coming?" Think about the 2007–2008 market crash or the 2011 Fukushima nuclear disaster in Japan.

Interestingly, even the blackest of Black Swans will generally have been foreseen by someone, at least in broad terms, as with maverick economist Hyman P. Minsky's insight that in modern economies "stability is destabilizing."[1] So when British prime minister Gordon Brown lauded the stability of his country's economy, predicting an end to the cycles of "boom and bust," knowledgeable investors should have headed for the hills.[2] They didn't, because most had forgotten what Minsky (who died in 1996) had said, if indeed they had ever heard of him or his warnings.

Black Swans, Taleb concluded, generally create negative, unwelcome, and above all systemic impacts. A bit further along the color spectrum, we find Gray Swans. They display many of the same characteristics as Black Swans, but differ in that they can be anticipated, at least to a degree. Gray Swans, according to the president of the Population Institute, Robert J. Walker, are "unlikely occurrences that are just likely enough that they should be anticipated."[3] While they can—indeed ought to—be seen coming, it can still be very hard to get a grip on their implications and potential impact before they happen.

Walker argued that "a confluence of events—including climate change, population growth, debt loads and the world's rising demand for food, energy and water—are dramatically increasing the overall levels of risk in the world." Exactly the sort of world, you might conclude, in which both Black and Gray Swans proliferate, and in which capitalism and democracy come under existential pressure.

Pushing the slider further along the spectrum, we come to what we might call "White Swans"—sets of exponential dynamics that could take us either toward breakdown or breakthrough. Like whiteboards, White Swans are templates that can be filled in by people with good, bad, or ugly intentions.

Further along still we find the "Green Swans" of our story. At one level, they show very similar characteristics and dynamics to their typically degenerative cousins, Gray and Black. They too take the world by surprise, in large part because of their exponential character and because they produce outcomes previously considered to be not just improbable but impossible. But rather than driving degeneration like many Gray and Black Swans, they spur regeneration. And regeneration is now our task, across our economies, our societies, our natural environment, and, perhaps most important of all, our politics. The role of politicians, governments and public policy will be critically important in determining the pace, direction and success of our collective change efforts.

Green Swans, it turns out, often evolve as responses to earlier Black or Gray Swan problems and impacts. By way of a public health warning, just as even the very worst of Black Swans may sport a few green feathers, or upsides, so even the most welcome of Green Swans can grow black feathers—and in some cases even black wings.

Consider electric vehicles, part of one of the most notable current Green Swan dynamics in the world of mobility. They generally depend on batteries, and these, in turn, require materials like cobalt. This is where this Green Swan starts to sprout darker feathers, with some 70% of the global supply of cobalt coming from the Democratic Republic of Congo, one of the poorest, most corrupt, and intensely violent places on Earth.[4]

THINKING DIFFERENT

A central challenge identified in what follows is to create the market, policy, governance, and cultural conditions in which Black and Gray Swans are identified and tackled early on, and that promote and support more, bigger, and better Green Swans. Much needs to happen for this to become the new normal.

It is human nature, for example, to dismiss or ignore what we fail to understand. And we are particularly inclined to do so when confronted with people and ideas that threaten our sense of reality, our hard-won certainties, and our identities. Too often, we dismiss ideas or information that cut across our current sense of reality as crazy. This is as true in business and financial markets as it is in our day-to-day lives. Most people find it hard enough getting their brains around Black Swans, so Green Swans can be an even tougher sell—seeming to stray into the realm of miracles.

My favorite explanation of what a miracle is in today's world comes from Charles Eisenstein of Yale University.[5] He concludes that transformations of the sort we now need will be characterized as miracles. But he provides a very different take on what miracles are. In his view, they are events that seem impossible from an old worldview (an old story) but that become eminently possible within an expanded, new story.[6] So what is a modern miracle? He explains:

> It is not the intercession of a supernatural being into material affairs, not an event that violates the laws of the universe. A miracle is something that is impossible from one's current understanding of reality and truth, but that becomes possible from a new understanding.
>
> A miracle is more than an event: it is an invitation. It says, "The universe is bigger than you thought it was." It invites us to step into a larger world, in which new things are possible. A miracle can blow apart our world if we accept it. Indeed, sometimes we do not accept it; sometimes we relegate it to the category of "that was weird," an exception to life, and we preserve normalcy and think and live as we always have, as if nothing had happened. When faced with an event that defies our usual explanations, we discard the event to preserve the explanation.

So people on the far side of such mental divides, who have passed through some sort of looking glass, are typically viewed with intense suspicion. Still, picking up on Apple's inspirational "Think Different" ad campaign, quoted earlier, where some see crazy people, others see genius.[7] Where some see "misfits, troublemakers, and round pegs in square holes," they may be looking at—but still be blind to—some of the most important people in today's world and tomorrow's. As blind both to Black and Gray Swan futures some of those crazy people are warning about as they are to possible Green Swan opportunities.

We will explore how new forms of wealth are being created tomorrow by people previously seen as marginal, irrelevant even. Ultimately, the genius of capitalism links to Adam Smith's "invisible hand," with the individual self-interest of businesspeople driving the innovation and production that potentially serve the interests of the many. Ideas that start on the margins can push—or be sucked—into the mainstream. Failed experiments are allowed to die, with the most productive capitalist economies allowing for a certain amount of failure.

That, at least, is the theory. The real world can be very different. This book bears witness to decades of the close-quarters work I've done at Volans, and earlier on with Environmental Data Services (ENDS) and then SustainAbility, with some of the world's biggest and most successful corporations and brands. This work has spanned a literal A-to-Z roster of companies and financial institutions—in the latter case from Aviva Investors to Zouk Capital.

True, other advisors could make similar claims, but what perhaps distinguished my approach over time was that I sought to channel a radically different—and potentially highly disruptive—future into boardrooms and C-suites. In the process, I have come across many examples of capitalism's "invisible elbow," so to speak, a bit of our economic anatomy much given to triggering painful—and sometimes catastrophic—unintended consequences.

Most business advisors, sensibly, aim to be professional, objective, and neutral. By contrast, I have long told clients that my colleagues and I aspire to be objective in terms of the change agenda some ten to fifteen years into the future. Neutrality be damned. Working with leaders focused on making incremental changes to the status quo, I have encouraged them to move from the tactical to the transformational, expanding their horizons to embrace an exponentially mutating "future quo." A future reality where their existing business models, organizational cultures, teams, and mind-sets will no longer be fit for purpose.

Over decades, we have brought leading changemakers, seen by some as troublemakers, into the control centers of business. We began with Amnesty, Greenpeace, and Oxfam campaigners, for example, and then opened up the invitation to social innovators and entrepreneurs, including the new breed of impact investors. Next came exponential innovators aiming for "10X, not 10%" change.

Unusually, too, we have warned our clients that if it ever came to the crunch, we would side with the troublemakers, not our corporate hosts. That gave some potential clients pause, given that some of the critics of capitalism-as-usual have argued that corporations, by their very nature, are pathologically deranged. On Monday, October 25, 2004, for example, I chaired the London launch of the film *The Corporation*—subtitled "The Pathological Pursuit of Profit and Power."[8] Among the panelists were Joel Bakan, who wrote the book, and Jennifer Abbott, who co-directed the film.

The film eventually scooped dozens of awards, posing a simple, if deeply provocative, question: If corporations are considered by law to be legal "persons," then what would happen if you put them on the psychiatrist's couch? What sort of persons might they turn out to be? The film crew had interviewed some forty insiders and critics, among them Milton Friedman, Noam Chomsky, Vandana Shiva, Naomi Klein, and Michael Moore. Their conclusion: At least as defined by law in the United States, corporations are psychopaths.

Shareholder activist Bob Monks, quoted by Bakan in the book, explained that the corporation is "an externalizing machine, in the same way that a shark is a killing machine"—not because it is malevolent but because that is the way it was designed. That is, the corporation imposes a spectrum of economic, social, and environmental costs on society because it makes commercial sense to do so, and, loosely interpreted, the rules of the game do not forbid it.

In my experience, most people who run corporations do not set out to promote waves of obesity and chronic disease, to flood the oceans with plastic waste, or to destabilize our climate. Most are horrified, some ashamed, when the consequences of their actions are spotlighted for all to see, even as they struggle to work out what they can do in response.

I have been involved in much of the work that has led to many of the world's biggest corporations becoming more transparent, responsible, accountable, and—at least by their own claims—sustainable. But in what follows we will take the advice given in the 1976 film *All the President's Men* to "follow the money." However much individual business leaders and businesses may want to be nicer to people or better for the world, the markets they operate in often have very different priorities.

As we say at Volans, there is little point in cleaning up corporate fish if we then release them back into dirty market waters. Profit remains the key motivating force in markets and business. But while current definitions of profit have served economists, accountants, and many investors well, they are clearly not fit for purpose in the Anthropocene. It's a remarkable fact that our era will be marked in the geological record by such things as nuclear fallout, plastics, and, of all things, leftover chicken bones. Who knew that the combined mass of the 23 billion chickens alive at any point in time now outweighs all other birds on Earth?[9] I didn't. We live in worlds that often bear little semblance to the realities that evolution has designed us to accept or ignore—the message of Donald Hoffman's extraordinary book *The Case against Reality*, subtitled "How Evolution Hid the Truth from Our Eyes."[10]

The single-minded pursuit of profit, it turns out, is no way to think of or run a planet for long-term health. To take just one illustration, none of the world's top industries would be profitable today if they had to pay for the unpriced natural capital they exploit.[11] On the upside, however, I believe that we are living through the early stages of another renaissance, at least in terms of our understanding of profit, impact, and, crucially, value and wealth. Like the first renaissance, it will be existentially unsettling.

PARADISE BURNING

Most of us now sense this emergent reality, not that we necessarily find it comfortable. A recent global study of public opinion revealed that 79% of those interviewed felt that the world was "changing too fast"—and 82% felt that we live in an "increasingly dangerous world."[12] How terrible—and how fitting—that Paradise, a California town, was recently consumed by flames in the most destructive fire in the state's history.

Some of our great historic successes are now turning into looming catastrophes. As environmental scientist Jonathan Foley has put it:

> Just think about this for a second: During the last 50 years, we doubled the world's population, grew our economic activity eight-fold, and started using two to three times more global resources than ever before. Put another way, our society changed more in the last 50 years than at any other time in history. More startling, **we changed more in the last 50 years than in the *entirety of human existence*.**[13]
>
> [Original author's emphases.]

There are commercially successful super optimists on the theme of where all of this is taking us. People like Steven Pinker and the late Hans Rosling have argued that we are living in the most peaceful times ever, statistically speaking. In the last hundred years, we have seen the average human life expectancy nearly doubled—indeed, as I wrote these words, my father was ninety-eight, my mother ninety-six. Such things do not go on forever, however.[14] And the threat of the Anthropocene epoch is that our species, so successful in improving its own life expectancy and living conditions over a generation or two, may so disrupt the wider world that the very foundations of nature and civilization crack.

Many scientists now track the beginning of the Anthropocene epoch back to 1950, when the multiple exponential curves tracked in the work of the likes of the Stockholm Resilience Centre ("Planetary Boundaries"[15]) and the International Geosphere-Biosphere Programme (the "Great Acceleration"[16]) all began to rocket skyward. But two scientists suggest a strikingly different starting date, underscoring just how tightly coupled our species has become with its global habitat over recent centuries. In their book *The Human Planet: How We Created the Anthropocene*, University College London professors Simon Lewis and Mark Maslin argue that the Anthropocene began with the European colonization of the "New World" back in the sixteenth century.[17]

How so? Well, it is now estimated that the diseases that those migrants carried with them, combined with the genocidal use of then advanced technologies, led to the deaths of between 50 million and 80 million indigenous people in the Americas. Unimaginable. A true Black Swan from the viewpoint of those whose worlds were torn apart. Then as the original peoples faded from the landscape, trees grew back. And as the forests recovered, they sucked carbon dioxide out of the atmosphere—with carbon dioxide levels reaching a distinctive minimum around the year 1610.

Who knew that our species could have impacts of this nature and scale so long ago? But, however momentous those changes may have been, those we have now set in motion threaten to have effects that will be many orders of magnitude greater.

So how can we rethink today's market realities and assumptions? How can we learn to think the previously unthinkable? And how do we learn to do things previously thought impossible? These are just some of the questions to which we must now urgently find answers.

RECALLING THE TRIPLE BOTTOM LINE

Such questions drove me to do something intuitive, even if counter-intuitive for many. The publication of *Green Swans* was always intended to coincide with the twenty-fifth anniversary of the triple bottom line, a concept I coined in 1994. This idea went into the language, particularly after the publication of my book *Cannibals with Forks* in 1997. This was subtitled "The Triple Bottom Line of 21st Century Business." The term became a mantra for champions of sustainable business.

Meanwhile, however, the "software" controlling capitalism today includes the millions of algorithms that churn away constantly, out of sight and out of mind, but it also includes the values and assumptions of generations of economists. Their focus on financial value above all other forms has delivered huge rewards for those in capitalism's driving seats, but also burned through unconscionable amounts of natural, social, and human capital along the way.

That was the reality that the triple bottom line was intended to challenge. For those unfamiliar with the concept, the triple bottom line is a management framework designed to examine a company's social, environmental, and economic impact. In 1995, I followed up with the simplified "People, Planet & Profit." Together, these terms have been among the more successful new entrants to the business lexicon over the past quarter century. So why recall them? After all, since the 1990s, the sustainability sector has grown rapidly, though at somewhere between one and two billion dollars in annual revenues globally, it is no giant.[18]

Still, market research suggests that future markets for its products and services could be huge, with the UN Sustainable Development Goals forecast to generate market opportunities of over $12 trillion a year by 2030—and that's considered a conservative estimate.[19] But it is far from clear to whom that new wealth will go. At the same time, success or failure on sustainability goals cannot be measured simply in terms of profit and loss. It must also be measured in terms of the well-being of billions of people and the health of our planet, and the sustainability sector's record in moving the needle on those goals has been decidedly mixed. While there have been unquestionable successes, our climate, water resources, oceans, forests, soils, and biodiversity are all increasingly threatened.

It is time to either step up or to get out of the way. In that spirit, it is clear that the triple bottom line, variously shortened to TBL, 3BL or the 3Ps (People, Planet, Profit), has been a powerful element of the genetic code of the sustainability agenda. A decade ago, *The Economist* was already signaling that the term had become part of the business lexicon.[20] As the magazine explained, the approach "aims to measure the financial, social and environmental performance of the corporation over a period of time. Only a company that produces a TBL is taking account of the full cost involved in doing business."

Well yes, but the original idea was wider still, encouraging businesses to track and manage *economic* (not just financial), social, and environmental value added—or destroyed. The basic idea later inspired platforms like the Global Reporting Initiative and Dow Jones Sustainability Indexes, influencing corporate accounting, stakeholder engagement, and, increasingly, strategy.

Critically, though, the triple bottom line was never designed to simply be an accounting tool. It was supposed to provoke deeper thinking about capitalism and its future, even if many early adopters understood the concept as a balancing act, adopting a trade-off mentality. With the financial (sic) element seen as dominant, social, or (even more likely) environmental, trade-offs were only to be expected.

As it happens, the concept surfaced exactly 500 years after Luca Paccioli published the world's first treatise on double-entry bookkeeping, the cornerstone for single bottom line thinking. It is now clear that the advent of the triple bottom line was a key branching point. It helped inspire and was followed by Double and Quadruple Bottom Lines; Social Return on Investment; multiple capital models; Full Cost Accounting; ESG (a framework focusing investors and financial analysts on Environmental, Social, and Governance factors); the Environmental Profit & Loss approach pioneered by Trucost, Puma, and Kering; Net Positive; Blended and Shared Value; Integrated Reporting; Impact Investment; and a range of proprietary versions, including consultancy BCG's Total Societal Impact framework. That's even before we get into next-generation concepts like Carbon Productivity, the Sharing Economy, the Circular Economy, and Biomimicry.

Such experimentation is clearly essential and can spur a proliferation of potential solutions. But too often the sheer range of options, this Tower of Babel we have been building, provides business with yet another alibi for inaction. Worse, we have conspicuously failed to benchmark progress across these options on the basis of their real-world potential, impact, and performance. That work must be done urgently if we are to improve them, and choose among them.

Fundamentally, we have a hardwired cultural problem in business, finance, and markets. Whereas CEOs, CFOs, and other corporate leaders move heaven and earth to ensure that they hit their profit targets, the same is very rarely true of their people and planet targets. Clearly, the triple bottom line has failed to bury the paradigm of the single bottom line.

But a profound paradigm shift is now underway, toward a global mind-set based on one-planet thinking. Its impacts will become increasingly evident in the 2020s and 2030s. Through this coming decade, our environmental, economic, social, human, and, above all, environmental challenges will be greater than at any time in recorded history. But at the same time, there will be unprecedented opportunities for those offering workable solutions to such challenges. They will create novel forms of wealth that, outside of science fiction, are pretty much unimaginable today.

Yes, I am encouraged by the progress made since the early 1990s. I am genuinely proud and delighted that thousands of B Corporations have embraced the triple bottom line agenda, including two that I cofounded, SustainAbility and then Volans. But no idea is perfect and mantras can be distracting.

So, in 2018, I announced what I was told was the first ever "product recall" of a management concept.[21] Ironically, it was announced in the *Harvard Business Review* (*HBR*). The irony lies in the fact that, several years earlier, *HBR* had published its latest ranking of CEOs—and listed Novo Nordisk's then CEO as the world's best business leader. Novo Nordisk had been the first large company in the world to formally re-charter itself around the triple bottom line.

While much of capitalism is becoming more responsible and less destructive per unit of production or profit, it must now become radically more economically inclusive, socially just, and—crucially—environmentally restorative. This, in turn, means rebooting our thinking about profit and profitability. A real challenge, given that most businesspeople only wake up to the need for radical change when their corporate reality bubbles are punctured by an unexpected crisis, or when they experience a personal epiphany, go on a transformative learning journey, or, in some cases, retire from the daily cut and thrust of serving Mammon.

This challenge is off-the-scale more demanding than anything most leaders have yet taken on board. Some will argue that our suggested solutions are literal impossibilities, but we see them not just as possible but, often, as inevitable. Indeed, we assume that something that already exists is unlikely to be impossible.

As my favorite living science fiction author William Gibson famously put it, "The future is already here—it's just not evenly distributed." Yet. But, while exciting and necessary, early experiments in breakthrough wealth creation are far from guaranteed to evolve at the necessary pace and scale. To do so, they require active, intelligent, and sustained government, public, and—crucially—investor engagement.

That may prove problematic when much of the evidence now points in different, darker directions. Traditional forms of politics and regulation are failing. If cancer is life run riot, then plastic-clogged oceans, obscene wealth divides, the undermining of democracy, and accelerating climate-induced societal collapse are symptoms of our current forms of capitalism running riot. Like it or not, the generational task of containing—and then radically redesigning—capitalism is now our central challenge.

Just as we try to contain nuclear fission processes with layers of concrete and lead, or to contain fusion reactions with magnetic fields, so the destructive power of capitalism must be contained and constrained by well-enforced laws, widely accepted standards, and deep-rooted values to stop it from blowing up in our faces.

EXPLORING THE EXPONENTIAL FRONTIER

To help support those moving in this direction, Volans and PA
Consulting joined forces some years back with the United Nations
Global Compact, the world's largest sustainable business platform, to
create Project Breakthrough.[22] In the process, Volans developed what
we call the "Breakthrough Compass" to map the emerging landscape of
risk and opportunity (Figure 2).

The horizontal axis in the Compass ("impact") tracks the spectrum
of outcomes created by business, from extremely negative to extremely
positive. The billion-people-impacted scale, either positively or nega-
tively, may seem far-fetched, but two brothers I have met over the years
have helped me define the outer limits here. Google's Larry Page invests
in solutions that potentially benefit up to one billion people, while his
brother Carl (at the Anthropocene Institute) focuses on problems that
could disadvantage—even kill—up to one billion of us.

Meanwhile, the vertical axis ("scale") moves from incremental
change at the bottom to increasingly exponential outcomes at the top.
To address the realities of climate change and other ways in which we
are increasingly overrunning planetary boundaries, we must now shift
our mind-sets, technologies, and business models from left to right,
and from bottom to top—ensuring that a growing proportion of our
economies operate in the top, right-hand quadrant, the realm of breakthrough innovation.

As reflected in the Acknowledgments section (from page 251), we have
been privileged to work with a growing number of businesses and CEOs
determined to move into that top right-hand quadrant. As 2020 dawned,
for example, we were in Madrid, working with Acciona people from
around the world on a strategy for achieving "exponential sustainability."
Led by their visionary chairman, José Manuel Entrecanales Domecq, and
now guided by global sustainability director José Luis Blasco, the infra-
structure-to-energy company became carbon neutral some years back,
largely thanks to its powerful push into renewable energy. Many more
businesses will be following their lead in the coming decades.

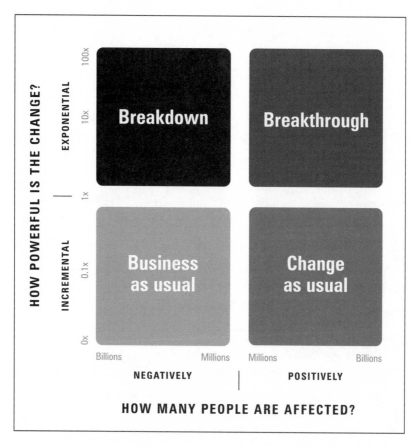

Figure 2: The Breakthrough Compass (Source: Volans and *Harvard Business Review*)

The "Breakdown" zone is the haunt of Black and Gray Swans, where bad exponentials push toward system collapse. Meanwhile, the "Breakthrough" zone is where we would expect to see a growing number of Green Swans hatching, fledging, and taking off. They may have started out as "Ugly Ducklings" in any of the other three zones, but their ultimate potential is to benefit millions—and ultimately billions—of people.

As Project Breakthrough evolved, we visited organizations like the XPRIZE Foundation, Google's X facility, and Singularity University— all at the cutting edge of exponential thinking. In the process, we were forcefully struck by their conviction that our global challenges will not be solved by hitting 1% (or even 10%) targets, but instead that business at large must embrace "10X" thinking—meaning, targets aiming for at least a tenfold improvement. This, we concluded, is the attitude now needed to make real progress on sustainability. Instead of simply pursuing incremental goals, we also need to set and deliver against goals that will have 10X (i.e., tenfold) or 100X the impact on anywhere between one million and one billion people.

Looking back now, I had been exploring the edges of exponential thinking for quite a while. In 2005, for example, I visited *Wired* magazine's founding editor Kevin Kelly at his home in California. His books *Out of Control* and *New Rules for the New Economy* had helped shift my vision of the future from a future of scarcity to one increasingly characterized, at least in some areas, by abundance. In a world increasingly marked by decreasing returns and limits to growth, he argued that new digital technology offered increasing—indeed exponentially accelerating—returns.

A few years later, Kelly wrote an influential blog post that captured the conundrum of shifting to an exponential mind-set:[23]

> [W]hile progress runs on exponential curves, our individual lives proceed in a linear fashion. We live day by day by day [. . .] Today will always be more valuable than some day in the future, in large part because we have no guarantee we'll get that extra day. Ditto for civilizations. In linear time, the future is a loss. But because human minds and societies can improve things over time, and compound that improvement in virtuous circles, the future in this dimension is a gain. Therefore long-term thinking entails the confluence of the linear and the exponential.

Shifting to an exponential mind-set is challenging for the reasons Kelly gave, and others. Most of us are not wired to think exponentially. But cracking such challenges is now vital for those very same reasons. Fellow

Californian Peter Diamandis, co-founder of the XPRIZE Foundation and Singularity University, has argued that technology can help create what he calls "a world of abundance."[24] The world, he insists, has lots of resources—water, energy, and so on—but we're hampered because we can't access them efficiently. But, he says, ultimately "technology is a resource-liberating force." If used properly, and that is an issue we will come back to repeatedly, it could help us solve our resource constraints.

I am a qualified optimist. Dark clouds, silver linings. Our species often does its best work after being backed—or backing itself—into a corner. We have now backed ourselves into what I often call the "mother of all corners." That is the really big picture. Come down a level or two and it is clear that our global economy is now heading into some sort of historic U-bend as illustrated in Figure 1 (page 4).

The links between this idea and Otto Scharmer's "Theory U" have not escaped me; indeed his work should be at the heart of any future attempts to cultivate Green Swans.[25] He aims to address Einstein's dictum that you cannot solve problems with the same level of thought that created them.

IT ALWAYS SEEMS IMPOSSIBLE . . .

All around, an old order is dying and a new one struggling to be born and find its feet. A couple of decades ago, in 2001, I heralded this in terms of an emerging "Chrysalis Economy."[26] A global economy that my generation had grown up in and taken for granted had turned out to be as destructive as a gigantic, global caterpillar. Now science suggests that it must be squeezed down into some sort of economic and political cocoon by resource and environmental constraints, triggering a profound process of metamorphosis.

Inside a normal chrysalis, I discovered, the once-insatiable caterpillar melts into a slurry of nutrients. These are then reassembled into a butterfly by so-called imaginal cells—living blueprints. The same, I concluded, would be true of the Chrysalis Economy, where the imaginal cells are people like innovators, business leaders, and city mayors. And the evidence suggests that, at least in some places, our economic chrysalis is beginning to crack open—a process that can only accelerate.

PANEL 1: THREE HORIZONS, TWO SCENARIOS, 2000-2100

How to dive into tomorrow? And how to track—and spur—the shift from a world of Black and Gray Swans to one increasingly populated by Green Swans? We asked Bill Sharpe of the International Futures Forum, who helps leaders engage the future in terms of three distinct horizons. All three, he noted, exist in the present. His framework has underpinned both our Tomorrow's Capitalism Inquiry[27] and the development of the *Green Swans* narrative.

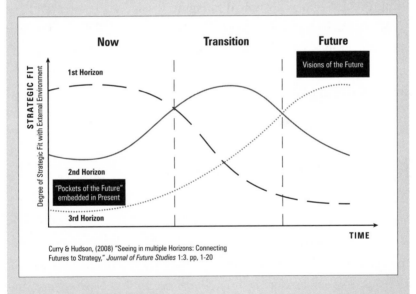

Curry & Hudson, (2008) "Seeing in multiple Horizons: Connecting Futures to Strategy," *Journal of Future Studies* 1:3. pp, 1-20

Figure 3: The Three Horizons

The first horizon—H1 (2000-2020)—dominates today, representing "business as usual." As the world changes, so H1 thinking and practice begin to feel out of step, no longer fit for purpose. In the end, they are superseded by new ways of doing things. The increasingly obvious shortcomings of the H1 system spur growing innovation, although much of this may be captured by the existing system, for example through mergers and acquisitions.

This creates a second horizon, H2. Eventually, the new, innovative approaches become more effective than the original system, creating an inflection point, a point of disruption. Clayton Christensen flagged this as the onset of the "innovator's dilemma": Should you protect your core business that is at risk, or instead invest in the innovations that look as if they might replace it?

Often, breakthrough innovations—including exponential Green Swan solutions—emerge at the edges of the current system. This is the domain of Apple's misfits, crazies, round pegs in square holes. Their H3 mind-sets seem light-years away from the H1 status quo, founded on very different assumptions. Easy to ignore, discount. This is the emergent third horizon, H3. It is the new way of thinking and doing things. Ignore it at your peril.

Bill Sharpe explains that H1 is the world of the *manager*, H2 of the *entrepreneur*, and H3 of the *visionary*. All have strengths and skills needed to make a successful transition to a better future. Note, however, that many elements of today's H1 reality, including the triple bottom line, were themselves H3 ideas back in the twentieth century.

In what follows, Horizons 1 (today) and 2 (2021–2030) frame the period when we might expect "Ugly Ducklings" to pop up all around, while Horizon 3 (2031–2100) will see a growing number of Green Swan solutions taking flight—and, in doing so, changing the system, for the better.

But it could be for the worse, which is the Black Swan Scenario. In this future we largely delay action to the point where unforeseen tipping points trigger exponential downward spirals. This is a world of breakdown and of increasing chaos. We have been there before, with bubonic plagues, religious conflicts, world wars, and the like.

The Green Swan Scenario takes us in a very different direction, though it is eminently possible to imagine a future that combines elements of both scenarios. Meanwhile, we have no real choice but to dive in. Throughout the process of producing *Green Swans*, we had in mind a saying often attributed to Nelson Mandela, but with roots stretching back to Roman naturalist Pliny the Elder: "It always seems impossible until it's done."[28]

CHAPTER 1

MIRACLES ON DEMAND

Making the Impossible Inevitable

"Any sufficiently advanced technology is indistinguishable from magic," science fiction author Arthur C. Clarke famously concluded. In much the same way, anything that cracks a major economic, social, or environmental challenge that had previously seemed impossible to solve is likely to be loosely described as some form of "miracle." And truth lurks in that loose use of language.

Miracles may have gone out of fashion, but they are exactly what we now need in the Anthropocene—as our species increasingly bangs up against the planetary ceiling. Some of the most interesting thinking about what constitutes a miracle has come from author Charles Eisenstein.[1] Here are some things he has said about miracles and the overarching story, or stories, shaping our understanding of the world we live in:[2]

- *You could say that [. . .] we are in the business of creating a miracle on Earth.*[3]

- *[A modern miracle is] something that is impossible from an old understanding of reality, but possible from a new one.*[4]

- *Stories, like all beings, have a life span. In their youth, their immune system is strong, but as time goes on they become increasingly unable to withstand the contrary evidence and experiences that pile up.*[5]

- *Working on the level of story has two dimensions. First is to disrupt the old, which says, "What you thought was real is just an illusion." Second is to offer a new [one], which says, "The possible, and the real, are much grander than you knew." The first, we experience as crisis and breakdown. The second, we experience as miraculous.*[6]

- *That's what a miracle is: Not the intercession of an external divinity in worldly affairs that violates the laws of physics, but something that is impossible from within an old Story of the World and possible from a new one.*[7]

- *A miracle is [. . .] both a glimpse and a promise.*[8]

I have developed antibodies to most forms of religious thinking, but there is something about this definition that attracts me. I am not suggesting that we teeter on the edge of a brave new world, where miracles will be available on demand—some form of miracles-as-a-service. Instead, the message is that our old "Story of the World," which Thomas Kuhn would have described as the prevailing paradigm in which our science, our societies, and our economies operate and evolve, is itself being transformed.

What follows is a glimpse into a future where the overarching paradigm is no longer as likely to produce Black or Gray Swan degenerations—and, in the process, massively increases the chances of Green Swan regenerations. This is not magical, "with one bound she was free" thinking. Instead it draws on a serious inquiry into the sort of psychological, cultural, political, and market conditions that massively enhance our chances of making exponential progress.

For skeptics, and there will be many, it is worth noting that we have been here before, though one current problem is that interest in history seems to be waning in some key societies, raising a real risk to democracy.[9] As far as our economies are concerned, some potential Black Swan events through history include the longer-term consequences of the 1929 and 2007–2008 market crashes. Societal Black Swans might include the Holocaust, though some foresaw it, and the profound impact of HIV/AIDS. On the environmental front, there is the catastrophic die-off of insects that some call "Insectageddon," and the glutting of the world ocean with plastic debris.

Now on to Green Swans. In the economic domain, recent Green Swan breakthroughs have included the rapid spread of cell phone technology and the internet, linking us in new ways and massively boosting the prospects for self-education, and the staggering cost reductions for solar and wind power systems. The accelerating shift to electric vehicles is a linked example, especially when coupled with the rapid evolution of battery technology and the impact of digitalization on autonomous vehicles, the internet of everything, and the sharing economy.

In the social domain, Green Swan trajectories have been followed by universal schooling in many countries, the evolution of vaccine technology (despite recent anti-vaccine rumors and propaganda), and the growth of social movements focusing on environmentalism, social enterprise, and impact investment.

When it comes to the environment, we have seen pollutants like asbestos, DDT, lead, and CFCs largely driven out of the economy, coupled with the emergence of concepts like sustainable development, the circular economy, and biomimicry. Equally impressive on the ground have been such ecosystem restoration projects as the progressive recovery of the Iraqi marsh ecosystems destroyed by Saddam Hussein's forces, and the progressive re-greening of China's Loess Plateau, a cradle of early Chinese civilization.[10] The scale of the regeneration in such places of past ruination has to be seen to be believed—and is hugely encouraging in terms of the longer-term prospects for our core task of planet-level regeneration. But to ensure we prevent future destruction of such ecosystems, we need a new crime of "ecocide," ranked alongside war crimes.

PLACEBO BUTTONS

Any breakthrough—or breakdown—of significant magnitude will have impacts across all three dimensions of wealth creation and destruction. Swans of whatever color create cascades of effects in our three dimensions and beyond. For a profoundly negative example of such interconnections, recall the European colonization of the Americas, already mentioned, resulting in between 50 and 80 million deaths among indigenous peoples, the collapse of a range of civilizations, and, as farms reverted to nature and the recovering forests drew carbon out of the atmosphere, the onset of the Little Ice Age in Europe.[11]

A positive example of a Green Swan, which surfaced as a response to Black Swan problems of widespread pollution and disease in cities, would be the spread of clean water, sanitation, sewerage, and related infrastructures. Still only a partial success globally, but nonetheless an extraordinary one. As it happens, our London office is in Somerset House, overlooking the River Thames, and alongside the Embankment—created in a massive project that reclaimed marshland by the river, created expensive new riverside property, and, critically, from the 1860s on included a huge new sewage system. Over time, such projects turned a river into which almost everything was dumped, and in which almost nothing could live, into something in which even environmentally fastidious salmon could, at least potentially, swim.

As technology evolves, the nature, pace, and reach of Green Swans evolve in surprising ways, as in the case of the so-called Blue Planet Effect. When the BBC screened Sir David Attenborough's TV series *The Blue Planet*, with its hard-hitting footage of wildlife caught in drifting plastic waste, the response was almost instantaneous—and hugely damaging for the international plastics industry.

But these are exceptions in a storyline that more typically sees change operating on the basis of too little, too late. Indeed, one key reason why I decided to announce that product recall for the triple bottom line was that I concluded that, at least in the context of the so-called wicked and super wicked problems haunting today's world, the concept was suffering from what we might call the Placebo Effect. Let me explain.

Every now and then you see or hear something that crystallizes a thought that has been nagging at your brain. That was my experience when I downloaded a CNN article that asked a simple question: *Have you ever pressed the pedestrian button at a crosswalk and wondered if it really worked?*[12] Many times, as it happens, not least because I worked on pedestrianization schemes way back when. And I have often suspected, as the article concluded, that "the world is full of buttons that don't actually do anything." It went on to say the following:

> They're sometimes called "placebo buttons"—buttons that are mechanically sound and can be pushed, but provide no functionality. Like placebo pills, however, these buttons may still serve a purpose, according to Ellen Langer, a Harvard psychologist who pioneered a concept known as the "illusion of control."

Langer pointed out that "doing something typically feels better than doing nothing." But what, I wondered, if many of the things we have been encouraging business leaders to do to create a better world are little more than market versions of the placebo button? What if their main effect is to make us all feel a bit better, while the real problems remain out of sight, out of mind, and, as a result, out of control?

Having worked closely with business since the late 1970s, helping CEOs and other corporate leaders to change their priorities and even their mind-sets, I saw this as a chilling possibility. People in the change industry increasingly discuss the impact they have in the wider world—but are we simply equipping cabinets, government departments, boardrooms, and C-suites with a plethora of handy placebo buttons? The answer, I believe, is an unstable mix of "yes," "it's too early to tell," and "no."

Yes, because the impact of all the effort invested by business has so far had a limited effect on the systemic challenges the world now faces.

As CDC Group CEO Nick O'Donohoe put it, "Today over 90 percent of major businesses have specific programs dedicated to Corporate Social Responsibility (CSR). Most CEOs talk about their organization's commitment to a wide range of philanthropic, employee engagement, and other benevolent activities at almost every possible opportunity."[13]

All well and good, but O'Donohoe, an investor who has advised the Bill & Melinda Gates Foundation, concluded, "As long as CSR stays fundamentally altruistic in its motivation it is unlikely ever to be considered as being core to business and is unlikely ever to scale or to provide lasting solutions to critical social challenges."

So, yes, we see placebo effects at work. But, on the other hand, and to the same original question, no—at least in the sense that momentous progress has been made since I began work in this space. Back then it was almost impossible to get companies to talk to outsiders about ethical, social, and environmental issues. When we set up Environmental Data Services (ENDS) in 1978, it took us nine months to get inside the first company—even though our parent company was highly respected in the world of industrial relations. Now access to the boardrooms and C-suites of major companies is pretty much taken for granted by serious change agents.

But, finally, what about that middle option, "it's too early to tell"? Well, the penny is beginning to drop. Leaders in the private, public, and citizen sectors increasingly see long-predicted problems becoming everyday realities. As a result, even some laggard leaders now talk about disruptive change driven by social and environmental factors. Growing numbers have committed their organizations to one or more of the expanding spectrum of business-to-business platforms launched to help companies address such issues at scale. But who is keeping a close eye on our—and their—progress overall?

As already mentioned, too often it seems as if we busy ourselves cleaning up corporate fish, only to release them back into murky market waters. We should ask the following questions: Have we picked the wrong unit, or units, of analysis? If so, how do we begin to think about changing the wider market environments within which businesses operate? Or, to use a rather different angle of attack: Have we been focusing too much on people like CEOs and other leaders, and spending too little time thinking about the market operating codes that drive corporate thinking, priorities, and behavior? The answer, I believe, is yes—even if business leadership remains crucial in all of this.

CORPORATIONS ON THE COUCH

In that context, how do today's business leaders really think? Where is the leading edge of their knowledge taking them? And what is it that they do not currently see that they need to be made aware of? In a moment we will look at prevailing business mind-sets through ten lenses provided by business terms that have been in common use for ages, but are now mutating and evolving as new change agendas surface.

In effect, it is time to psychoanalyze business. When asked what I did late in the last century, I would often reply, half seriously, that I was some sort of corporate psychiatrist, putting corporations on the couch. At a time when many business leaders were wondering if the wider world was going mad, with its calls for everything from human rights for future generations to apparently impossible cuts in greenhouse gases, I saw it as my job to help these leaders see that the world their MBAs and rapid rises through industry ranks had prepared them for was what psychologists would call a "false construct." A false—or at least seriously distorted—version of reality.

Just as some psychiatrists use word associations to probe minds, I have long been fascinated to listen to the words and phrases that business leaders used, particularly in private, to explain the business of business.

So now on to the ten business terms. To ensure we capture the original essence of each term, we will draw on definitions from the *Financial Times* (*FT*) online business lexicon,[14] hereafter simply called the *Lexicon*. It is intriguing to see the *FT* now offering an additional service, whereby you can sign up to a watchlist for relevant terms, perhaps ultimately enabling us to observe business language evolving in something like real time.

The ten terms spotlighted here are *Purpose, Business Model, Profit, Growth, Value, Impact, Liability, Materiality, Governance,* and *Stranded Assets.* None of these would seem to be obviously connected with the potential generation of market miracles, but together they offer a kaleidoscopic view of some of the profound changes now underway in the worlds of capitalism, markets, and business. They are addressed in this order because it helps tell the following story:

> The *Purpose* of a new business helps dictate and shape the *Business Model* it uses, although longer term the latter can come to powerfully shape the former. As we move the needle from unintentional Black Swan pathways to more intentional Green Swan pathways, the performance of a business model will still be measured in terms of *Profits,* or performance against the financial bottom line. But the bottom line calculus must now expand to embrace multiple forms of value and wealth creation.
>
> The so-called top line (measuring growth in gross sales and revenues) then takes us into the area of *Growth.* This is something that any market-oriented business pursues, not least because growth—and, crucially, future growth prospects—helps dictate the *Value* of the business.
>
> Along the way a business or industry creates various forms of *Impact.* Some of these may be intended, others not. Economists have talked of "economic externalities," whereas today people are more likely to talk of "unintended consequences." These may be positive, but they may also be negative, creating problems for people, for other economic actors, and for the planet.
>
> These problems may result in various forms of *Liability,*

undermining the future prospects of a business or market. To understand such risks better, growing numbers of businesses use *Materiality* tests as part of their corporate *Governance* processes.

The reason why we have left *Stranded Assets* to last—and this was the only term in the list not covered by the *FT Lexicon* when consulted—is that it provides a natural bridge to the subject of wicked and super wicked challenges. So, as seems fitting, we start with *Purpose*.

1. PURPOSE

Very few people, apart from villains in James Bond movies, actively set out to create Black or Gray Swan outcomes, but they may help create them nonetheless. Sometimes you get a front-row seat: One week before Lehman Brothers crashed in 2008, I was taking photographs out of their boardroom window in London's Canary Wharf, overlooking the Thames. There were no Black Swans visible on the river, at least that I remember, but I should have sensed them in the boardroom behind me.

I couldn't understand why I got a call, shortly after I got back to our offices, from the Lehman security people, threatening me with legal action unless I took the photos down from my website. Then, a few days later, the news broke, and I understood why they had been so agitated.

A decade later, elements of that drama were turned into an astounding trio of plays by Italian dramatist Stefano Massini, called *The Lehman Trilogy*.[15] They explore how the original purpose of Lehman Brothers changed as it evolved from the dry goods store founded by three Bavarian-Jewish brothers who had migrated to Montgomery, Alabama, via commodity dealing to finance. Along the way, the family lost control of the business. Its purpose changed from serving customers to increasingly abstracted financial dealings. Ultimately, a once-powerful business was wrecked.

The drama of the plot comes from the question, How did this

once-unimaginable Black Swan outcome happen? This is a question that now needs to be applied not just to failed businesses like Lehman Brothers but to capitalism as a whole. With a general weakening of government efforts to understand and rein in such excesses, the spotlight inevitably has slid back to what drives business—and to purpose.

THE OLD STORY

Given the degree to which debate around purpose has exploded in recent times, the *FT Lexicon*'s entry was disappointing, and somewhat circular: "Another name for mission statement." Dig a bit deeper and you found that a mission statement is "a short written statement made by an organization, intended to communicate its aims to customers, employees, shareholders, etc."

But for much of the past half century, corporate purpose has been powerfully shaped by the thinking of Milton Friedman. Among his best-known assertions are "The business of business is business," and "There is one and only one social responsibility of business—to use its resources and engage in activities designed to increase its profits so long as it stays within the rules of the game, which is to say, engages in open and free competition without deception or fraud."

Nor was he an enthusiast for government, or for raising taxes to fund government. One phrase attributed to him was, "If you put the federal government in charge of the Sahara Desert, in five years there'd be a shortage of sand." Hyperbole, of course, but this was very much the gist of his thinking.[16] On taxes, he had this to say: "I am in favor of cutting taxes under any circumstances and for any excuse, for any reason, whenever it's possible."

NEW STORIES

Reviewing a new book called *Prosperity*, by Colin Mayer of Oxford University's Saïd Business School, the *Financial Times* economics editor

Martin Wolf concluded that "profit is not itself a business purpose. Profit is a condition of—and result of—achieving a purpose. The purpose might be making cars, delivering products, disseminating information, or many other things. If a business substitutes making money for purpose, it will fail at both."[17]

Purpose has been much debated recently, but these efforts must increasingly be set in the context of the fact that, as Wolf himself has concluded, "capitalism is broken." On the upside, we see movements building around new concepts like the B Corporation. The idea here is that for-profit companies bearing the B Corporation certification should "meet the highest standards of verified social and environmental performance, public transparency, and legal accountability to balance profit and purpose." The founders of B Lab, the social enterprise behind the B Corp movement, argue that "B Corps are accelerating a global culture shift to redefine success in business and build a more inclusive and sustainable economy."[18]

Having co-founded the first two British B Corps in the UK, I am excited about the movement, but even the several thousand B Corps around the world still have a long way to go before they effectively tackle the market dynamics dramatized in *The Lehman Trilogy*. Otherwise, they risk being green feathers on much bigger—and largely oblivious— Black Swans. In that context, the Business Roundtable's announcement that it would increasingly turn its back on shareholder primacy is a useful signal that we may finally have reached peak Friedman.

PURPOSE WITH GREEN SWAN CHARACTERISTICS

Most of the discussion about purpose focuses on a given business or organization. System dynamics are typically defined as someone else's problem. So for your purpose to support the Green Swan agenda, it must embrace and promote the necessary systemic changes.

2. BUSINESS MODELS

If there is one change in business language that stands out for me in recent years, it is the shift from the use of the term *business case* (as in "what's the business case—not the moral case—for tackling ethical, social, and environmental issues?") to a growing interest in *business models*. To my mind, this signals a wider shift in the center of gravity of business thinking, from a defensive, show-us-why-we-should-do-this mind-set to a can-do, help-us-do-it approach.

But ask most people in business to draw their company's business model on the proverbial napkin and they struggle. One reason is that most people work for businesses founded by others, so the original design of the business model was done elsewhere. Another reason, perhaps, is that the weak business case for transformational change has been pretty much taken for granted by anyone who has chosen to be employed in the private sector, so there was little need to think about redesigning business models.

THE OLD STORY

A business model, according to the *Lexicon*, is "the method or means by which a company tries to capture value from its business. A business model may be based on many different aspects of a company, such as how it makes, distributes, prices or advertises its products."

More specifically, "the business model indicates how the firm will convert inputs (capital, raw materials, and labor) into outputs (total value of goods produced) and delivers a return to investors that is greater than the opportunity cost of capital. This means that a business model's success is reflected in its ability to create returns that are greater than the (opportunity) cost of capital, invested by its shareholders and bondholders."

Much of the recent interest in business models flows from California in general, and Silicon Valley in particular. One of the peculiarities of the thinking coming from such places has been that some of the business models that have been most successful often started out by burning cash for much longer than would once have seemed desirable or viable.

A prime case in point has been Amazon, where CEO Jeff Bezos has long argued that investing in future growth is much more important than hitting quarterly earnings targets, to the horror of many traditionalists on Wall Street. The obvious question is, If business models can be bent so far, apparently without breaking, how might tomorrow's breakthrough, and increasingly "future-fit," business models be designed, operated, and, crucially, sold to investors?

NEW STORIES

Tomorrow's business leaders understand that truly sustainable development is becoming a mainstream priority for a growing number of markets and, in the process, for an ever-extending list of companies. They sense that it is no longer just a matter of reputation and trust, but also of longer-term survival, security, and competitive advantage. Critically, too, it is about business model innovation. When we reviewed next-generation business models for the Business and Sustainable Development Commission,[19] we concluded that, as a minimum, leading-edge models now increasingly aim to achieve exponential progress in four key areas:

1. **Social:** They deliver both financial and extra-financial value[20] through positive impacts for people, in the present and in the future.

2. **Lean:** They optimize the use of all types of capital, from physical and financial through human and intellectual to social and natural forms.

3. **Integrated:** Increasingly, they are integrated, managing financial and extra-financial value creation across economic, social, and environmental systems.

4. **Circular:** And over time they must have the potential to become increasingly circular, sustaining inputs and outputs at their highest value in both technical and biological cycles.

BUSINESS MODELS WITH GREEN SWAN CHARACTERISTICS

If your purpose embraces system-wide change, then your business model, or models, must be designed to create value in ways that do not generate negative social and environmental problems for others. If they are to help drive Green Swan outcomes, then they must be designed with an eye toward the full impact spectrum and their potential for exponential scaling and replication.

3. PROFIT

The social responsibility of business, according to Milton Friedman, is to increase its profits. So with profits of some $5 billion a quarter, you would have thought that Facebook would be sitting pretty. But recent times have seen the social media company attacked from many directions. Indeed, late in 2018 *Wired* magazine listed Facebook CEO Mark Zuckerberg as one of the "Most Dangerous People on the Internet in 2018."[21] Zuckerberg appeared alongside people like Russian president Vladimir Putin and Min Aung Hlaing, head of Myanmar's (Burma's) armed forces.

The reason why Min Aung Hlaing made the list was that he had used social media to promote hate speech, inflaming the country's genocidal war against the Rohingya people. Myanmar's armed forces ran at least 425 Facebook pages, 17 Facebook groups, 135 Facebook accounts, and 15 Instagram accounts. An open-and-shut case of Black Swan thinking infiltrating social media, some might conclude. As *The New York Times* explained, Min Aung Hlaing's colleagues had "turned the social network into a tool for ethnic cleansing."[22] In effect, the same trick that Nazi propaganda minister Joseph Goebbels played with radio in the buildup to World War II. But there had been warnings well before this had happened, so perhaps this was a Gray Swan.

THE OLD STORY

The placebo button response from corporations here might be, "Most people are good and use our service as we intend it to be used. For any problems, consult the appropriate authorities." We can readily imagine a gun manufacturer using the same argument—an industry that has ridden out waves of mass shootings in the United States that seem unconscionable to many non-Americans, and most Americans, too.

Strip things back, however, and it is clear that the critical element in any company's calculation of its viability is the *bottom line*. This, notes the *Lexicon*, is "the last line of a profit and loss statement, after all income, costs, tax and other factors have been taken into account—normally the net profit or loss." But it goes on to note, "Business sustainability is often defined as managing the triple bottom line—a process by which companies manage their financial, social and environmental risks, obligations and opportunities. These three impacts are sometimes referred to as profits, people and planet." Well yes, though my original formulation of the idea was "People, Planet & Profit," putting the financial element firmly in third position.

NEW STORIES

My previous book, *The Breakthrough Challenge*, was co-authored with Jochen Zeitz, at the time chairman and CEO of the sportswear company PUMA.[23] Working with Trucost, they had pioneered in calculating an early Environmental Profit and Loss (EP&L) statement, which Zeitz saw as a stepping-stone to a full-blown triple bottom line accounting. PUMA's first EP&L report revealed that in the 2010 accounting year the total monetary impact of PUMA's direct and supply chain operations was valued at €145 million. This compared with net earnings of

€202.2 million. So if total costs had been taken into account, PUMA's profits would have been cut by around 70%.

The greatest negative impacts proved to be from the use of water and the generation of greenhouse gas emissions, at €47 million each. The conversion of land for agriculture for key raw materials such as leather, cotton, and rubber constituted the third-greatest impact at €37 million. Significantly, just 6% (€8 million) of the impacts arose in PUMA's own operations, with a further 9% (€13 million) caused by their direct (Tier 1) suppliers. This left an astonishing 85% of the impact outside of what could be considered areas in which the company has direct control or influence.[24]

As the world becomes more transparent, and however profitable their activities may be, will business leaders be able to turn blind eyes to such huge negative impacts? More importantly still, will they manage—alongside economists and accountants—to evolve our understanding of true value to the point where market pricing and other incentives reward not just the reduction of negative impacts but also the creation of a growing spectrum of positive impacts? Our performance against tomorrow's bottom and top lines will depend on the answer, as will the degree to which businesses, markets, cities, and countries can evolve and grow.

PROFITABILITY WITH GREEN SWAN CHARACTERISTICS

Even if its business model aligns tightly with an organization's purpose, it will only survive in the private sector if it is profitable. To pull this off in a future-fit way, a business's calculations of profitability must take into account the full range of negative (and positive) externalities and impacts created in the process.

4. GROWTH

There is a long-standing debate about the limits to growth, ranging from the 1972 report "The Limits to Growth"[25] to more recent work on planetary boundaries by the Stockholm Resilience Centre.[26] It is easy to counter-claim, a phrase often heard, that you can't make an omelet without breaking a few eggs, but what if the outcome involved the ultimate Black Swan, the cracking of the biosphere, the breaking of our planet?

THE OLD STORY

Governments and the financial markets remain obsessed with the economic growth rate and with GDP. That is understandable, given that GDP measures are deeply entrenched, and if the growth rate as measured in this way slows, or goes into reverse, the market and political consequences can be severe. But what are we really talking about here? Economic growth is fairly easy to define at one level. Indeed, the *Lexicon* does so as follows: "An increase in the value of goods and services produced in a country or area." By extension, the economic growth rate is "the annual rate of growth of the economy, normally measured by the change in gross national product (GNP) or gross domestic product (GDP)."

For several decades, the focus of activists was on potential limits to endless, exponential growth. Some experts—including Tim Jackson, with his book *Prosperity without Growth*[27]—have even argued for a "degrowth" strategy.[28] If the global population were declining—and business people were not needed on the journey—the idea might have attracted more attention than it has. But it isn't (yet) and they are, more than ever.

NEW STORIES

In recent years, as the global population has continued to explode, there has been a jump in interest in potential growth markets linked to various change agendas. The question increasingly asked is, How can we create multitrillion-dollar-per-year market opportunities by 2030? One answer: by meeting the United Nations' Sustainable Development Goals. These are a set of 17 ambitious goals and 169 related targets championed by the United Nations. In effect, the first crowd-sourced global market research study.

Encouragingly, experts conclude that meeting the goals in just four out of sixty sectors (the four are food and agriculture, cities, energy and materials, and health and well-being) could open up market opportunities worth up to $12 trillion a year by the early 2030s.[29]

To get there, however, we must break out of the zone of incremental change, what Volans has dubbed "change-as-usual." Incrementalism has its uses, of course, but it is worrying to see even committed business leaders treating the goals as an incremental change agenda. Their assumption: If we do more of what we have been doing, but a little bit faster and a little better, we can deliver many—if not most—of the goals by the target date of 2030. Mistake. Big mistake. Huge.[30]

Instead, a shift to a radically more future-fit economy demands exponential growth in the best-aligned sectors, while others shrink or are driven to extinction. Listen to Michael Liebreich, who over a decade ago came up with the idea of a Sustainable Energy Free Trade Area. That idea was torpedoed, but it is hard to disagree that what we need now is a huge dash of optimism and can-do thinking. His view: "Dramatic progress in low-carbon technologies over the past decade—energy efficiency, wind, solar, batteries, electric vehicles—suggest the vast bulk of [greenhouse] emissions from energy and transport can be eliminated over the coming few decades at modest or negative cost, even as modern energy services are cheaply brought to the last billion [unserved] people on the planet."[31] The ultimate Green Swan for energy, perhaps?

GROWTH WITH GREEN SWAN CHARACTERISTICS

The growth/no growth debate is misguided so long as it restricts itself to black-or-white thinking. We must learn to be (much) more discriminating. Yes, Black Swan growth takes us inexorably toward unpredictable disasters, but if we act too precipitately we create other crises. And ditto if we act too

continued

late. Green Swan growth is now urgently needed and will be for generations to come. We need exponentially less of the degenerative forms of capitalism and exponentially more of the increasingly resilient and regenerative forms.

5. VALUE

We have Oscar Wilde to thank for the idea that we may simultaneously know the "price of everything," yet understand "the value of nothing." The *Lexicon* defines value as "what something is worth—financially or otherwise." And it is that "otherwise" that we too often forget. Cracking this nut will be a critical factor in determining whether our economies, societies, and natural environment get through the present century in good order.

THE OLD STORY

There have been many experiments in accounting for "real" or "true" value. When I was learning to be a city planner, for example, we were encouraged to reflect on the value of a Norman church standing in the way of a planned motorway. How, we were asked, do you put a meaningful value on a thousand years of history and community life? On memories and cultural identity? Later, I also learned about the "existence value" some economists wanted to attach to major landscape features like the Grand Canyon. This experiment asked people who had never visited the Grand Canyon—and probably never would—to say how much they would pay to keep it in its natural state.

Other approaches have included fair value accounting, which seeks to capture changes in asset and liability values over time. The International Accounting Standards Board defines fair value as "an amount at which an asset could be exchanged between knowledgeable and willing parties in an arm's length transaction."

Assets and liabilities are re-measured periodically to reflect changes in their value, with the resulting change impacting either net income or other income for the period. The result is a balance sheet that better reflects the current value of assets and liabilities. The downside can be greater volatility in reported performance caused by changes in fair value.

NEW STORIES

A more recent approach is "shared value," originally pioneered by Nestlé as part of its "Creating Shared Value" initiative, and then developed and promoted by Michael Porter and Mark Kramer. As the *Lexicon* explains:

> Creating shared value (CSV) conveys the idea that a business must do two things simultaneously to be successful in the long term: *create* economic *value* for both the company and the society. The CSV definition of the role of business in society has emerged with a clear focus on long-term thinking and aligning the interests of shareholders and societies for mutual benefit. CSV carries the idea that in order to overcome the profound and harmful disconnect between the needs of society and business, a business must *create value* for society alongside *creating value* for shareholders in order to be successful in the long term.

All well and good, but I fought a polite, yearlong battle with Porter and Kramer inside Nestlé, where all three of us were involved in the Swiss food giant's Creating Shared Value Advisory Council. As we met each other in places like Colombia, Indonesia, and the Côte d'Ivoire, we debated whether shared value effectively trumped sustainability, as Porter argued, or whether shared value itself was just part of the wider quest for sustainable development.

A nano-victory, perhaps, but in the end Nestlé took my line, talking about shared value *and* sustainable development. My conclusion: The sort of win-win outcomes sought by shared value advocates are only part of the system change story—there will be many win-lose and even lose-lose outcomes, too. At a time when we are all encouraged to measure and report on our personal and organizational impact, I am not totally sure how best to measure the impact or value of that "and" in the Nestlé definition of its mission and purpose! Not a Green Swan—a great leap—but perhaps a small, useful step away from incremental thinking on how to tackle systemic challenges.

If we are to fully embrace the potential of tomorrow's Green Swan solutions, a central task will be to ensure that economics, the master discipline of capitalism, is fit for the twenty-first century. For those rare people who have yet to come across the work of Kate Raworth, she should be an early port of call,[32] alongside such post-Friedman economists as Mariana Mazzucato, Thomas Piketty, and Joe Stiglitz.

Early in 2019, I returned to my second alma mater, University College London (UCL), to debate Mazzucato[33] on how best to deliver innovation aligned with the sustainability agenda. To be honest, I felt something of a fraud, having given up economics partway through my first degree in 1968, because it seemed to have so little to say on the great issues of the day, at least as it was taught then.

Whatever the UCL debate organizers may have had in mind, Mazzucato and I ended up agreeing energetically. I had been asked to argue that the private sector is the key driver, she that the public sector is the key. On the day, we both rapidly concluded that truly sustainable and inclusive value and wealth can only be produced for the overwhelming majority of people if the private, public, and citizen sectors are all actively, creatively, and productively involved, and from the very outset.

Do make time to read her report to the European Commission, *Mission-Oriented Research and Innovation in the European Union*.[34] She argues for EU-wide missions to drive innovation-led, sustainable growth in such areas as climate change, cancer, obesity, and dementia care. Actual or potential Black Swans, all of them. She underscores the necessity of bold, inspirational, societally relevant, targeted, measurable, and time-bound missions that are cross-disciplinary and cross-sectoral, and promote bottom-up solutions. Sounds to me like the beginning of a more generic White Swan template for exponential evolution.

> ## VALUE WITH GREEN SWAN CHARACTERISTICS
>
> Both Black and Gray Swan calculations of value mislead because they largely discount the sort of impacts on value and valuations that will emerge in the longer term. Green Swan value may be equally hard to calculate, but becomes more likely where societies and their economies embrace a vision of, and targets for, positive transformation. And the likelihood is that discounting with Green Swan characteristics will be a real shock to many capitalists.

6. IMPACT

For businesspeople, not to be able to speak the language of impact these days is a bit like not being able to speak at least some form of English in business. Unfair, perhaps, at least in terms of the current predominance of English, but increasingly true of both. When I began work in the early 1970s, my focus on impact revolved around carrying out environmental impact assessments on major development projects in Egypt and Singapore. The spotlight was mainly on the negative impacts—bad things—including traffic congestion, pollution, explosion risks, and the loss of natural habitats. How things have evolved since then.

THE OLD STORY

Use the word *impact* today and many people will assume that you are talking about positive impacts, good things. So the main focus is on how you can "replicate" and "scale" the processes that produce them. Working with Swiss pharmaceutical giant Novartis, for example, we have been involved in efforts to quantify and value impacts across the triple bottom line agenda. Here's how the company described that work in its 2018 *Novartis in Society* report:[35]

The Novartis financial, environmental and social (FES) impact valuation is our approach to measuring the social and environmental impact our business activities have on society, in addition to our economic value. We first developed, tested and applied our methodology in 2016.

Since then, we have further developed the approach, significantly expanding the scope. In 2017, this approach showed that our activities contributed USD 84 billion to the global gross domestic product (GDP), as well as an estimated 830,000 jobs beyond those held by our own employees. In addition, our human capital impact—including employee development, occupational safety and living wages—was valued at USD 7.0 billion, with USD 6.6 billion coming from the social impact of living wages in our own operations and the entire supply chain, and USD 0.4 billion coming from employee development and occupational safety. At the same time, we are taking steps to minimize our negative environmental impact, as measured by the carbon, other air emissions, water and waste impacts of our own operations and supply chain, which were valued at USD 4.7 billion. For the first time in 2017, we calculated the social impact of a large part of our Innovative Medicines portfolio in 29 countries, amounting to USD 72 billion.

In the same report, I explained why this work was important:

There is growing market awareness that impact valuation—the quantifying of impacts in monetary terms—can bring key social and environmental value into the equation. Challenges once seen as peripheral are becoming financially "material"—a trend illustrated by BlackRock CEO Larry Fink's call in 2018 for urgent progress in this area [. . .] The work Novartis is doing in the space goes beyond what most companies aspire to. In addition to publishing data on its impacts, both positive and negative, Novartis is openly sharing its evolving impact valuation methodology through detailed case studies. That's a huge boost for the entire field.

But the biggest story of all in this space has been that of the rise of *impact investing*. As the *Lexicon* puts it, "The term 'impact investing' is used informally by many in the investment community but there is increasing demand from investors to develop a global standard as set out by the Global Impact Investing Network, or GIIN. Impact investing is generally accepted to describe investing that intentionally seeks *measurable* social and environmental benefits. It differs from socially responsible investing which traditionally avoids investments that are inconsistent with the values of the investors, such as tobacco and arms, or investments that might be associated with poor labor rights."

NEW STORIES

Even so, many of those who attended the annual summit of the Global Steering Group for Impact Investing in Delhi during 2018 must have been stunned to hear the language used by former-refugee-turned-multimillionaire investor Sir Ronald Cohen. "Comrades," he began, albeit with tongue firmly in cheek, "it's clear that capitalism in its present form has fundamental flaws. It's not delivering on its promise to share prosperity and to bring social progress for all."[36]

Then his language became even more provocative. "We have persisted through many crises with the view that the system can be tinkered with," he said. "But we have now reached the stage where the scale of these challenges is so daunting that even the most skeptical are saying that something must be done. Nothing less than a revolution will enable us to achieve solutions at a scale that can improve billions of lives and our planet." A head-on assault on Black Swan capitalism and, at least by implication, Black Swan democracy.

One way I have tried to get a grip on all of this over the years is to think of the 2 x 2 matrix shown on page 35, with the horizontal (x) axis running from negative impact on the left to positive impact on the right. Then the vertical (y) axis runs from incremental change at the bottom to increasing magnitudes of exponential change at the top.

As we have seen, Carl Page of the Anthropocene Institute worries about one billion or more people dying or disadvantaged by pandemics, nuclear exchanges, or asteroid strikes. Potential Black Swans, all of them. His younger brother Larry, meanwhile, has talked in terms of improving the well-being of up to a billion people through the use of radical new technologies. Potentially Green Swan territory. As cofounder and former CEO of Google, you might think that he knows of what he speaks.

IMPACT WITH GREEN SWAN CHARACTERISTICS

We are getting better at measuring and valuing the negative impacts created by our businesses, markets, and economies. But we still struggle to master the task of predicting and valuing the positive impacts associated with Green Swan trajectories. This is a core challenge, among others, for the rapidly expanding impact investment sector. It also now needs to push even more forcefully into the investment mainstream. Currently worth around $500 billion, impact investment could reach over $25 trillion if it mainstreams properly.[37]

7. LIABILITY

Oh, to be a lawyer. Liability comes in an almost infinite array of forms, all of them potential sources of sumptuous legal fees. But groups such as Client Earth are paving the way for very different liability regimes by suing on behalf of the planet and those most dependent on its health.[38] What might happen, for example, if the fossil fuels industry were to be taken to court en masse for the untold damage it has helped cause to the climate?[39]

Like the tobacco industry before it, the fossil fuel industry might argue that it had no clue as to the scale of the devastation it was causing, but the facts prove otherwise. Intriguingly, Exxon's climate scientists accurately predicted as long ago as 1982 that the atmospheric content of carbon dioxide would rise to over five hundred parts per million, driving temperatures up by more than two degrees.[40] Thirty-seven years later, more or less exactly on the track sketched by the old company's "high case" scenario, we hit 415 ppm. As *Scientific American* explained at the time:

> Another climate milestone soared by last weekend when scientists announced that atmospheric carbon dioxide levels hit 415 parts per million for the first time ever (*Climatewire*, May 7). It's the latest in a long list of broken records, and like the others, it promises to hold the title temporarily. Atmospheric CO2 is rising at accelerating rates—currently climbing at close to 3 ppm each year, and getting faster. Every year, the world sees new levels that were previously unrecorded in modern human history. The last time CO2 concentrations hit 415 ppm was likely close to 3 million years ago.[41]

Even if we were able to turn off the tap today, the impacts would continue building for quite some time. *Scientific American* again:

> Even if humans stopped emitting all carbon today, it would still take decades or even centuries for global temperatures to stabilize, and perhaps between 1,000 and 2,000 years for the climate system as a whole—including the response of the world's ice sheets, sea levels, ecosystems and so on—to reach a point of equilibrium.

THE OLD STORY

Scrolling through the *Lexicon*, you find that key forms of liability include *product liability*, when the maker of a product is responsible for any damage or injury that the product causes; *criminal liability*, when there is responsibility for injury or damage that is serious enough to be covered by criminal law; *civil liability*, "when responsibility for injury or damage is not serious enough to be covered by criminal law"; and *joint and several liability*, "when a number of parties make a joint commitment under a contract and agree to be liable as a group as well as individually (jointly and severally) for that obligation to be fulfilled."

That is just the beginning. Such threats to their bottom lines and futures are why businesses are often formed as *limited liability* companies. Also, why businesses often resort to increasingly sophisticated liability insurance to cover any claims that might be imposed on them for damage or injury caused by negligence.

A typical placebo button response here would be, "Our lawyers haven't raised the issue, so we think we'd better let sleeping dogs lie." If you want to watch this story playing out in real time, keep an eye on what is happening to major peat, coal, and oil companies.

NEW STORIES

Many years ago, I was bawled at by then Exxon CEO Rex Tillerson over the heads of several hundred baffled Norwegian fossil fuel professionals at an event in Stavanger. I was speaking from the stage about Exxon's deliberate disruption of the climate debate when Tillerson strode into the room with his entourage. "That's a goddamn lie!" he yelled from the back of the room. In the end, we reached an armed truce as he took his seat in the auditorium and I went on.

How interesting then, years later, to see New York filing a lawsuit against ExxonMobil, alleging that the company had deceived investors for years by deliberately downplaying the climate risks to its business and long-term financial health.[42] The lawsuit, filed by Attorney General

Barbara Underwood, was the culmination of a multiyear investigation into Exxon's actions and communications about climate change. The suit alleged, "This fraud reached the highest levels of the company to include former chief executive Rex Tillerson, who left the company in 2017 to become President Trump's first Secretary of State."

Underwood continued, "Investors put their money and their trust in Exxon, which assured them of the long-term value of their shares, as the company claimed to be factoring the risk of increasing climate change regulation into its business decisions." "Instead," she concluded, "Exxon built a facade to deceive investors into believing that the company was managing the risks of climate change regulation to its business when, in fact, it was intentionally and systematically underestimating or ignoring them, contrary to its public representations."

In the end, ExxonMobil won this round, but as the climate continues to warm, expect the legal challenges to accelerate, and the financial claims against Big Oil and other climate-destabilizing industries to build—indeed, to go exponential. One area that can only become more contentious is the growth in state subsidies for the fossil fuels industry. The world spent an appalling $4.7 trillion on fossil fuel subsidies in 2015, for example, which grew to $5.2 trillion in 2017.[43] China was "by far, the largest subsidizer" in 2015 at $1.4 trillion, with the United States spending more on such subsidies than it did on its bloated Pentagon budget. Clearly, there are many future dramas to be made featuring Black Swan CEOs and investors ending up in the dock.

But until they are blocked from doing so, many incumbent industries and businesses whose futures are threatened will continue to resort to what Alex Steffen has called "predatory delay." As he describes the process, predatory delay involves "the blocking or slowing of needed change, in order to make money off unsustainable, unjust systems in the meantime." This is not delay resulting from the absence of action, but delay as a plan of action—a way of "keeping things the way they are for the people who are benefiting now, at the expense of the next and future generations."[44]

LIABILITY WITH GREEN SWAN CHARACTERISTICS

The use of legal liability regimes to drive divestment from sectors of the economy that are pushing us toward Black or Gray Swan outcomes will grow, inspired by the work of initiatives like Client Earth. Think of Bayer, which acquired Monsanto for $63 billion, only to find itself facing some 13,000 lawsuits in relation to the health impacts of Monsanto's Roundup herbicide. Just one of those ended in a payment of $2 billion to an elderly couple suffering from non-Hodgkin's lymphoma after years of exposure to Roundup.[45] Fossil fuel companies are also under increasing legal pressure because of the costs of climate change.[46] There will also be liability claims as Green Swan trajectories elbow aside incumbent industries, going both ways. We must work out how to protect Green Swan pioneers from such claims, particularly when they are brought to slow down progress, to cause "predatory delay."[47]

8. MATERIALITY

If everything is significant, they say, then nothing is. So how can business leaders get a grip on the issues that should be prioritized—and those that can be tackled later? One answer is to use a "materiality matrix." The concept of materiality is something that has been clicked on and dragged across from the world of accounting and auditing.

There it implies that certain things are more important than others, at least financially. So, for example, mistakes in minor expenses may be immaterial as far as the general health of the business is concerned, while others—like the misvaluation of an acquisition target like Autonomy by an acquirer like HP—can have multibillion-dollar consequences.

THE OLD STORY

When materiality matrixes (or is it matrices?) first started appearing in corporate nonfinancial or sustainability reports, they were a welcome relief from all the verbiage that had once clogged these publications.

Once again, a typical materiality matrix plots issues in two dimensions. First, there is the importance or attractiveness of a given issue to external stakeholders. Second, there is the issue's importance to the company in terms of the likely impact on financial considerations like profitability and valuations.

The *Lexicon* illustrates this by referring to Allianz, the insurance company. Like a growing number of companies, Allianz analyzes megatrends internally and carries out regular stakeholder surveys to create its annual matrix. In 2010, for example, climate change and employee satisfaction emerged as priority issues both for Allianz and its stakeholders, while issues such as "social disparities" are thought to be of much less concern to the company and its stakeholders.

With populism having run riot in recent years, one wonders how accurate some of these materiality assessments really are now.

NEW STORIES

As we step from one paradigm and linked market reality, where Black Swans have been an occupational hazard, to another, increasingly designed to promote Green Swan dynamics, our interpretations of impact, value, materiality, and liability must evolve rapidly. Keeping up with the emerging trends will tax leaders in both the private and public sectors up to—and often beyond—the limit. Risk analysts and accountants, in particular, have a ferociously steep learning curve to climb.

MATERIALITY WITH GREEN SWAN CHARACTERISTICS

Materiality looks very different in the Black and Green Swan scenarios. In the first, the Brazilian mining company Vale did materiality assessments that failed to prioritize the sort of risks that produced the Mariana tailings dam collapse in 2015.[48] Nineteen people died. Vale explicitly studied the concept of Black Swans following that tragedy, presumably concluding that because they considered the collapse some sort of Black Swan, it

continued

was not their fault that it was not predicted. It is hard to imagine the sort of gyrations in their thinking in 2019 when the collapse of their Brumadinho tailings dam drowned nearly 300 people in toxic sludge. Just because such companies talk knowledgeably about materiality does not mean they understand the risks to their business and the wider world. By contrast, Green Swan materiality assessments must take into account any opportunities for exponential upsides.

9. GOVERNANCE

Shortly after the turn of the century, on the top floor of the Ford global headquarters in Dearborn, Michigan, I was taken to task by a well-known corporate lawyer. He was a man of a certain age, with white curly hair and sporting a colorful bowtie. His beef was that "people like you" imagine that issues like climate change, human rights, and the like are part of the corporate governance agenda, he told me. Not so, he insisted.

THE OLD STORY

Well maybe not then, or not with that particular lawyer and his particular practice. But my understanding then was—and still is—that corporate governance is, to quote the *Lexicon*, "the way a company is managed at the highest level." In effect by the people who occupied the top floor we found ourselves on that day. If such people ignore new types of risk, whatever their logic, they potentially betray their key stakeholders, including their shareholders. Even Milton Friedman might have balked at that.

NEW STORIES

Today the situation has changed very significantly, in the wake of numerous major reviews of the ethical, social, and environmental aspects of corporate governance, including the Cadbury Code, launched in

Britain in 1992. As a result, issues once seen as peripheral have stormed their way into boardrooms and C-suites.

As I was drafting this section, the globetrotting Carlos Ghosn, still (just) chairman of Renault, Nissan, and Mitsubishi, was languishing in a Japanese prison, accused of various financial misdemeanors.[49] By the time the book was finished, Ghosn had escaped Japan. Whatever the final outcome, his ongoing adventures—and misadventures—underscore how the governance agenda is both intensifying and expanding.

Having spent an afternoon in the Nissan boardroom in Tokyo years ago, I wondered how much the nature of the discussions in that exalted space had changed over time—particularly in the wake of Ghosn's arrest. I would love to have been a fly on the wall of the ExxonMobil boardroom, for example, when news broke of the New York lawsuit against the company. After such events it is easy to ask, "Really, what were they thinking?"

GOVERNANCE WITH GREEN SWAN CHARACTERISTICS

Many boards now recruit risk specialists and others who can help them try to predict future Gray and even Black Swans. But very few manage to pull in people who can help them think through potential Green Swan dynamics that could revolutionize their mind-sets, business models, and markets. One approach more innovative organizations are now taking is to expose their leadership teams to emerging and potentially exponential opportunities through participation in courses offered by the likes of Singularity University[50] or the learning journeys offered by the likes of Leaders' Quest.[51] If your top team has yet to dip its toes into exponential waters, maybe it is time to give it a go.

10. STRANDED ASSETS

Some of the most important work in the world is done, and some of the most important new business concepts and language are introduced by, not-for-profit organizations. One of my favorites has been the Carbon Tracker Initiative. Among other things, they repurposed the concept of *stranded assets* to get people thinking about the structural implications of global warming for our economies and for particular industry sectors and companies.

Such market activism is likely to transform company and industry sector valuations in the coming decade, with huge implications for business leaders, investors, and those whose careers, tax revenues, or pensions are increasingly at risk.

THE OLD STORY

Intriguingly, the online *Lexicon*, at least when consulted, failed to offer an entry for the term. Instead, having defined an asset as "something belonging to an individual or a business that has value or the power to earn money," it went on to distinguish between *tangible assets*, "that have physical form, such as plant and equipment," and *intangible assets*, which "have no physical form but are considered valuable resources of the business, e.g. patents, trademarks, goodwill, brand names, licenses, franchises, etc."

It did, however, mention *wasting assets*, "such as property or a business, that is losing money over time," and *toxic assets*, "the value of which has fallen significantly and may fall further, especially as the market for them has frozen. This may be due to hidden risks within the assets becoming visible or due to changes in the external market environment, or both."

Many of the problems experienced by major banks in the financial crisis of 2007–2008 were due to such toxic assets, including "securitizations of subprime mortgages, where the original creators of the securities failed to take into account the real rate of mortgage default and the extent to which it would be contagious across securities."[52] Assets previously rated as AAA "suddenly looked like junk bonds and were worth a fraction of their previous value, if indeed it was possible to find a price at all in a market where no one wanted to buy them."

NEW STORIES

The stranding of an asset can have regulatory causes, due to changes in legislation; economic causes, due to relative shifts in costs and prices; and physical causes, due to distance or environmental factors like drought or flooding.[53] The race to tackle the climate emergency, when it really gets going, will strand flotillas, indeed entire armadas of once-valuable assets. Governments may struggle to keep global warming within a two-degree ceiling, but the idea of a global carbon budget is likely to stick—with huge implications for climate-intensive industries.

Mark Carney, the Bank of England governor who chaired the Financial Stability Board Task Force, warned that a carbon budget consistent with a 2°C target "would render the vast majority of [fossil fuel] reserves 'stranded'—oil, gas and coal that will be literally unburnable without expensive carbon capture technology, which itself alters fossil fuel economics."[54]

A future, then, bustling with potential Gray—and even Black—Swans. But that will mean plenty of incentives to develop the next generation of Green Swans, which from today's viewpoint would still look like market miracles.

ASSETS WITH GREEN SWAN CHARACTERISTICS

Black and Gray Swan trajectories boost the risk of assets becoming stranded, including many of those spotlighted in Part I of this book. Green Swan trajectories will strand unsustainable assets, too, but they will also "float," or refloat, other types of assets, affording them radically new valuations. Such considerations are now surfacing in boardrooms and top team sessions in both the private and public sectors. There are a number of ways in which we can tilt tomorrow's capitalism, democracy, sustainability agenda, and market dynamics toward Green Swan outcomes. In the process, the evolution in the business lexicon is likely to go into overdrive. Literally, watch this space.

PART I

THE BLACK SWAN BLUES

An Age of Consequences

CHAPTER 2

A WICKED WORLD

Bad Exponentials

Green Swans are like Black Swans in the sense that they often evolve gradually, then suddenly.[1] Throughout human history people have failed to see or understand potentially existential threats—and the same is true of the sort of market and societal opportunities that Green Swan dynamics bring.[2] Given that Green Swans often emerge in response to Black or Gray Swan threats, however, we will explore the world of bad exponentials before asking how good exponentials are best created and harnessed.

Some bad exponentials threaten to take us in directions so dire that they need new language to describe them. The first time I recall hearing the phrase "wicked problem" was around the turn of the century, when we were working with the Ford Motor Company in Dearborn, Michigan. A third-generation Ford employee, Dave Berdish, used the words in a meeting. Although I have long considered him a friend, my initial reaction was to wince. The term seemed self-conscious, as if trying too hard to be noticed.

Yet the deeper we dug into the giant auto company's challenges, the more relevant the phrase seemed. Bill Ford, our ultimate client, once summed it up for me. He reflected that the tobacco industry had known for decades that smoking caused health problems, including cancer. But it had covered up the bad news to defend its so-called sunk capital. Or, to use today's terminology, to protect assets that risked becoming stranded when market expectations and demand began to shift.

So when the lawyers and judges eventually came after the Big Tobacco companies, as Bill noted, they had a field day—levying fines totaling hundreds of billions of dollars. With a deep family and personal involvement in Ford, Bill had a much longer-term perspective than most CEOs I had worked with to that point. He was genuinely concerned that the auto industry risked going down the same road as Big Tobacco. That it was conjuring Black Swans without planning to do so, or even being particularly conscious of what it was doing in that regard.

Here, again, the industry had long known that emissions from its vehicles' tail pipes contributed to a range of problems. These included childhood asthma, lung disease, damage to property and plants, and— the really big one—climate breakdown. How long would it be, Bill wondered, before the lawyers came after Ford and the rest of the auto industry? He hazarded a guess that it might be between fifteen and twenty years.

The court cases began just a few years after we had that conversation. The process continues today. While I was sketching this chapter, former California governor Arnold Schwarzenegger disclosed that he was in talks with private law firms to help bring a major lawsuit against Big Oil.[3] He argued that oil companies were "knowingly killing people all over the world" by helping trigger and exacerbate global warming. He even went so far as to claim that by contributing to impending "climate chaos," oil company CEOs were guilty of first-degree murder. Dramatic language, certainly, but many would see it as justified by the fast-developing climate emergency.

Perhaps equally alarming for the oil majors, Schwarzenegger also insisted that any product produced or processed using fossil fuels, which these days is pretty much everything we buy, should have a warning label on it. (A WCKD tag, perhaps, an idea we explore in the next chapter.)

He explained the logic as follows. "Because to me it's absolutely irresponsible to know that your product is killing people and not have a warning label on it, like tobacco," he offered. "Every gas station [should have a warning label], every car should have a warning label on it, every product that has fossil fuels should have a warning label on it." Clearly, the tide is changing. As I look back, it is now clear that Ford knew it was already enmeshed in challenges that fully merited the label "wicked."

People then wanted—and many still want—cars and trucks. Increasingly, too, they wanted bigger cars, many based on truck designs and chassis. Indeed, the demand for so-called sport utility vehicles, better known as SUVs, seemed to have no limit. Investors insisted Ford sell more and more of ever-bigger SUVs. Why? Well again the logic was simple: Companies like Ford made far greater profits on gas-guzzling SUVs than they did on more fuel-efficient compact models. So we saw a worsening industry and consumer lock-in to forms of automobility that appeared to guarantee future climate-induced societal collapse.

Then along came Elon Musk. The breakthrough success of his firm, Tesla, helped reboot the prevailing industry mind-set, turning electric vehicles from an apparent impossibility into a virtual inevitability. While there have been many criticisms of Musk's personality and business approach,[4] the market shock waves caused by his work continue to spread. As I write, more electric charging points are being installed around the area where I live in London. Truly, Musk has been an entrepreneur with Green Swan characteristics.

Still, though complicated, the auto industry's problems are hardly the wickedest to be found in this increasingly complex, interlinked, and challenging world of ours. To get a better sense of which challenges might merit the term, we will now consider the nature of wicked problems.

GRADUALLY, THEN SUDDENLY

Few people understand the technology-driven future, and communicate about it, better than Tim O'Reilly, founder of the eponymous

O'Reilly Media. He has identified a key characteristic of the world we are moving into: Things that seem to move slowly have a tendency to accelerate in unexpected ways. He explained this unsettling reality by referring back to Ernest Hemingway's novel *The Sun Also Rises*.

In the book, a character named Mike is asked how he went bankrupt. "Two ways," he answered. "Gradually, then suddenly." O'Reilly noted, "Technological change happens in much the same way. Small changes accumulate, and suddenly the world is a different place."[5] He recalled that he had tracked and helped foster a bunch of "gradually, then suddenly" transitions, including "the World Wide Web, open source software, big data, cloud computing, sensors and ubiquitous computing, and now the pervasive effects of AI and algorithmic systems on society and the economy."

So what are some of the things that O'Reilly sees as in the midst of "gradually, then suddenly" transitions today? His analysis signals crucial shifts in the realities that leaders in every sector will need to respond to. They include the following:

- The rapid spread of artificial intelligence and algorithms is heralding new relationships between man and machine, spurred by neural interfaces used to augment our ability to control machines—with a huge impact on education via online learning.

- The rest of the world is leapfrogging the United States because emerging economies are not locked in by obsolete infrastructures and technologies.

- As a result, China will do to the United States what the United States did to Britain, taking over as the world's dominant superpower.

- Africa,[6] accelerated by incoming Chinese investment, will emerge as the "next factory of the world."

- Agriculture will be transformed by new technologies, business models, and diets.

- Climate chaos will rush headlong toward its own "suddenly" moment.

- The undermining of government in the United States and elsewhere could not be coming at a worse moment, given the role of the public sector in such key sectors as education, innovation, infrastructure, and the provision of social safety nets.

Interestingly, the tenth and final theme that O'Reilly flagged was the need to reinvent the discipline of economics, the master discipline of capitalism. Among the books he had been reading were Kate Raworth's *Doughnut Economics*, Mariana Mazzucato's *The Value of Everything*, and Russ Roberts's *How Adam Smith Can Change Your Life*.

Just in case his readers thought that the last book was another hymnal to Smith's "invisible hand," O'Reilly underscored the fact that the main point of reference in the book was not Smith's 1776 book, *The Wealth of Nations*, but *The Theory of Moral Sentiments*, which Smith had published seventeen years earlier. The key argument in that work was that social norms play a crucial role in reining in self-interest.

Growing concerns about the nature and excesses of increasingly untrammeled capitalism would be troubling enough in ordinary times, but these are extraordinary times. The Anthropocene epoch, coupled with burgeoning human populations, particularly in Africa, will trigger a growing number of "gradually, then suddenly" breaches and cascades in what we take for granted as normality. Central to those dynamics will be new types of wicked and even super wicked problems. They are the nuclei around which tomorrow's Black Swans are already evolving.

SO, WHAT IS A WICKED PROBLEM?

Answering this question is central to everything that follows. But finding an answer is not easy. Still, there are clues to how such problems can be spotted and addressed. One of the most interesting articles I have read on the subject appeared in the *Harvard Business Review* back in 2008—as the global financial crash threatened to trigger a new economic depression.

"Wicked problems often crop up when organizations have to face constant change or unprecedented challenges," concluded the article's author, John Camillus, the Donald R. Beall professor of strategic management at the University of Pittsburgh's Joseph M. Katz Graduate School of Business.[7] So, you might conclude, they crop up in times very much like our own.

Camillus then filled in some of the details. Such problems, he explained, "occur in a social context; the greater the disagreement among stakeholders, the more wicked the problem. In fact, it's the social complexity of wicked problems as much as their technical difficulties that make them tough to manage. Not all problems are wicked; confusion, discord, and lack of progress are telltale signs that an issue might be wicked." Fine, but where did the term first originate—and what was it meant to imply?

The first thing to recognize, Camillus continued, was that "wicked issues are different because traditional processes can't resolve them." This point had been central to the argument made back in 1973 by Horst W. J. Rittel and Melvin M. Webber, professors of design and urban planning at the University of California at Berkeley.

"A wicked problem has innumerable causes, is tough to describe, and doesn't have a right answer," as Camillus summed up. "Environmental degradation, terrorism, and poverty—these are classic examples of wicked problems. They're the opposite of hard but ordinary problems, which people can solve in a finite time period by applying standard techniques. Not only do conventional processes fail to tackle wicked problems, but they may exacerbate situations by generating undesirable consequences."

Rittel subsequently spotlighted no less than ten characteristics that he considered central to a problem's "wickedness."[8] Here they are, with my own commentary to link each characteristic with the main argument of *Green Swans*:[9]

1. **Wicked problems have no definitive formulation**

   "The problem of poverty in Texas is grossly similar but discretely different from poverty in Nairobi," Rittel noted. "So no practical characteristics describe 'poverty.'"

   Alternatively, think of the different ways in which people from different world regions see climate change. Even though it is one of the countries most likely to be hit by climate-induced societal collapse,[10] India has long insisted that it is its right to burn fossil fuels to tackle the needs of its immense population—arguing that America should lead the way in squeezing carbon out of the economy, and then share the resulting clean technologies to compensate for the damage American growth has already caused.

2. **It's hard, perhaps impossible, to measure or claim success with wicked problems because they bleed into one another**

   This is very different from traditional problems, Rittel noted, which can usually be articulated or defined. Sticking with climate breakdown, it is clear that there are hugely complex linkages between global warming and other challenges such as water security, human migrations, ocean acidification, the bleaching of coral reefs, and the spread of tropical diseases like malaria to former temperate zones.

3. **Solutions to wicked problems can be only good or bad, not true or false**

   Since there is no idealized end state to arrive at, we are told, approaches to wicked problems should try to *improve* a situation rather than solve it. Maybe that is why a number of leading countries have published sustainable development strategies and visions over the years, but most have later quietly let them drop. Trying to imagine the world in 2030 or 2050 is tough, let alone when you are trying to factor in ways of controlling climate breakdown. But that does not mean we should give up—indeed the very opposite is true.

4. There is no template to follow when tackling a wicked problem, although history may provide a guide

Teams that approach wicked problems must literally make things up as they go, Rittel argued. This is why organizations like Tesla, the XPRIZE Foundation, Singularity University, and Google's X facility are so intriguing today. Unlike giant incumbent companies, they start with a relatively clean slate—and, crucially, have no reason yet to fear cannibalizing their existing businesses or agendas.

5. There is always more than one explanation for a wicked problem

If you take a challenge like extreme poverty, the explanations that will be offered may include regional differences in the availability of natural resources, the health of those resources, the effectiveness of national and local governance systems, the prevalence of bribery and corruption, and so on. Such multiple explanations not only confuse, but they may also provide a ready alibi for inaction for those already inclined to do little or nothing.

6. Every wicked problem is a symptom of another problem

What do you do in a situation where everything furiously links to everything else? Where trying to solve one problem creates others? Rittel observed, "The interconnected quality of socio-economic political systems illustrates how, for example, a change in education will cause new behavior in nutrition."

7. No mitigation strategy for a wicked problem has a definitive scientific test

Humans invented wicked problems—and science, Rittel argued, exists to understand natural phenomena. Some social scientists would dispute this point, with many characteristics of wicked problems clearly economic, social, and political—and therefore eminently suitable subjects for scientific scrutiny. But this part of the challenge has been aggravated by the growing willingness of populist politicians to ignore science when its conclusions and recommendations are uncomfortable. Witness President Trump's surprisingly successful efforts to defang the US Environmental Protection Agency.

8. Offering a "solution" to a wicked problem frequently is a "one shot" effort

A significant effort to tackle a wicked problem can sometimes affect the ability of innovators elsewhere in the system to learn from trial and error. On the other hand, the nature and scale of the systemic challenges we now face dictate that we try multiple experiments at the same time—given that no single "black box" solution yet exists.

9. Every wicked problem is unique

Each of these challenges is by its very nature unique, in the sense that our species has never had to accept responsibility for dealing with it before. This is as true of the issue of plastics in the ocean as it is for the global obesity pandemic, growing antibiotic resistance among disease agents, or the clogging of space with debris from past launches and other events.

10. Those trying to address wicked problems must be fully responsible for their actions

Intentionally or not, this tenth characteristic provides a bridge to four elements of an even more complex form of wicked headache, "super wicked" problems. These were subsequently identified during efforts to get a grip on the climate emergency.

NEXT, SUPER WICKED PROBLEMS

As I dug deeper into the field of wicked problems, I stumbled across a special class of such challenges, so-called super wicked problems. In a 2007 conference paper, Kelly Levin, Benjamin Cashore, Graeme Auld, and Steven Bernstein distinguished between wicked and super wicked problems. Considering what they saw as the clearly super wicked case of climate change, they defined such problems as having four additional characteristics:[11]

1. **Time is running out**

   The shift of many of our most urgent problems onto exponential—even super exponential—trajectories is radically shrinking the timescales in which we must act.

2. **There is no central authority**

   A range of international institutions, many of them established in the wake of the Second World War, are officially chartered to deal with selected wicked problems. The real problem is that there is no *effective* central authority to deal with such problems. As we have seen, too many actors have a vested interest in stalling or subverting timely collective action.

3. **Those seeking to solve the problem are also causing it**

   The combination of globalization, hyper-capitalism, and rampant consumerism means that anyone reading this book will likely be a significant contributor to many or most of the problems some of them are trying to solve. Me too. Problematically, and inescapably, we are part of the system we are trying to change. I recall a line flashing unbidden into my mind back in the 1970s: "The harder we work, the closer we are to buying ourselves out of the system we are in the process of creating."

4. **Current policies discount the future irrationally**

   Ultimately, this is the beating heart of the matter. Behind our policies lie not just our politics and priorities but also the immense power of the so-called invisible hand of economics and the discipline of discounting the future. The need to reimagine and reinvent Adam Smith's "dismal science" is now clear to a growing number of economists—but they, too, are trapped (for example, by the dynamics of academic tenure) in a system that many see as dangerously dysfunctional.

There is another thing we should remember, or perhaps learn, about wicked problems: While their number and intensity can go up and down, there are periods when they proliferate like rabbits. Our current century, it is increasingly clear, is one of those periods. A key reason for that is that we are moving into an unprecedented, exponentially charged era in Earth's evolution.

WELCOME TO THE ANTHROPOCENE

One thing to know about the Anthropocene epoch is that we are likely to be in it for as long as human numbers are measured in the billions. As our population numbers push up against the capacity of our planet to nurture us and absorb the damage we inflict upon it, the potential for wicked problems, for Gray and Black Swans, goes off the scale.

Like many baby boomers, I was born (just) in the earlier Holocene geological epoch, at least as the boundaries are currently understood, with the Anthropocene considered to have started in 1950. By geological standards, the Holocene is—or as many scientists now argue was—remarkably young. While most epochs last for millions of years, the Holocene (or "Recent") epoch started some 11,500 years ago, when the glaciers began to retreat. As the ice went, so the forests expanded. Then, not long afterward, they began to retreat again as humankind's appetite for timber and agricultural land exploded.

Science is catching up with this reality. Indeed, probably the single most interesting issue of *The Economist* I recall reading appeared on May 26, 2011.[12] Early on, it noted the following:

> In 2000 Paul Crutzen, an eminent atmospheric chemist, realized he no longer believed he was living in the Holocene. He was living in some other age, one shaped primarily by people. From their trawlers scraping the floors of the seas to their dams impounding sediment by the gigatonne, from their stripping of forests to their irrigation of farms, from their mile-deep mines to their melting of glaciers, humans

were bringing about an age of planetary change. With a colleague, Eugene Stoermer, Dr Crutzen suggested this age be called the Anthropocene—"the recent age of man."

Many people still find it unimaginable that we mere humans could be influencing something as big as our planet. But we are. "The Earth is a big thing," *The Economist* observed. If you divided it up evenly among its 7 billion inhabitants, "they would get almost 1 trillion tonnes each. To think that the workings of so vast an entity could be lastingly changed by a species that has been scampering across its surface for less than 1 percent of 1 percent of its history seems, on the face of it, absurd. But it is not. Humans have become a force of nature reshaping the planet on a geological scale—but at a far-faster-than-geological speed."

Here is an extraordinary fact: You know, of course, that one way we can tell what eon or epoch a given geological layer dates back to is by the fossils it contains. Many of us have watched with wonder as scientists retrieved the fossilized remains of dinosaurs and other long-gone animals from their rocky surroundings. Now imagine this: We live in a period of geological time identifiable by the fossils not just of individual—or groups of—animals but of *entire cities*. *The Economist* again:

> The most common way of distinguishing periods of geological time is by means of the fossils they contain. On this basis picking out the Anthropocene in the rocks of days to come will be pretty easy. Cities will make particularly distinctive fossils. A city on a fast-sinking river delta (and fast-sinking deltas, undermined by the pumping of groundwater and starved of sediment by dams upstream, are common Anthropocene environments) could spend millions of years buried and still, when eventually uncovered, reveal through its crushed structures and weird mixtures of materials that it is unlike anything else in the geological record.

Some scientists are still debating whether we should talk in terms of the Anthropocene, but the signs increasingly suggest that this is the term that future scientists will use. If they do, it is very likely to be dated back to 1950, despite efforts to move the date back to the 1600s.

Finally, *The Economist* moved from a discussion of how the dawn of the Anthropocene could herald a fundamental rebooting of our entire climate system, in ways that would spell the end of civilization as we know it, to a rather more positive framing:

> Better to embrace the Anthropocene's potential as a revolution in the way the Earth system works [. . .] than to try to retreat onto a low-impact path that runs the risk of global immiseration.
>
> Such a choice is possible because of the most fundamental change in Earth history that the Anthropocene marks: the emergence of a form of intelligence that allows new ways of being to be imagined and, through co-operation and innovation, to be achieved. The lessons of science, from Copernicus to Darwin, encourage people to dismiss such special pleading. So do all manner of cultural warnings, from the hubris around which Greek tragedies are built to the lamentation of King David's preacher: "Vanity of vanities, all is vanity [. . .] the Earth abideth for ever [. . .] and there is no new thing under the sun." But the lamentation of vanity can be false modesty. On a planetary scale, intelligence is something genuinely new and powerful. Through the domestication of plants and animals intelligence has remade the living environment. Through industry it has disrupted the key biogeochemical cycles. For good or ill, it will do yet more.

We will see a lot more ills before the balance shifts conclusively to the sort of Green Swan pathways that do not lead to "global immiseration." But before going exponentially positive, let's take a closer look at five real-world wicked problems, exploring how they have evolved and, increasingly, cast lengthening shadows across our future. If the past is any guide, tomorrow's Green Swan thinking, science, and technology will evolve from our attempts to tackle such challenges, gradually—and then suddenly.

CHAPTER 3

BLACK SWAN CAPITALISM

Five Global Crises

We urgently need better ways to track and transform the human activities—commercial, economic, social, and political—driving us toward Black and Gray Swan breakdowns. Ideally, too, we would be able to closely monitor and spur the evolution of Green Swan breakthroughs, allowing us to support and direct them more effectively. So how might this best be done?

First, imagine how financial markets could embrace the challenge. Anyone tracking businesses listed on the world's stock exchanges, with a view to calculating their performance in terms of profits and dividends or assessing their longer-term prospects, needs a way to identify a given stock among the blizzard of other listings. Which is where so-called tickers come in. For most of us the term *ticker* has to do with clocks, hearts, or bombs, but for anyone familiar with stock market capitalism, the term suggests the unique code assigned to each security traded on a given stock market.

AAPL, for example, denotes Apple Inc.; BAC means Bank of America; while F stands for the Ford Motor Company. Our proposal is for a secondary ticker to be applied by governments and stock exchanges to all companies vulnerable to risks—or well positioned for opportunities—associated with the sort of wicked problems introduced in the previous chapter. The obvious ticker symbol, whether on the Wall Street, London, or Shanghai stock exchanges, would be WCKD.[1]

The value of anything marked in this way would be discounted in equity, bond, or insurance markets depending on the gravity of emerging threats to its sector, or enhanced where the relevant opportunities and capabilities were greatest. Does it contribute to the delivery of the United Nations' Sustainable Development Goals, analysts might ask, or not?

As we have seen, wicked problems are those that are difficult, even impossible, to solve because of incomplete, contradictory, or changing requirements that are difficult to recognize and understand. In other words, the term denotes resistance to resolution, not evil intent. Another way to think of a wicked problem is "a problem whose social complexity means that it has no determinable stopping point." Worse, because of complex interdependencies, efforts to solve a wicked problem can reveal or even create other problems.

Imagine, simply as a thought experiment, a future where WCKD is added to existing tickers, with the direction of travel indicated by arrows pointing up or down. These would be based on the company's perceived value based on how it is, or is not, addressing wicked problems.

We might then see AAPL-WCKD with a green arrow pointing up, suggesting the Cupertino company, on balance, is now solving for its most significant future risks and opportunities, and is therefore more valuable to investors. Or F-WCKD with a red arrow pointing down, suggesting Ford, in this example, is not yet headed in the right direction. Or, alternatively, a green arrow pointing upward, suggesting that it is.

Which shares would we then want to sell, hold, or buy? Here are five initial suggestions of sectors where investors might want to take a closer look at the stocks and bonds in their portfolio. Let's start with an everyday material that has become so ubiquitous in this world of ours that we often take it for granted in the same way we take oxygen for granted in the air we breathe.

WICKED PROBLEM 1: PLASTIC OCEANS

Once plastics were the future, but now they are under a global cloud. While researching this chapter I was invited to a showing of the film *A Plastic Ocean*[2] and was fascinated to hear how the project helped to expose the growing threat posed by the global polymers industry. Producer Jo Ruxton had joined an expedition to the so-called Great Pacific Garbage Patch in the North Pacific Gyre, 1,500 miles off the coast of San Francisco. Her aim was to get a sense of what was going on. When the expedition unexpectedly discovered free-floating micro-plastics instead of an anticipated solid mass that could be contained, Jo knew the world had an even bigger problem than imagined and that she had to make the film.

In their day, plastics were miracle materials, indeed still are. They came into their element when they helped the Allies win the Second World War, later becoming the backbone of modern industry and con-sumer lifestyles. Today we hardly notice them, even as they morph and mutate into endless new applications, in an ever-extending rainbow of colors and textures.

To understand how important they have been in modern times, it helps to recall what we did before plastics came along. A good place to start this part of the story is with one of our earliest, simplest, and yet most useful tools: the comb. These were once so important in our lives that some people were actually buried with them. Here is how Susan Freinkel conjured up the pre-plastic world in her fascinating book *Plastic: A Toxic Love Story:*[3]

> Combs are one of our oldest tools, used by humans across cultures and ages for decoration, detangling, and delous-ing. They derive from the most fundamental human tool of all—the hand. And from the time that humans began using combs instead of their fingers, comb design has scarcely changed, prompting the satirical paper the *Onion* to publish a piece titled "Comb Technology: Why Is It So Far Behind

the Razor and Toothbrush Fields?" The Stone Age craftsman who made the oldest known comb—a small four-toothed number carved from animal bone some eight thousand years ago—would have no trouble knowing what to do with the bright blue plastic version sitting on my bathroom counter.

For most of history, combs were made of almost any material humans had at hand, including bone, tortoise-shell, ivory, rubber, iron, tin, gold, silver, lead, reeds, wood, glass, porcelain, papier-mâché. But in the late nine-teenth century, that panoply of possibilities began to fall away with the arrival of a totally new kind of material—celluloid, the first man-made plastic. Combs were among the first and most popular objects made of celluloid. And having crossed that material Rubicon, comb makers never went back. Ever since, combs generally have been made of one kind of plastic or another.

Interestingly, anyone interested in wildlife conservation back then might well have welcomed plastic with open arms as a life-saving gift to elephants, walruses, and other animals sporting tusks. Ivory was widely used at the time for everything from buttonhooks and boxes to piano keys and billiard balls. In relation to the latter, Freinkel recalled the following:

> Billiards had come to captivate upper-crust society in the United States as well as in Europe. Every estate, every man-sion had a billiards table, and by the mid-1800s, there was growing concern that there would soon be no more elephants left to keep the game tables stocked with balls. The situation was most dire in Ceylon, source of the ivory that made the best billiard balls. There, in the northern part of the island, *The Times* reported, "upon the reward of a few shillings per head being offered by the authorities, 3,500 pachyderms were dispatched in less than three years by the natives."

The story of how John Wesley Hyatt developed the first plastic, celluloid, tracks back to the aftermath of the American Civil War. It has to be one of the most extraordinary sagas in the entire history of invention. He mixed a range of ingredients—some of them highly explosive—to create his prototype materials. Used to make billiard balls, they soon proved overly exciting, making a noise like a shotgun blast when they hit one another. One Colorado saloonkeeper wrote to Hyatt to say that "he didn't mind, but every time the balls collided, every man in the room pulled a gun."[4]

That was then, when anything plastic was a novelty. Today, by contrast, plastics are ubiquitous, cheapened by overfamiliarity. From birth to death, ours is an increasingly plastic world. In the same way that scientists now conclude that *Homo sapiens* were domesticated by dogs and cats, you could also argue that we have been domesticated by endless new species of plastic.

So how should we think about these materials? Ask an expert to explain what's going on and at some point they are likely to get technical, splitting plastics into two main types of plastic: thermoplastics and thermosets.[5]

The first sort can be re-melted, returning to their original state. They include polyethylene, polypropylene, polyvinyl chloride, polystyrene, nylon, polycarbonate, and others. The second group are typically produced and formed into products simultaneously, so they cannot easily be returned to their original state. They include vulcanized synthetic rubber, acrylics, polyurethanes, melamine, silicone, epoxies, and others. So far so complicated—and it gets worse.

Next come engineered plastics. Designed to offer better mechanical properties and greater durability. Polycarbonates, for example, resist impact. Polyamides like nylon resist abrasion—and have found their way into everything from stockings and cooking tongs to parachutes. And then there is an ever-growing list of other materials made from combinations of plastics, such as the incredibly tough material ABS, acrylonitrile butadiene styrene.

Nor is that the end of the matter. Next come the plastic fibers. Some of the best known are spun from polyester, nylon, rayon, acrylic, or spandex, although there are many more. And all that is before we get to the world of coatings, adhesives, elastomers, and rubbers—including, to underscore their versatility, materials used, remarkably, to coat the outside of the Space Shuttle.

So plastics are everywhere. But their source varies widely. Many, indeed most, are made from fossil fuels. But rayon is made from cellulosics derived from trees, just as rubber is made from tree sap. Meanwhile, whatever the source, does anyone know how much plastic we have produced to date? Well, in the first global study of the production, use, and fate of all plastics, researchers found that by 2015 we humans had generated 8.3 billion metric tons of plastics, 6.3 billion tons of which had already become waste. Of that waste total, only 9% was recycled, 12% was incinerated, and 79% accumulated in landfills or the natural environment.[6]

If current trends continue, we are told, a further 12 billion metric tons of plastic waste will end up in landfills or in the natural environment by 2050. For comparison, 12 billion metric tons is about 35,000 times as heavy as the Empire State Building. Even so, what makes the plastics challenge so wicked? One answer was given in a major survey on plastics by *The Economist*:

> Often, as with disposable coffee cups, drinks bottles, sweet wrappers and other packets that account for much of the plastic produced in Europe and America, this happens after a brief, one-off indulgence. If the stuff ends up in the sea, it can wash up on a distant beach or choke a seal. Exposed to salt water and ultraviolet light, it can fragment into "microplastics" small enough to find their way into fish bellies. From there, it seems only a short journey to dinner plates.[7]

I first drafted this section while in Brasilia, working with Nestlé—where I was one of a number of people standing down from the company's Creating Shared Value Advisory Council, in my case after nine years. Our event focused on water. The company produces a huge range of products, but is particularly well known for its bottled waters. Indeed, an earlier CEO, Peter Brabeck-Letmathe, who had originally invited me to join the council, had been a leading champion of better water stewardship worldwide.

So in a public panel discussion featuring Nestlé's new CEO Mark Schneider, I asked him how worried we should be about plastics in the oceans and, a media story that had broken days earlier, microplastics in bottled water. By way of background, here's a sample of the sort of coverage that had appeared in *The Guardian* on the first day of our Brasilia event:

> The World Health Organisation (WHO) has announced a review into the potential risks of plastic in drinking water after a new analysis of some of the world's most popular bottled water brands found that more than 90 percent contained tiny pieces of plastic. A previous study also found high levels of microplastics in tap water.
>
> In the new study, analysis of 259 bottles from 19 locations in nine countries across 11 different brands found an average of 325 plastic particles for every litre of water being sold. In one bottle of Nestlé Pure Life, concentrations were as high as 10,000 plastic pieces per litre of water. Of the 259 bottles tested, only 17 were free of plastics, according to the study.[8]

We soon learned that Nestlé scientists had been unable to reproduce the findings reported in the media. But Schneider, in public and on-air, noted that even though the science was complex his strong sense was that such issues could only become more urgent over time. The following day, when the council convened again, he even used the "wicked" word to describe the nature and scale of the problem.

As with our four other cases, we will return to the question of what can be done to tackle such systemic problems later. But, first, to get a sense of the scale of the challenge we now face with plastics, here is a final quote from that *Economist* survey:

> Even if the flow of plastic into the sea, totaling perhaps 10m tonnes a year, was instantly stanched, huge quantities would remain. And the flow will not stop. Most of the plastic in the ocean comes not from tidy Europe and America, but from countries in fast-developing East Asia, where waste-collection systems are flawed or non-existent. Last October scientists at the Helmholtz Centre for Environmental Research, in Germany, found that ten rivers—two in Africa and the rest in Asia—discharge 90 percent of all plastic marine debris. The Yangtze alone carries 1.5m tonnes a year.

Forever the contrarians, the *Economist* team then wondered aloud whether the plastics-in-the-ocean problem was really worth worrying about when we also face challenges like climate breakdown. But the wickedness of this challenge stems from the fact that the world ocean is not just under assault from plastics. It also is under growing stress from overfishing; from other forms of pollution, with massive dead zones forming off major estuaries impacted by the runoff of fertilizers and insecticides from farming areas; and—both linked to global warming—from rising water temperatures and acidification.

THROUGH THE GREEN SWAN LENS

Plastics are probably with us in perpetuity. But they will increasingly need to be based on renewable raw materials and incorporated in closed loop systems. At the same time, we must work out ways to get plastics out of the oceans in the same way we must now get greenhouse gases out of the atmosphere. An important initiative in this space is the New Plastics Economy program run by the Ellen MacArthur Foundation.[9]

WICKED PROBLEM 2: KILLER CALORIES

Highly profitable calories underpin some of the biggest businesses in the world. But calories in modern diets are now triggering a global health crisis. They are increasingly linked to obesity, for example, and to a growing range of chronic diseases. One thing that makes obesity not just a wicked problem, but also potentially a *super* wicked problem, is the fact that it can spread through social networks. We are learning that it can be transmitted across generations, from parents to their children. And also, it seems, between people who have never physically met, via social media.

I am not a scientist. Indeed I gave up science when in my early teens because I refused to dissect frogs. But I have long loved science. That said, I readily confess that I have struggled to understand calories—in fact, I suspect that most of us suffer from the same problem—except at the most basic level, of understanding that more calories are good, up to a certain point, after which they can become bad.

So here is the clearest explanation I have yet come across of the complicated world of calories, as told in *Scientific American*:

> Food is energy for the body. Digestive enzymes in the mouth, stomach and intestines break up complex food molecules into simpler structures, such as sugars and amino acids that travel through the bloodstream to all our tissues. Our cells use the energy stored in the chemical bonds of these simpler molecules to carry on business as usual. We calculate the available energy in all foods with a unit known as the food calorie, or kilocalorie—the amount of energy required to heat one kilogram of water by one degree Celsius. Fats provide approximately nine calories per gram, whereas carbohydrates and proteins deliver just four. Fiber offers a piddling two calories because enzymes in the human digestive tract have great difficulty chopping it up into smaller molecules.[10]

One thing I learned from this piece was that analyzing the way calories affect us is an infernally difficult task, however scientific you may be. "To accurately calculate the total calories that someone gets out of a given food," the article explained, "you would have to take into account a dizzying array of factors, including whether that food has evolved to survive digestion; how boiling, baking, microwaving or flambéing a food changes its structure and chemistry; how much energy the body expends to break down different kinds of food; and the extent to which the billions of bacteria in the gut aid human digestion and, conversely, steal some calories for themselves."

So where does that leave us? *Scientific American* concluded, "Nutrition scientists are beginning to learn enough to hypothetically improve calorie labels, but digestion turns out to be such a fantastically complex and messy affair that we will probably never derive a formula for an infallible calorie count." Scrape that complexity aside for a moment and it is increasingly clear that some key features of our modern diets are wickedly problematic, in the full sense of the term.

A global survey reported some years ago in *Newsweek* underscored the sheer scale of the challenge. The research, which reviewed 325 dietary surveys, covering almost 90% of the world's population, is thought to have been the largest study to date of international eating habits.

On the upside, between 1990 and 2014, roughly the same timescale as that adopted by the study, the number of hungry people worldwide dropped by 209 million to 805 million. That is still an incredibly large number of hungry people, but the upside is that previously unimaginable progress is being made.

The downside, however, is that the quality of the world's diet has deteriorated substantially in recent decades. Poor countries in sub-Saharan Africa and Asia are seeing the fastest increases in unhealthy food consumption, according to Dariush Mozaffarian, dean of the Friedman School of Nutrition Science and Policy at Tufts University.[11]

The globalization of Western diets—with a small group of food and agriculture companies now having quite disproportionate power to decide what they produce and we consume—is partially to blame for this shift to unhealthy eating. Processed foods high in sugar, fat, and starch are at the epicenter of this seismic shift, but are also now seen to be a particular challenge to our health and well-being.

So how does all this play out regionally? China and India, with more than a billion people apiece, recorded some of the highest increases in unhealthy food consumption. Making things rather more complicated, some countries in Europe and Latin America saw an increase in both healthy and unhealthy food consumption.

So where did calories fit in? "Most global nutrition efforts have focused on calories—getting starchy staples to people," Mozaffarian told the Thomson Reuters Foundation. "We need to focus on the quality of calories for poor countries, not just the quantity."[12] Perhaps unsurprisingly, older people displayed better eating habits than the young in most of the 187 countries covered. The flip side: Many young people are growing up with much worse diets than their parents or grandparents.

But what turns all of this into our second wicked problem? The answer is that a key result of poor diets is the rapid spread of obesity worldwide. The World Health Organization (WHO) defines overweight and obesity as "abnormal or excessive fat accumulation that may impair health."[13] Such fat accumulation, in turn, brings in its train a whole spectrum of chronic diseases. According to WHO, "Overweight and obesity are major risk factors for a number of chronic diseases, including diabetes, cardiovascular diseases and cancer. Once considered a problem only in high income countries, overweight and obesity are now dramatically on the rise in low- and middle-income countries, particularly in urban settings."[14]

WHO also warns, "Obesity has reached epidemic proportions globally, with at least 2.8 million people dying each year as a result of being overweight or obese. "

In 2016, more than 1.9 billion adults aged eighteen years and older were overweight. Of these, over 650 million adults were obese. That same year, 39% of adults aged eighteen years and over (that is, 39% of men and 40% of women) were overweight. Overall, staggeringly, about 13% of the world's adult population (11% of men and 15% of women) was obese in 2016.[15] The worldwide prevalence of obesity nearly tripled between 1975 and 2016.

Now, to make matters much worse, it is cascading down the age scale. In 2016, an estimated 41 million children under the age of five years were overweight or obese. In Africa, the number of overweight children under five has increased by nearly 50% since 2000. Obesity can slow people down, even stop them doing exercise altogether. But it is also a significant risk factor to a number of serious health disorders—including cardiovascular disease and diabetes.[16] Other problems it can cause include osteoarthritis, liver and kidney disease, sleep apnea, and depression.

Interestingly, one of the leading health-care companies in the world, Denmark's Novo Nordisk,[17] is among those now calling for obesity to be classified—and treated—as a chronic disease in its own right.

The total number of diabetics has passed 450 million and is expected to reach 693 million by 2045, if current trends continue.[18] The high price of dealing with the disease—with the global cost of the disease estimated in 2016 to be $850 billion a year—reflects not only the cost of medicines but also the cost of managing a range of complications, among them limb amputations and eye disease.

Paradoxically, Novo Nordisk, one of the companies that have been doing most to tackle this evolving wicked problem, is well placed to benefit from the spread of obesity and diabetes. So why is it working, in effect, to shrink its own longer-term market? One key reason is that it concluded years ago that the accelerating global spread of obesity and diabetes could potentially collapse public health-care systems in some countries.

THROUGH THE GREEN SWAN LENS

Calories are only part of the story of obesity and chronic disease. Over time, we will also see growing understanding of the role of our genetics and intestinal microbiology. Meanwhile, better information, coupled with wise "choice editing"[19] by supermarkets and governments, can help slow the spread of diabetes and other diseases. Ultimately, Green Swan thinking must favor new diets, lifestyles, and exercise regimes.

WICKED PROBLEM 3: ANTIBIOTICS BREED DEADLIER BUGS

Antibiotics have been highly profitable, including—controversially—in farming. One thing that links obesity and antibiotics, our third wicked problem, is the fact that the latter have often been used to promote growth and body weight in farm animals destined for the table. In the process, unintentionally, farmers have helped drive growing antibiotic resistance in microbes and other organisms.

Like many people alive today, I would have been dead long ago without antibiotics. Indeed, they probably saved my life a couple of times. Unlike most people, however, I have had the privilege of visiting some of the places where these semi-miraculous medicines are developed and made. In the 1980s, for example, I was taken around factories producing antibiotics in the United Kingdom, the United States, and Japan.

The more I learned about these extraordinary substances, the deeper I wanted to dig into their history. Like many people, I probably thought that the whole story began in a messy laboratory sink in London. But I discovered that our use of antibiotics to treat infections stretches back over millennia. For most of that time, we humans had no idea why what we were doing actually worked—or at least worked sometimes. So, to set the scene, here's a whistle-stop tour of the world of antibiotics, as told by the Microbiology Society:

Various moulds and plant extracts were used to treat infections by some of the earliest civilisations—the ancient Egyptians, for example, applied moldy bread to infected wounds. Nevertheless, until the 20th century, infections that we now consider straightforward to treat—such as pneumonia and diarrhoea—that are caused by bacteria, were the number one cause of human death in the developed world.

It wasn't until the late 19th century that scientists began to observe antibacterial chemicals in action. Paul Ehrlich, a German physician, noted that certain chemical dyes coloured some bacterial cells but not others. He concluded that, according to this principle, it must be possible to create substances that can kill certain bacteria selectively without harming other cells. In 1909, he discovered that a chemical called arsphenamine was an effective treatment for syphilis.

This became the first modern antibiotic, although Ehrlich himself referred to his discovery as "chemotherapy"—the use of a chemical to treat a disease. The word "antibiotics" was first used over 30 years later by the Ukrainian-American inventor and microbiologist Selman Waksman, who in his lifetime discovered over 20 antibiotics.[20]

Only at this point does the legendary Alexander Fleming step into the spotlight. Like many brilliant people, and indeed like many of the rest of us, he appears to have been somewhat untidy in his habits. In the now-mythic story, when he returned to his laboratory after a holiday in 1928, he spotted something odd.

It was concluded later that a natural fungus, *Penicillium notatum*, had probably floated in through an open window—contaminating a culture plate of *Staphylococcus* bacteria that Fleming had accidentally left uncovered when he left for his holiday. But what was so special about that accidental contamination? The answer—and it took a highly skilled eye to see it—was that the fungus had created bacteria-free zones wherever it grew on the plate. Excited, Fleming set to work to isolate the mold and grow more of it.

To his delight, he discovered that *P. notatum* was extremely effective, even at very low concentrations, and could prevent the growth of deadly *Staphylococcus* even when diluted 800 times. Better still, it was less toxic than the disinfectants used at the time for the same purpose. The story kept getting better, as the Microbiology Society explains:

> After early trials in treating human wounds, collaborations with British pharmaceutical companies ensured that the mass production of penicillin (the antibiotic chemical produced by *P. notatum*) was possible. Following a fire in Boston, Massachusetts, USA, in which nearly 500 people died, many survivors received skin grafts which are liable to infection by *Staphylococcus*. Treatment with penicillin was hugely successful, and the US government began supporting the mass production of the drug. By D-Day in 1944, penicillin was being widely used to treat troops for infections both in the field and in hospitals throughout Europe. By the end of World War II, penicillin was nicknamed "the wonder drug" and had saved many lives.

All of which might suggest that in the modern day we would be treating antibiotics with huge respect, as some form of planetary treasure—but far from it. Instead, through carelessness, laziness, ignorance, and greed, we have squandered the extraordinary power they have given us over once-deadly diseases. Once again, yesterday's Green Swan is being transformed into a Black Swan.

To some degree, Fleming saw it coming. So a Gray Swan, perhaps. England's chief medical officer, Dame Sally Davies, explained, "Well, it was predicted in 1945 by Alexander Fleming, when he accepted his Nobel Prize for penicillin. And he said resistance will occur, and it will cause deaths."[21] Even so, the scale of today's resistance problem would have shocked and saddened him. Dame Sally again: "Worldwide, at least 700,000 people die a year. Let's make it real for the United States: the equivalent of a Boeing 747 dropping out of the sky every week in the United States, 25,000 deaths. The same in Europe. Take India: 60,000 newborn babies dying of infections that are resistant to drugs every year."

As a result, the World Health Organization warns that we now face a global health crisis of potentially epic proportions. Here's how they summed up the problem:

> Antibiotic resistance is rising to dangerously high levels in all parts of the world. New resistance mechanisms are emerging and spreading globally, threatening our ability to treat common infectious diseases. A growing list of infections—such as pneumonia, tuberculosis, blood poisoning, gonorrhoea, and foodborne diseases—are becoming harder, and sometimes impossible, to treat as antibiotics become less effective [. . .]
>
> Without urgent action, we are heading for a post-antibiotic era, in which common infections and minor injuries can once again kill.[22]

Dame Sally also spotlighted the level of our almost criminal neglect in the wider world: "So there's a river in India which has levels of ciprofloxacin, which is a very important antibiotic, of the level that we would like to see in the blood. It is just quite shocking how runoff from intensive farming, high-use hospitals—and the Chinese and Indians are alleged to have the highest use in their hospitals—from factories making pharmaceuticals or their precursor models are running into our environment and poisoning our environment."[23]

Even given such insane levels of exposure, how can microbes develop resistance to antibiotics so fast? Part of the answer is that these antimicrobial substances were developed by microorganisms themselves over many millions of years. For example, I recently saw South American leaf-cutter ants doing what such insects naturally do, using fungi and bacteria to produce natural antibiotics. Some of these compounds now show promising results against superbugs like MRSA. And researchers are investigating how these bacteria function, in the hope that they may provide clues to how new types of antibiotics can be developed.

The fact that such antibiotics have been in existence for such a long time suggests that there will have been plenty of opportunities for other organisms exposed to them to develop resistance mechanisms. And, as the ciprofloxacin example shows, the exposure of wild organisms to antibiotics has gone off the scale in recent decades. All of this reflects the fact that we have learned to produce antibiotics in types, quantities, and purities that Fleming and other pioneers would have found genuinely mind-boggling.

Then we have broadcast them into the wider world, among other things through our sewage systems. As a result, a wide range of microbes have now developed—or remobilized—resistance mechanisms that mean that once-powerful drugs struggle to keep up with their rapidly evolving foes.

So whom should we blame? WHO is in no doubt about what has produced this crisis. "Antibiotic resistance is accelerated by the misuse and overuse of antibiotics," it concludes, "as well as poor infection prevention and control."[24] Furthermore: "Where antibiotics can be bought for human or animal use without a prescription, the emergence and spread of resistance is made worse. Similarly, in countries without standard treatment guidelines, antibiotics are often over-prescribed by health workers and veterinarians and over-used by the public."

I gained a powerful sense of the evolving battle against antibiotic-resistant "superbugs" when I visited the London Science Museum's exhibition *Superbugs: The Fight for Our Lives*.[25] The museum explained why we should all be worried:

We share our world with bacteria. Trillions live on and inside you, and although many are harmless they can also cause infection and death. Thanks to antibiotics, millions of people each year are cured of previously untreatable bacterial diseases. But bacteria have fought back, evolving into super-bugs resistant to antibiotics. Today superbugs kill almost 700,000 people a year globally and by 2050 this could rise to 10 million.

The microbial point of view on all of this was illuminated by twelve real-life bacteria colonies, including nine deadly bacteria that WHO classifies as a significant threat to human health. Grown by bioartist Anna Dumitriu, the bacteria included *Escherichia coli*, often the first microbe to colonize newborn babies' stomachs; *Staphylococcus aureus*, one of the earliest superbugs identified; and *Neisseria gonorrhoeae*. The exhibition also introduced visitors to *Bdellovibrio bacterivorous* (a bacterium that eats other bacteria) and bacteriophages (viruses that infect bacteria), both of which are increasingly being used to fight superbugs.

At the human scale, we also heard from Geoffrey, a former patient who was in isolation for five months after antibiotics failed to treat a bacterial infection he contracted during surgery. As the exhibition's curator Sheldon Paquin put it, "For over seventy years antibiotics have been essential to medicine, helping save hundreds of millions of lives." Now that some infections can no longer be treated by first-line antibiotics, more expensive medicines must be used, if and where available.

As patients live and suffer for longer, and need more treatment, often in hospitals, we are seeing significant increases in health-care costs, as well as in the economic impact on families and societies. Various remedies are suggested, but truly the wickedness of what we are doing with the antibiotics is breathtaking.

THROUGH THE GREEN SWAN LENS

We will probably develop alternatives to the most abused antibiotics, although perhaps not in time to avoid major health crises. But the resistance issues that dog these extraordinary medicines will come to haunt those alternatives, too. The Hippocratic Oath, requiring doctors to "do no harm,"[26] must be expanded to include harm to all forms of life—and extended to cover intergenerational timescales. Seemingly impossible today? Yes. Inevitable tomorrow? Again probably, if we can prescribe and administer the right policy remedies.

WICKED PROBLEM 4: CARBON BRINGS PLANET TO BOIL

The fossil fuel industries have been among the most profitable in human history—and among the most environmentally destructive. This thought was in my mind as I perched on the twenty-seventh floor of the Grand Kempinski Hotel in Shanghai, a city of 24 million people at the time, looking down at the barges, ferries, floating cranes, and police boats surging back and forth along the huge Huangpu River. I felt a sense of vertigo, in multiple dimensions. The scale of the economic activity suggested by this throbbing artery, part of the immense Yangtze River system, is—not a word I often use—awesome.

I was in the city to speak at the Tongji University Sustainable Development Forum, co-hosted by the German materials company Covestro—and my message was designed to disconcert, at least to begin with. I wanted to disconcert because I was disconcerted. As I looked down on the river and city, my brain tried to fuse two very different views of Shanghai's future, one without runaway climate breakdown, and one with.

As Shanghai reaches for the skies, with more building activity than I remember seeing anywhere else in the world, the latest science suggests that a two-degree Celsius warming trajectory could flood land in the city that currently houses 11.6 million people. A four-degree warming, which some scientists now argue is a "locked-in" outcome, could impact 22.4 million. Forget the decimal places. No one really has a true grip on the scale of the devastation, and Shanghai is spending billions in attempts to moderate the likely impact. But, really, what sort of species would pour so much time, energy, and investment into cities destined to become twenty-second-century versions of Atlantis?

This question was given greater urgency by two things I had read on the flight across from London. One was Mohsin Hamid's stunning novel *Exit West*, portraying a world where the climate emergency has turned most of us into migrants.[27] A world where London's once-fabled Green Belt, now called the "London Halo," is being bulldozed for swarming refugee camps. Nor is London alone: The same phenomenon also disfigures places such as California's once-delightful Marin County, the next stage in the main protagonists' journey.

The second thing I read as I winged east was a Louis Klee blog post, "Unthinking Modernity,"[28] written in response to Amitav Ghosh's book *The Great Derangement*.[29] Ghosh is a world-class novelist, though his 2016 book switched from fiction to fact, arguing that modern literature, history, and politics often betray us when it comes to the looming consequences of climate chaos.

All three make a set of assumptions, hinging on uniform and gradual processes rather than catastrophes and cataclysms. As a result, they render climate-induced societal collapse unthinkable. Ghosh asks the question head on: Are we deranged? He concludes that we must be, because our cultures and imaginations simply fail to grasp and engage emergent realities. As Klee had put it in his review, "Words buckle under the unthinkability of the crisis."[30] Or, as Ghosh argued, we increasingly suffer from "a crisis of the imagination."[31]

His conclusion, as summarized in a blurb by his publishers, is that "hundred-year storms and freakish tornadoes simply feel too improbable for the novel; they are automatically consigned to other genres. In the writing of history, too, the climate crisis has sometimes led to gross simplifications; Ghosh shows that the history of the carbon economy is a tangled global story with many contradictory and counterintuitive elements."

Helpfully, other voices are also calling out the risk of climate catastrophe. Alongside writers such as Margaret Atwood, who argues that this isn't just about our climate changing, but also about *everything* changing, Mohsin Hamid has also risen to the challenge. Weirdly, though, I can't recall global warming being mentioned directly even once in *Exit West*. Perhaps it's a reflection of the challenge being too well known by then to name?

Another striking climate change novel, albeit in an even more apocalyptic vein, is Omar El Akkad's *American War*.[32] Here, fossil fuel bans help trigger a second American Civil War, in the same way that the proposed abolition of slavery did back in the 1860s. In energy terms, almost an exact parallel.

The Greek goddess Cassandra gave apocalyptic warnings a bad name, but that should not stop us from pointing decision takers and policy makers to evidence that catastrophic climate change is, at least in historical terms, just around the corner. Thinking the unthinkable may be beyond most of our pay grades, but one reason I have returned to reading the latest science fiction is that sci-fi writers are people who have learned how to think around corners.

You don't need to be a sci-fi fan to know that the business of business is changing all around us—with perhaps the most worrying wicked problem of all being the shriveling of the natural world as our numbers grow and our reach spreads. Meanwhile, literally over our heads, and even higher than the realm where greenhouse gases are working their increasingly malign magic, another wicked problem is evolving in the silent vacuum of space.

THROUGH THE GREEN SWAN LENS

Carbon is the most magical of substances, the very stuff of life. Yet most people understand little of the carbon cycle—or of the implications of our distortion of the cycle and the potential for climate-induced societal collapse. This area of knowledge must become central to every aspect of education, at every age and every level. Trust in science must be rebuilt where it has been—and is being—eroded. Carbon pricing, meanwhile, must move from a political improbability to an integral, taken-for-granted part of our economic operating systems and markets. And fast.

WICKED PROBLEM 5: SPACE JUNK HITS CRITICAL DENSITY

For a long time, space exploration was very far from profitable. It was done for science, or to control a new set of commanding heights as the superpowers competed to control the planet and our future. But the wicked problems came just the same, particularly in the form of space debris. Some years back Brian Weeden, a technical advisor for the Secure World Foundation, even described space junk as a "super wicked problem."[33]

Interestingly, one thing that links antibiotics to space is the fact that antibiotic resistance research has now itself gone into orbit.[34] It was already known that bacteria found on the International Space Station (ISS) were more resistant, for some reason, than bacteria isolated at the Antarctic Research Station, Concordia. Now, for the first time, antimicrobial resistant genes have been detected in bacteria taken directly from the ISS. Samples were taken from places like the dining table and the foot platform of an exercise device. Tests have shown that *Enterobacter bugandensis* strains (a novel species isolated from the ISS) were resistant to all antibiotics tested, while *Staphylococcus haemolyticus* (an important pathogen in hospital-acquired infections) was resistant to none.

Genomic analysis then revealed that out of 518 known antibiotic resistance genes, 123 were contained in the ISS bacterial samples.

Strikingly, it seems that our adventures in space are driving the evolution of our microbial crewmates, in ways that may well come back to haunt us down here on Earth. This process represents a mere eyeblink in the vast timescales of evolution but suggests how rapidly wicked problems can develop when the circumstances are right, or wrong.

Our fifth wicked problem is a powerful demonstration of how this process is taking place, literally, over our heads. Since the Soviets launched Sputnik 1 in 1957, our species has polluted the once-empty space around Earth with various forms of debris, to the point where it is becoming deadly dangerous. "We're at what we call a 'critical density,'" says Donald Kessler, a former NASA scientist who used to run the agency's Orbital Debris Program Office, "where there are enough large objects in space that they will collide with one another and create small debris faster than it can be removed."[35]

He predicted that eventually there will be so much space junk that leaving Earth to explore deep space will become highly risky, if not impossible. That, someone might want to tell Elon Musk and Jeff Bezos, might also eventually rule out sending manned missions to Mars. Anyone who has seen the film *Gravity* will have some sense of where all of this could now be headed. Talk about a wicked problem with super wicked characteristics. So how do serious space people themselves view the space junk challenge? Here's how NASA sums up the problem:[36]

> Space debris encompasses both natural (meteoroid) and artificial (man-made) particles. Meteoroids are in orbit about the sun, while most artificial debris is in orbit about the Earth. Hence, the latter is more commonly referred to as orbital debris.
>
> Orbital debris is any man-made object in orbit about the Earth that no longer serves a useful function. Such debris includes non-functional spacecraft, abandoned launch vehicle stages, mission-related debris and fragmentation debris.

There are more than 20,000 pieces of debris larger than a softball orbiting the Earth. They travel at speeds up to 17,500 mph, fast enough for a relatively small piece of orbital debris to damage a satellite or a spacecraft. There are 500,000 pieces of debris the size of a marble or larger. There are many millions of pieces of debris that are so small they can't be tracked.

Even tiny paint flecks can damage a spacecraft when traveling at these velocities. In fact a number of space shuttle windows have been replaced because of damage caused by material that was analyzed and shown to be paint flecks.

I wondered what the biggest threat is now to space vehicles, crewed by humans or not. "The greatest risk to space missions comes from non-trackable debris," explained Nicholas Johnson, NASA chief scientist for orbital debris. That said, with so much orbital debris whizzing around over our heads, and at astonishing speeds, there have been surprisingly few disastrous collisions to date.

In 1996, though, a French satellite was hit and damaged by debris from a French rocket that had exploded a decade earlier. Poetic justice, perhaps, but also a warning of what is to come. Then on February 10, 2009, a defunct Russian satellite collided with and destroyed a functioning US Iridium commercial satellite. The collision added more than 2,000 pieces of trackable debris to the inventory of space junk.

Next, while I was in that country, China carried out its 2007 anti-satellite test, using a missile to destroy an old weather satellite. This single act, unlikely to be welcomed by future space travelers, added more than 2,300 trackable pieces of junk, more than 35,000 pieces larger than a thumbnail, and perhaps hundreds of thousands of pieces too small to track.[37]

So who has the worst space-littering record to date? Well, in 2015, it was discovered that while Russia had the most objects in space, more than 6,500 of them, it was not the biggest contributor to space junk. Instead, at the time, the United States held the title of the dirtiest country in space, even if by a whisker. Russia had 3,961 pieces of detectable space debris compared to the 3,999 pieces of trackable space trash in orbit created by the Americans.[38] Perhaps we should call it a tie?

China, meanwhile, had only just increased its space efforts. Even so, it ran a close third with 3,475 pieces of space junk, much of it the result of that 2007 anti-satellite test. Obvious questions to ask include whether this stuff falls back to Earth—and, if it does, should we be worried or relieved? NASA explains, "The higher the altitude, the longer the orbital debris will typically remain in Earth orbit. Debris left in orbits below 600 km normally fall back to Earth within several years. At altitudes of 800 km, the time for orbital decay is often measured in decades. Above 1,000 km, orbital debris will normally continue circling the Earth for a century or more."[39]

And how much of it gets back to Earth? Here NASA advises, "A significant amount of debris does not survive the severe heating that occurs during re-entry. Components which do survive are most likely to fall into the oceans or other bodies of water or onto sparsely populated regions like the Canadian Tundra, the Australian Outback, or Siberia in the Russian Federation. During the past 50 years an average of one cataloged piece of debris fell back to Earth each day."

Anyone hurt? "No serious injury or significant property damage caused by re-entering debris has been confirmed," NASA reports. Meanwhile, the big space agencies that have dominated space for years are no longer the only game in orbit. A couple of years ago, for example, I visited Planet Labs in San Francisco. They are part of a very different space industry now challenging NASA, the European Space Agency, and their Russian, Chinese, and Indian counterparts for space dominance. Clearly, all this activity is bound to have an impact on the amount of space junk. Here's how *Wired* magazine put it:

Just how much bigger will the problem get? SpaceX alone plans to send up nearly 12,000 small internet-beaming objects over time. OneWeb has designs on some 700 similar sats. Planet [Labs] just launched around 100 that take pictures of the Earth's entire landmass every day. And those are just the heaviest hitters. Little orbiters—especially the smallest types, CubeSats and NanoSats—are within reach of research scientists, government agency experiments, smaller companies, and even individual humans. Take the private Breakthrough Starshot project, which eventually plans to send diminutive spacecraft to Alpha Centauri star system (really). It just launched six "Sprites": the world's smallest satellites, measuring 3.5 centimeters on a side.[40]

All of which suggests that space junk is already a wicked problem—and, if space warfare ever breaks out, potentially a super wicked problem in the making. If others follow the Chinese lead and fire missiles at satellites or other space vehicles, as India has, the situation could get much worse, fast. When India followed suit, NASA head Jim Bridenstine described the act as "a terrible thing."

Then there is a weird wrinkle in the story that again links a couple of the wicked problems already spotlighted here: Those predictions of how fast space objects come back into Earth's atmosphere critically depend on where the atmosphere is. New research suggests that the carbon dioxide we are pumping into the atmosphere, paradoxically, is cooling the thermosphere and so contracting it.

"This contraction, in turn, will reduce atmospheric drag on satellites and may have adverse consequences for the orbital debris environment that is already unstable," concluded a 2012 *Nature Geoscience* paper.[41] No one said life would be easy, but who knew that it could be this complicated? As our numbers expand and our technologies become increasingly sophisticated, the potential for surprises also grows exponentially.

THROUGH THE GREEN SWAN LENS

This issue has the potential to become radically worse before we are forced to turn it around. An event like the destruction of a space station, as depicted in Alfonso Cuarón's 2013 film *Gravity*, could force our hand—or even a war in which enemy satellites and installations are targeted, spraying debris every which way. Whatever it is that wakes us up, decluttering space will be a critical task for decades. One way of incentivizing the process might be to offer a bounty for innovators who work out how to dispose of space waste, based on the size, speed, and likely impact of given pieces of debris.

So, in the face of problems like these, what do we—and business in particular—need to do to become seriously fit for the future? How do we evolve the skills necessary to detect Black Swans before they overwhelm us—and create the Green Swan solutions that most corporate top teams still see as fantasy, or at least as science fiction? That is the question to which we now turn.

Happily, events already seem to signal the dawn of a decade of exponentially positive change. European Commission President Ursula von der Leyen announced a €1 trillion Green Deal for the European Union. There will be skeptics, inevitably, but this is exactly the sort of Green Swan initiative we now need to shift our economies toward social responsibility and inclusion—and, even more importantly, environmental resilience and regeneration.

PART II

BLACK VERSUS GREEN

Becoming Future-Fit

CHAPTER 4

SWANNING ROUND BOARDROOMS

Views from the Top Floor

Once swans are in your mind, you see them everywhere. We were sitting on the top floor of the Neste HQ building on the outskirts of Helsinki, Finland, with travel brochure views of lakes and forests. Inside, we were talking to the CEO and other top team members from the oil-company-in-transformation about their plans for shifting the business model toward renewable fuels and the circular economy. Outside, the sun was bright; indeed it was the first day when migratory birds were returning for the summer. Then, literally out of the blue, two whooper swans (aka common swans) flew across the great expanse of water outside, coincidentally in exactly the same formation as shown in an image Moscow-based Brazilian designer Silvio Rebêlo had developed for me as part of the early promotion of the Green Swan story and agenda.

I am not particularly superstitious, but I took this as an encouraging sign.

Over the decades, much of my work has involved getting into the minds of people in boardrooms and on the top floors of high-rise buildings. In São Paulo, I have even arrived on the top of a skyscraper, by helicopter, and gone straight down into the top floor boardroom. It is only too easy to imagine how, over time, this elevated perspective and lifestyle might give people delusions of grandeur.

Sometimes the sense of being inside a reality bubble is palpable. During the protests against the World Trade Organization in 1999, I recall being encouraged to literally look down on the activists in the street below from the boardroom of the International Finance Corporation in Washington, DC. Someone asked, "What has gotten into them?" The implication was that while sane people worked calmly within the building, outside crazy people prowled the streets.

Having been in a number of demonstrations myself over the years, that is not how I look at it. Indeed I once stood outside the Shell HQ in London, after a memorial service for Body Shop International founder Anita Roddick, with Greenpeace UK director John Sauven and activist Bianca Jagger, noting, "Shell are one of our clients." Our view of the world really does vary enormously depending on who we are and where we happen to be standing at the time.

It is easy to assume that people in power are rational and powerful and can exercise that power as they see fit. But as the Gershwin song concluded, "It ain't necessarily so." The CEO of a major international company once told me that he felt anything but all-powerful. Among other things, he felt hemmed in by competitors, by the financial markets, by regulators, by campaigners, by the media, by the interests of employees and communities, by the company's history and earlier decisions, and—crucially—by events. His company was Monsanto, eventually sold to Bayer, with dire results for the latter.

If your work takes you regularly into the world's boardrooms and C-suites, it really is hard to miss the reality distortion fields such places generate. Black and Gray Swan risks seem remote, almost certainly covered by insurance policies or the responsibility of governments, while Green Swan opportunities are the stuff of speculation by delusional do-gooders. Such reality distortion shapes incoming information in both direct and indirect ways, creating worldviews that may differ considerably from those held by other people elsewhere in the same organization, let alone in the wider world.

Once inside that rarefied world, you are often struck by the silence. In part, this results from fewer people working in larger spaces, but it also reflects deference for those in authority—plus the pervasive white noise effect of air-conditioning systems. My self-appointed role has been to disrupt all that, to bring activist agendas, and sometimes the activists themselves, into the conversation. To be grit in the corporate oyster. The task is to deliver inconvenient and sometimes irritating intelligence that rocks hard-won certainties, challenges assumptions, and, perhaps most disruptively of all, forces leaders to think wider, deeper, longer, different.

NO LAUGHING MATTER

Over time, I have learned to sugarcoat the pill a little, at least to begin with. I was once asked by a board member of 3M, a company I have long admired, why I used humor when challenging her board, and others. My reply was that I could never remember jokes, so any humor had to be situational, playing off what people said around the table. She had a psychology background, it turned out, and her analysis was that mine was a dangerous tack to take but that, at least in her view, I had made it work. Where it did work, she told me, it did so for two key reasons:

First, because it relaxed people, by signaling that I was not a missionary—and could be playful with my own change agenda. Second, she suggested, it disrupted the normal power dynamics. My humorous interventions were read by those around the table as an expression of confidence, suggesting that the change movement under discussion was potentially more powerful than they had imagined.

To be clear, I am not recommending that everyone in a boardroom situation use humor. Far from it. For me it comes naturally, whereas few things are worse than forced playfulness. Instead, the point here is that it can be a mistake to simply rely on numbers, PowerPoint slides, name-dropping, and forceful handshakes. Most people in boardrooms and C-suites are human and are best engaged with that fact in mind.

The organizations I have co-founded have used a shifting cast of characters to play out the change agenda, inviting in activists and NGOs, social innovators and entrepreneurs, impact investors, and more recently people from the world of exponential change. The aim has been to communicate one unvarying message, that deep-seated changes are afoot, that they have major implications for the business and its stakeholders, and that they hint at even deeper trends.

The term "paradigm shift" is often misunderstood, but that is what is now underway. Indeed, if I had to name the single book that had the biggest impact on my own early thinking, it would be Thomas Kuhn's 1962 book, *The Structure of Scientific Revolutions*. I read it a year or two after its first publication, when I must have been fourteen or fifteen, and it totally changed the way I saw the world.

Kuhn's focus was on science. He compared the worlds of biology and evolution, on the one hand, and, on the other, of wider science and technology. Like many people, I had thought of the world as something that generally changed incrementally, uniformly. But Kuhn concluded that science, like the natural world, goes through periods of radical disruption. Periods of what evolutionary biologists call "punctuated equilibrium."

Once you know this, again, you see punctuations everywhere. Kuhn also introduced the terms "paradigm" and "paradigm shift" to capture the process by which our understanding of reality evolves. A paradigm, simply stated, is the overall model that shapes our thinking about what the key challenges are and how they might best be solved. So while Kuhn had science in mind, we will expand the concept here to embrace economic and business paradigms.

A paradigm shift, where an old model dies and a new one emerges, proceeds in five main stages. Before the first one, which Kuhn called "Normal Science," there is what he called "Pre-Science," where there is no effective paradigm at all. That has long been the case with the sustainability agenda. The previous paradigm, which we all grew up within, steered our species through the Industrial Revolution, two World Wars, the Great Depression, the Cold War, and so on.[1] But over time any model enters a period of "Model Drift," where a growing number of anomalies surface that current mind-sets struggle to spot and understand, let alone tackle.

Reality distortions ensure that early, weaker signals of change are filtered out. Ultimately, however, even those who are most invested in the existing model are forced to admit that it is breaking, or already broken. The moment of "Model Crisis." This is what is now happening with current forms of capitalism, democracy, and, I believe, early notions of sustainability. These are times of growing anguish for those whose training and experience lead them to believe that the world works in ways that it no longer seems to. Now the stage is set for a "Model Revolution," where a new model evolves.

Generally, this new way of thinking is very hard for most incumbents to take seriously—because it is so radically different. But however tough it may be to get our brains around, the evidence suggests that we are now living through the final stage of this Kuhn Cycle, "Paradigm Change." Our sense of what is normal is being turned upside down, inside out. To put it in a nutshell, our thinking and priorities are now having to catch up with the fact that living in the Anthropocene epoch changes the business environment profoundly and likely forever, at least in market terms.

GETTING FROM REJECTION TO REGENERATION

But try downloading all of that for a busy CEO or CFO, in front of their colleagues, some of whom are waiting for the first sign of weakness to pull their rival down and trigger a battle for succession. These people are struggling to play the game they know, with little appetite for new rules, let alone new games. And, time and again, I have seen evidence of Goethe's conclusion: "People only hear what they understand." Over time, though, I have learned to spot—and work around—five distinct stages in major change processes.

First comes *Rejection*, also seen in Kuhn's "Pre-Science" phase, when the new reality is so different that people literally cannot see it or take it in. Where they do wake up, many fight back, working to ensure that the new reality is stillborn. Interestingly, people are as likely to dismiss the prospect of Green Swan outcomes as they are the possibility of Black Swans.

Second, there is our equivalent of the "Normal Science" era, *Responsibility*. Most leaders do not want to be actively or noticeably irresponsible, but one problem here is that the relevant agendas keep expanding as the failures of the old order become more obvious. This can be an excuse, an alibi, for tokenism or inaction. Responsibility is a key, necessary condition for progress but can never be a sufficient condition for turning around Black Swan trajectories or building Green Swan ones. And it is an issue wherever there are human beings, whether they are operating in the private, public, or citizen sector. The repeated sex-for-aid scandals that have rocked Oxfam are proof enough of that.[2]

Third, as the change agenda expands, leaders recognize that they cannot do this on their own, however large and well-endowed their organization may be. This, essentially, is Kuhn's "Model Drift" stage. The pioneers seek out partners and join change-minded business-to-business initiatives. They want others to help them do what they have been forced—or volunteered—to do. This is our *Replication* stage. Over time, however, such replicators will need to expand their efforts to the next two stages.

Fourth, in the *Resilience* stage, and despite all the responsibility-focused efforts to date, the consequences of the new, disrupted, and disruptive order start to press in, as the climate emergency is now doing. True leaders begin to think about how to make their operations more resilient. They consider the resilience of the communities, cities, and countries where they operate. Kuhn called this the "Model Crisis" phase. This will be crucial in the Anthropocene as we move into future realities with pronounced Black Swan characteristics.

Then, fifth, there is the *Regeneration* stage. Most people's understanding of what is meant by sustainability and the triple bottom line
would fit quite comfortably in the previous stages. The challenge now
is to change our overall operating economic and political systems en
route to regenerating our economies, societies, and, crucially, the natural world. This is the insight that sits at the heart of today's emerging
change paradigm.

So where are you, and where is your organization, in this progres-
sion? What might be the implications of moving to the next stage? To
get a better sense, we will now walk through the five stages, probing
how top teams see and understand the relevant trends. In the process,
it is worth remembering that the process is rarely linear as outlined
here—and the Green Swan agenda will increasingly focus on the fourth
and fifth stages, Resilience and Regeneration.

Stage 1: REJECTION

This opening stage sees rejection working in several directions. Black
Swans? *What are you on?* Green Swans? Same question. Critics of the
existing, dysfunctional system reject key aspects of the way it works,
while those locked into the system reject such criticism as naïve, irrational, socialist, or, the ultimate put-down for insiders, "communist." The
closer we get to an inflection point, where change goes into overdrive,
the more bitter the exchanges can become.

It is all too human to deny or ignore evidence that suggests tomorrow will be radically different. After all, if that were true much of what
we think, much of what we do, and much of what we are valued for
would no longer apply. We would be cast adrift, awash in uncertainties.
Significantly, science tells us that the human mind often shuts down
when stressed, rather than flipping into more creative modes.

Which is a concern, given that these are already frightening times
for business leaders, with a succession of leaders of well-known company heads being toppled. WPP founder Sir Martin Sorrell was one

conspicuous casualty; Carlos Ghosn of Renault-Nissan-Mitsubishi was sent to prison in Japan, awaiting trial; and Sacha Romanovitch, admired for her social change agenda at auditors Grant Thornton, was fired—with some colleagues dismissing her as "a socialist."[3]

Nor was it simply high-profile CEOs losing their footing. Anyone tracking the largest companies would have seen major shifts in the rankings between 2009 and 2018. ExxonMobil, which had topped the chart in 2009, fell to ninth place by 2018, and a similar fate hit companies like Walmart (dropping from second to thirteenth position), P&G (fourth to twenty-third), and Coca-Cola (tenth to twenty-fifth).[4]

Intriguingly, the top four by 2018 were Apple, Amazon, Alphabet, and Microsoft, with Facebook—not even listed in 2009—in sixth position, ahead of long-established companies like Johnson & Johnson, ExxonMobil, and Bank of America. The top-tier carnage has been even more striking than might at first appear, according to the McKinsey Global Institute team that compiled the rankings.

About half of the top 10% of companies fell out of the top tier every business cycle, with 40% of these dropouts falling all the way down to the bottom 10%.[5] Such shocking market volatility may have opened up some minds to the threats of disruption, but it has also shut others down—or at least focused them even more intensely on ramping up business-as-usual.

It also encourages manipulative behaviors. Consider cell phones. There is now clear evidence that radiation from cell phones causes cancer, according to one of the largest studies ever conducted. Yet, not surprisingly, there is also clear evidence that such findings have been actively suppressed by the industry. Britain's *Observer* newspaper reported the following:

> Not one major news organisation in the US or Europe reported this news. But then, news coverage of mobile phone safety has long reflected the outlook of the wireless industry. For a quarter of a century now, the industry has

been orchestrating a global PR campaign aimed at misleading not only journalists, but also consumers and policymakers about the actual science concerning mobile phone radiation. Indeed, big wireless has borrowed the very same strategy and tactics big tobacco and big oil pioneered to deceive the public about the risks of smoking and climate change. And like their tobacco and oil counterparts, wireless industry CEOs lied to the public even after their own scientists privately warned that their products could be dangerous, especially to children.[6]

Not everyone lies, of course, even in industries under pressure. But the market and political force fields operating on top teams skew outcomes in many different ways, some good and some bad. Worse, as an industry sinks into difficulties, internal critics often quit, or are fired, with those replacing them typically having more relaxed views about their change obligations—coupled with much shorter timescales.

Take Samsung. For more than a decade, the South Korean company robustly denied that hundreds of workers had fallen ill in its factories making chips and LCD displays. The struggle to force the company to accept blame took off in 2007, when taxi driver Hwang Sang-ki refused a settlement for his twenty-two-year-old daughter, who died of leukemia after working for four years at a Samsung plant. Over time, about 260 Samsung workers developed serious diseases following exposure to toxic chemicals.[7]

For years, Samsung aggressively fought claims through the courts. But that ended in 2018, when the company finally admitted responsibility—and offered a compensation plan of up to $132,000 to each worker who had contracted cancer or other serious diseases while working at its plants since 1984.[8]

You see pretty much the same pattern of denial at county, city, and country levels. To take just one example, Johnson County, Indiana, which voted overwhelmingly for Donald Trump as president, has

experienced full force the impact of his rollback of health and environmental regulations. Children there have been hit by a wave of cancers,
spread by a carcinogenic plume spreading underground from an old
industrial site.[9]

Even self-declared responsible businesses sometimes lobby against
efforts to clean up the planet. Take Tetra Pak, the Scandinavian packaging company. Some years ago, I did three consecutive sessions with
senior Tetra Pak executives from around the world. Each time, some
fifty or sixty of them would troop into the conference center, sitting
on real grass imported into the space. Some even went barefoot as we
discussed the evolving sustainability agenda.

But as the tide has built against plastic packaging, the same company was reported to be lobbying to head off bans of the plastic straws
it uses on the sides of its drink packs. Tetra Pak's head of sales and
marketing told customers that it was trying to develop paper straws but
faced "significant challenges" in making them work with its cartons.[10]
In effect, it was saying, *Slow down, back off. Trust us. Give us time.*

Even where companies embrace the responsibility agenda, rejection remains part of their armory.[11] The likelihood that they will be
conflicted grows massively where their basic business is not—or not
yet—fit for the future. But perhaps the most powerful factor behind
the inability to see what lies ahead is the very different nature and scale
of what is now coming at us. Business leaders are being told that the
global economy is heading for the mother of all downturns as the carbon bubble bursts.[12]

This process, largely driven by disinvestment from fossil fuels and
the exponential growth of new technologies in renewable power generation and electric vehicles, could ensure that the oil industry's vast
reserves turn into stranded assets, undermining pension funds heavily
invested in old forms of energy—and triggering both mass unemploy-
ment and, as a consequence, new waves of populist politics.

Recall that the financial crisis of 2008 was triggered by the loss of
$0.25 trillion, then imagine what might happen when this coming

energy transition wipes somewhere between 1 and 4 trillion dollars from the global economy.

Stage 2: RESPONSIBILITY

Fifty years ago, as already mentioned, Chicago economist Milton Friedman famously declared that the "one and only" social responsibility of business is to create profits. Ever since, variants of these words have become the mantras of capitalism, corporations, and business schools—with a growing range of consequences, many of them unintended. Gray and Black Swan outcomes have proliferated because of Friedman's ideology.

It is now fashionable to attack Friedman for market myopia. But it is worth recalling again what he went on to say: "In [a free economy] there is one and only one social responsibility of business to use its resources and engage in activities designed to increase its profits so long as it stays within the rules of the game."[13]

Too often, we forget that last bit: *So long as it stays within the rules of the game.* The notion that these rules were set by governments and enforced by regulators was taken for granted. But our politicians and governments increasingly underperform, partly because of the corrosive impact of globalization on traditional forms of democracy, partly because established political models are running out of steam, and partly because so many political leaders fail to recognize the magnitude and import of what is now happening as we move deeper into the Anthropocene.

As a result, thoughtful business leaders and investors accept that the values and mind-sets that many Friedman-inspired mantras promote are dangerously out of touch with emerging realities. Even so, you can picture some business leaders rolling their eyes when Pope Francis told the heads of major oil companies that there was "no time to lose" in addressing the climate emergency.[14] You can also picture some shrugging when the Church of England joined forces with the State of New

York to call on ExxonMobil, the world's largest listed oil company, to set targets for cutting its greenhouse emissions.[15]

Even some tough CFOs paid at least momentary attention, however, when the call to action came from Laurence D. Fink, chief executive of BlackRock, the world's largest investor. Fink, whose firm managed more than $6 trillion in assets at the time, used his annual letter to call on the chief executives of the world's largest public companies to "not only deliver financial performance, but also show how it makes a positive contribution to society."[16]

Warning that he saw "many governments failing to prepare for the future, on issues ranging from retirement and infrastructure to automation and worker retraining," Fink widened the focus to include issues like the climate emergency, noting that "society is increasingly turning to the private sector and asking that companies respond to broader societal challenges."

The point Larry Fink was making was not that profits are bad but that having a well-thought-through social purpose is now inextricably linked with a company's longer-term profitability and wider success. Meanwhile, what was once a single-issue set of agendas is now converging in powerful new ways. Indeed, a recent McKinsey survey concluded that leading companies are increasingly formalizing their responsibility and wider sustainability programs.[17] Nearly six in ten respondents said that their organizations were more engaged with the agenda than they had been a couple of years earlier, with just 9% saying that engagement had actually declined.

So how are top teams handling all of this? One clue came when 70% of McKinsey's respondents said that they had a formal sustainability governance in place, compared with 56% back in 2014. A small but growing number, 16% rather than 12%, also reported that their companies now had a board-level committee dedicated to sustainability issues.

It is still difficult to judge from outside whether a given company is living up to its public commitments. Think of Germany's Volkswagen

(VW), praised as the sector leader in the 2015 Dow Jones Sustainability Index survey, a few weeks before the company found itself mired in the multibillion-euro "Dieselgate" scandal.[18] Even VW itself later accepted that its activities had been "wrong, unethical and repulsive."[19]

Or consider Carillion, the UK outsourcing company. They collapsed in 2018, at a considerable cost to taxpayers, after a process that a committee of MPs concluded was a "story of recklessness, hubris and greed."[20] But listen to what their chief sustainability officer was saying not long before the company ran off the rails:

> Businesses without visionary engagement, inspiring stories, responsible compliance or public trust are businesses without competitive futures. For Carillion, sustainability is how we shape our competitive future, how we add value and how our people create even more inspiring stories for a better tomorrow.[21]

Who wrote those words? What did they mean by them? Would they still stand by them? Did they see the writing on Carillion's wall even as they signed off on this propaganda?

Nor is it just businesses in such everyday sectors getting into trouble. Take Facebook again. As 2019 dawned, the company was still in the dock after what the media described as a "tsunami of crises." Speaking on behalf of the company he founded as recently as 2006, CEO Mark Zuckerberg protested the following:

> We're a very different company than we were in 2016, or even a year ago. We've fundamentally altered our DNA to focus more on preventing harm from all our services, and we've systematically shifted a large portion of our company to work on preventing harm.[22]

That is a seriously charitable—some might argue self-serving—picture of what has actually been going on as Facebook scrambled to protect and grow its $5 billion of profit each quarter. As the company has been forced to employ swarms of so-called moderators, to filter posts on the network, so the flaws in its evolving rulebook have attracted growing criticism. Pity these poor people, in places like the Philippines, forced to continuously view some of the most offensive viewing ever produced.

The New York Times was provided with more than 1,400 pages from Facebook's rulebooks, leaked by an employee concerned that the company was exercising too much power—and making too many mistakes. For example, the moderators were once told to remove fundraising appeals for volcano victims in Indonesia because a co-sponsor of the drive was on Facebook's internal list of banned groups.[23]

Tracking and managing a company's responsibilities is hard enough in normal times, but the world now being conjured by the likes of the so-called FAANGs, made up of Facebook, Apple, Amazon, Netflix, and Alphabet's Google, is far from normal. As they have bulldozed their way to the pinnacles of today's economy, they have triggered cascades of unintended consequences. Now people and their governments are pushing back.

But, at the same time, a profound paradox is at work—we increasingly want to see business leaders, including the CEOs of the FAANG companies, filling the vacuum left by governments. As a result, we now live in the age of the "activist chief executive." Here is how columnist Rana Foroohar put it:

> Such industry titans are willing to take an unusually public stand. Think of Merck chief Kenneth Frazier's resignation from Donald Trump's American Manufacturing Council in response to the US leader's handling of racial violence in Charlottesville. Or Unilever head Paul Polman's leading a charge on climate change as the US government was pulling out of the Paris accord. Or any number of corporate leaders, from Apple's Tim Cook to Salesforce's Marc Benioff, threatening to move business out of US states that do not respect LGBT rights.[24]

Exciting times, but we should be wary of simply leaving it to companies to handle the great challenges of tomorrow. Listen to a former managing director of Larry Fink's BlackRock. Tellingly, Morris Pearl is a board member of the Patriotic Millionaires, a group that went countercurrent by arguing against Trump's tax cuts for the wealthy. "We have a really good system for making the changes that we as a society feel are important," Pearl cautioned. "It's called voting. I don't think it's the job of business to decide what issues to take on. It's the job of the public to decide that, and then to tell business how to act."[25]

Stage 3: REPLICATION

Successful solutions need replication and scaling. Some businesses achieve this, but many do not. As a result, the upper reaches of corporate responsibility and sustainability rankings tend to feature the same companies, often over considerable timescales. Why? Because leadership in the early stages of a paradigm shift takes immense vision, courage, and stamina. But once a business leader has switched on, steering their organization onto a new change trajectory, they often discover that others, particularly in their value chains, are not moving as fast—if they are moving at all.

The logical next step is to look for ways to build the necessary critical mass for change. The obvious place to begin is the world of industry federations and associations, which have often been extreme laggards. Like convoys, it is often said, they protectively move at the speed of their slowest, most lumbering and potentially disadvantaged members. The result is that they not only drag their collective feet but also often actively lobby to slow or stall change.

As the number of "activist CEOs" has grown, however, there has been a proliferation of new business-to-business platforms committed to co-evolving new agendas, new codes and standards, and new forms of best practice. The competitive landscape for such replicators is constantly shifting, with new actors spotting potential opportunities and launching new initiatives.

Take RE100, launched in 2014 by the Climate Group and CDP, formerly the Carbon Disclosure Project. CDP runs an evolving global disclosure system enabling companies, cities, states, and regions to measure and manage their environmental impacts. By its own calculation, its network of investors and purchasers represents over $100 trillion of assets and activities.[26] RE100, however, goes beyond disclosure—and beyond the other business-to-business platforms mentioned—by actively pursuing market creation. It unites more than 100 influential businesses committed to using 100% renewable electricity, pushing toward massively increased demand for—and production of—renewable energy.

Companies in the commercial and industrial sector account for two-thirds of the world's end-of-use of electricity, according to IRENA, the International Renewable Energy Agency. Switching this demand to renewables will accelerate the transformation of the global energy market, aiding the transition to a low-carbon economy. A key part of the RE100 effort involves communicating the increasingly compelling business case for renewables, including greater control over energy costs, increased competitiveness, and delivery of emissions goals. It showcases relevant business action and encourages wider supplier engagement. Critically, too, it also works to tackle barriers that block or slow companies that might otherwise reap the benefits of going 100% renewable.

An A to Z of companies have joined RE100, with AkzoNobel, Apple, Allianz, AstroZeneca, Autodesk, Aviva, and AXA just some of those whose names start with A. Signatory companies set a public goal to source 100% of their global electricity consumption from renewable sources by a specified year. They then disclose their electricity data annually, and RE100 reports on their progress.

Facebook, Citigroup, and Ikea are among those moving in similar directions and at similar speeds. Facebook planned to cover 100% of its electricity needs from renewable energy by the end of 2020.[27] The company's demand for electricity is growing rapidly, but its data centers, which have to run 24/7, cannot risk losing power when the wind drops or the sun sets. The solution is to sign "green tariff" deals with local power utilities.

The aim is to ensure these purchases lead to additional capacity, rather than replacing or rebadging other clean energy investments that would have happened anyway. The sense of critical mass can be contagious, with member companies feeling they are part of something much bigger, something that can really move the needle. And this approach is itself now replicating.

Backed by around-the-world sailor Ellen MacArthur, the Circular Economy 100 is another precompetitive innovation program enabling organizations to realize their circular economy ambitions faster. It brings together corporates, governments and cities, academic institutions, emerging innovators, and other stakeholders.

Some such initiatives seek to "push" change by moving the supply lever, while others try to "pull" change, by moving the demand lever. Some, too, seek to do both. But as these networks spread, we must keep a close eye on what they are doing—and on the level of impact they are creating. The recent ban of waste imports to China, for example, underscored just how poorly founded many recycling, and so-called circular, projects can be.

China, which imported more than seven million tons of waste plastic in 2016 alone, according to the China Scrap Plastic Association, began enforcing rules that banned the import of twenty-four grades of solid waste, including waste paper and plastic.[28] Countries like Britain, which had shipped some 2.7 million tons of plastic waste to China since 2012, have since struggled to find alternative places to dump the stuff.

On the other side of the world, in Australia, the general manager of Suez Western Australia, an affiliate of the French utility company, noted that the Chinese move had "taken out effectively 50% of the global capacity for recyclable material to be re-manufactured—it's removed it overnight."[29] Such crises are likely to be a continuing feature of the global economy as it gradually works its way toward various forms of future fitness. But, remember, such Black Swan problems often create the preconditions for Greener Swans to hatch and take flight.

Stage 4: RESILIENCE

When I first heard the fourth R-word, *resilience*, in the early 1970s, it was in relation to the Florida Everglades. Before they were massively engineered for water control and agriculture, they had a natural resilience that was increasingly being compromised. Then, early in the new century, I sensed the word mutating—as I heard consultants on the lawns in front of the World Economic Forum's headquarters, overlooking Lake Geneva, arguing that the word *resilience* was bound to supplant *sustainability*.

It didn't, of course, but it did become an increasingly important part of the sustainability agenda and lexicon. Many such terms bubble up on the edges of such gatherings. Many wither on the vine, but sometimes events and wider trends push once-marginal concepts into the mainstream. That certainly happened with resilience, as a growing number of natural disasters hit major cities and battered and tangled global supply chains.

One moment when this new normal forcibly impressed itself on businesspeople came when manufacturers of products like car parts and computer hard drives were hit by massive floods in Thailand during 2011.[30] Billions of dollars of damage resulted, putting some 650,000 people at least temporarily out of work.

Japanese car makers that were only just recovering from an earlier earthquake and tsunami in their home country, that had massively disrupted their domestic supply chains, now found a key alternative manufacturing base in Southeast Asia in disarray. Companies like Toyota and Honda were forced to cut back production at plants as far away as North America because their Thai suppliers were literally underwater. Making the situation worse were the increasingly tight links that global companies have forged in their supply chains to minimize the need to hold expensive inventories and utilizing "just in time" manufacturing. When one link breaks, it can disrupt production on a global scale.

In the Anthropocene, such pressures will build on a growing range of economies, sectors, and businesses. It is reassuring that pioneers like Kongjian Yu are helping to turn a growing number of China's cities into "giant sponges"[31] to ensure greater resilience to flooding, but there is a limit to how far such measures can ward off the rising tides.

The insurers—and the reinsurers who insure the insurers—have been in the front line of all this for a while. The way they see it, things keep getting worse. This will have consequences for the premiums they charge and the insurance conditions they impose. At the same time, too, much of the resulting premium income is invested in the world's stock markets, so the referred pain will progressively shape market pressure on listed companies—and, in the process, create radically different market opportunities.

This Black Swan trend has been building for a while. Back in the last century, for example, I chaired the first environmental foundation set up in the City of London, the capital's financial center.[32] The original funding came from insurance syndicates that had underwritten a range of emerging risks in the United States. Among areas covered were asbestos, radioactive waste, and contaminated land. Everything had looked manageable at the time, but then the US Superfund legislation was introduced to drive the cleanup of sites contaminated with hazardous substances and pollutants, radically changing the liability regime and landscape.

Despite warnings that underwriting such risks on the basis of a half-day audit, at a time when those seeking insurance had every reason to dissemble, was a recipe for disaster, the market had boomed. Then it hit the Superfund wall—and something like 20% of the losses that almost brought down Lloyds, the London-based insurance market, were linked to claims in related areas. Luckily, the foundation had already been endowed, but I was left acutely aware of the financial implications of such environmental risks.

Now, almost forty years on, there have been signs that the cycle is repeating itself. Global markets for "alternative capital" for underwriting natural catastrophe risks have been flashing alarm signals. Indeed, the head of Swiss Re, the giant reinsurance firm, drew parallels with the signals that appeared ahead of the US mortgage crisis a decade earlier.[33]

So-called catastrophe bonds also boomed, with investors attracted by the fact that such bonds paid reasonable returns and were not correlated with other financial markets. But it turned out that they had their own problems as a series of natural disasters forced big payouts. The evidence suggests this new normal will cost us all dearly. Here's how the *Financial Times* described the natural disasters of 2018:[34]

> While fires are common in some parts of the world such as California and Australia, what is unusual about this year is that these disasters are happening in different places, catching people unawares. Fires burning inside the Arctic Circle are the result of drought and heat that have made forests there unusually combustible. Peat lands in the UK, traditionally protected from blazes by moisture, have also been burning amid a heatwave. In the US, the annual average number of fires has doubled since the 1970s, and this week Yosemite Valley, a national park in California, was evacuated due to a nearby fire.

All of this was before the apocalyptic fire hit Paradise, California, the deadliest fire in the state's history. With at least eighty-six people dead and huge areas of forest turned to cinders, the catastrophe had a fatal impact on the finances of the power utility PG&E.[35] It was soon facing at least $30 billion in liabilities for fires in 2017 and 2018, after evidence that the Paradise fire was sparked by one of its facilities. That figure did not include penalties, fines, or punitive damages. With its shares down 49% in three months, PG&E was soon considering bankruptcy protection for some—or maybe all—of its businesses. In the end, it did declare bankruptcy.[36]

Clearly, life in the Anthropocene is unlikely to be any form of busi-ness-as-usual. We seem to be moving into a world where the resilience of our economies and societies will be tested to the limit. If the planet exceeds the two-degree warming target on which most economic analy-ses are now based, the results will likely include massive storm damage, acute water shortages, mass displacements of populations, and, as a result, growing tensions, volatility, and conflict.

Increasingly, resilience will be in the minds of boards and C-suites. In parallel, a growing number of cities and countries are taking the resilience agenda on board too. One of the most interesting initiatives in recent years was the 100 Resilient Cities initiative launched by the Rockefeller Foundation. It explained the background as follows:[37]

> By 2050, 75% of the global population is expected to live in cities.
>
> Because of the collision of globalization, urbanization, and climate change, not a week goes by that there's not a disrup-tion to a city somewhere in the world: a cyber attack, a natu-ral disaster, or economic or social upheaval. Meanwhile, cities face acute stresses, such as poverty, endemic crime and vio-lence, or failing infrastructure, that weaken a city over time.
>
> While cities can't predict which disruptions will come next, they can plan for them, learn from them, and generate additional benefits through the same investments, such as opportunities for economic growth or improved parks for city residents. In other words, they can achieve "resilience dividends" that can make cities better places to live not just in times of emergency, but every single day.

Then, more or less out of the blue, the Rockefeller Foundation announced that it planned to end this side of its work, although that will most certainly not end the challenge faced by the world's cities.[38]

Someone who specializes in advising CEOs and corporate boards is Roger Martin, whom I first met through the Skoll Foundation for Social Entrepreneurship. So what does he have to say on resilience? His view is that we would be far better off focusing on resilience than on efficiency, including resource efficiency, and here is his explanation of why, published in the *Harvard Business Review*:

> Eliminating waste sounds like a reasonable goal. Why would we *not* want managers to strive for an ever-more-efficient use of resources? Yet as I will argue, an excessive focus on efficiency can produce startlingly negative effects, to the extent that superefficient businesses create the potential for social disorder. This happens because the rewards arising from efficiency get more and more unequal as that efficiency improves, creating a high degree of specialization and conferring an ever-growing market power on the most-efficient competitors. The resulting business environment is extremely risky, with high returns going to an increasingly limited number of companies and people—an outcome that is clearly unsustainable. The remedy, I believe, is for business, government, and education to focus more strongly on a less immediate source of competitive advantage: resilience. This may reduce the short-term gains from efficiency but will produce a more stable and equitable business environment in the long run.[39]

The problem with the way much of the global economy is headed, Martin argues, is that it is increasingly consolidated, with fewer and fewer companies controlling a growing slice of value creation. The advantages to the rich and powerful are clear, but the downsides are potentially catastrophic—with super-concentrated systems being much less resilient than more diverse systems.

Here is the way he sums up his argument: "Resilience is the ability to recover from difficulties—to spring back into shape after a shock.

Think of the difference between being adapted to an existing environment (which is what efficiency delivers) and being adaptable to changes in the environment. Resilient systems are typically characterized by the very features—diversity and redundancy, or slack—that efficiency seeks to destroy."

Which now brings us to the fifth stage, *Regeneration*. If millions of businesses worldwide are still stuck at the *Rejection* stage, and tens of thousands have arrived at least at the foothills of the *Responsibility* stage, the numbers energetically and coherently working on the *Replication* and *Resilience* stages are in the thousands, at best. Those so far working on *Regeneration* are fewer still—but, like it or not, this is where our best hopes for a better future now lie.

Stage 5: REGENERATION

Green Swans, in essence, are about regeneration—of our societies, economies, and, most fundamentally, of the biosphere. This is where things must now go seriously exponential, in a good way. Just as a few leaves swirling in the wind can herald an approaching storm, so a few mentions of a word can herald a profound shift in the change agenda. In the same way that I heard the word *resilience* surfacing in a new sense well over a decade ago, so in recent years I have increasingly heard the words *regeneration* and *regenerative*.

When major branding agencies start to pick up on such things, you know there is something stirring in the zeitgeist. We should always be wary of dipstick polls, but one that caught my eye was carried out in the United Kingdom, the United States, Australia, and China. Ad agency JWT's Innovation Group had commissioned the study from its research unit, Sonar. Sonar kicked off by saying, "Doing less harm is no longer enough. The future of sustainability is regeneration: replenishing and restoring what we have lost and building economies and communities that thrive, while allowing the planet to thrive too."[40]

The sample size was tiny, just over 2,000 adults, but the results were suggestive. Consumers, the study concluded, "are already operating from a sustainability mindset, even if they struggle to make it a lifestyle." Key findings included the following: 92% of "consumers" (but note again the sample size) said that they were trying to live more sustainably, with 54% thinking they could be doing more; similarly, 92% of consumers insisted that sustainable business practices should be standard, and 86% of consumers agreed that companies and brands that continue to deplete finite resources are, in effect, "stealing from the future."

That "doing less harm is no longer enough" line is central to the emerging change agenda. It tracks back to the thinking of people like architect Bill McDonough and his colleague Michael Braungart.[41] Braungart, a former Greenpeace director, is German, while McDonough is American—and it is striking how much of the regenerative economy thinking has been coming out of the United States, even during the Trump regime.[42]

Take Paul Hawken with his Project Drawdown, described as "the most comprehensive plan ever proposed to reverse global warming."[43] As the Drawdown team explained, "We did not make or devise the plan— the plan exists and is being implemented worldwide. It has been difficult to envision this possibility because the focus is overwhelmingly on the impacts of climate change. We gathered a qualified and diverse group of researchers from around the world to identify, research, and model the 100 most substantive, existing solutions to address climate change."

The conclusions were extraordinary.[44] "What was uncovered," the Drawdown team reported, "is a path forward that can roll back global greenhouse gas emissions within thirty years. The research revealed that humanity has the means and techniques at hand. Nothing new needs to be invented, yet many more solutions are coming due to purposeful human ingenuity. The solutions we modeled are in place and in action. Humanity's task is to accelerate the knowledge and growth of what is possible as soon as possible."

This is part of an emerging counterrevolution within the wider sustainability movement. At a time when much of the "sustainability industry" remains focused on countering the Rejection strategies of major industries and on promoting the Replication of a wide range of Responsibility strategies, all important tasks, the more challenging Resilience and Regeneration strategies are also now evolving at a rapid pace, albeit from a much lower base.

Both Hawken and our mutual friend and colleague Janine Benyus, the world's leading champion of biomimicry,[45] have been major influences on the carpet tile maker Interface. No accident, then, that Interface has been developing a revolutionary experiment in resilience and regeneration, in which it seeks advice not from McKinsey or other consultants but from nature, and forests in particular.

Ever since Interface founder Ray Anderson read Hawken's book *The Ecology of Commerce*, and was jolted into the realization that his generation of business leaders could eventually be seen as eco-criminals, "stealing from the future," the company has looked to nature for inspiration. As it happens, Interface first embraced sustainability in 1994, the same year the triple bottom line launched. Different roots, or routes, but the same source code.

One of the first questions Anderson asked was, "If nature designed a company, how would it function?" This early thinking helped his top team work toward a redesigned business that would have no negative impacts and, critically, an increasingly restorative influence. Working with Benyus's organization Biomimicry 3.8,[46] Interface evolved a methodology to transform facilities such as factories from "zero footprint" to providing the same environmental benefits as high-performing ecosystems.[47] In effect, this "factory-as-a-forest" (or, for the technically minded, FaaF) approach means that any Interface facility would produce the same environmental services as its site would if occupied by a forest.

Another American, and one whose thinking has forcefully influenced the Volans agenda, is John Fullerton, founder and president of the Capital Institute. Previously, he was a managing director of JPMorgan, where he worked for over eighteen years.[48] At JPMorgan, he managed various capital markets and derivatives businesses around the world, then shifted to private investments—and was subsequently chief investment officer at LabMorgan, following the merger with Chase Manhattan.

After experiencing the horrors of 9/11 firsthand, Fullerton became an impact investor, while investigating our multiple interconnected systemic crises. That, in turn, led to the launch of the Capital Institute in 2010. The core idea driving his work on "Regenerative Capitalism," which closely links to that of people like Benyus, Braungart, Hawken, and McDonough, runs as follows:

> Our conventional economic and financial theory, whether liberal or conservative, is grounded on flawed and often unquestioned critical assumptions. Like using an inaccurate map, we are unable to see what we need to see. We are lost. Our flawed assumptions include: exponential growth of material throughput on a finite planet, the all-knowing "invisible hand" of markets [. . .] the statistics underlying modern portfolio theory, value at risk, and on and on.[49]

Fullerton concludes that "regeneration goes well beyond sustainability. In fact, sustainability as an outcome is only possible if the system as a whole is regenerative." This is very far from the case today. So the next question is how we can develop a route map that is better designed for the Anthropocene. A key next step is to take a closer look at the financial markets, where John Fullerton was involved for so long. Before getting to that, though, we need a better framework within which to think about and address such challenges. So it is time to zero in on the Future-Fit change agenda.

CHAPTER 5

GETTING FUTURE FIT

A Blueprint for Tomorrow's Capitalism

S o what does the Green Swan genetic code look like? How does it differ from the code shaping Black and Gray Swans? And how can we create Green Swan dynamics in every sector of the economy, enabling us to move exponentially toward a more resilient and regenerative future for all? Such questions have been at the heart of my self-directed learning journey. A fair few initiatives claim to have the answers, but for my money the most interesting currently is the rapidly evolving work of the Future-Fit movement.[1]

Stand by for a deep dive into a future world where markets and businesses will be encouraged to measure their progress toward a planetary "break-even point"—and the best of our politicians, business leaders, and investors will work tirelessly to move beyond that break-even point toward genuine regeneration of our economies, societies, and biosphere.

Some readers may be feeling a little skeptical by now. Most of us aspire to be fit, of course, whatever our current state of health. But we know that what we do about it can be another matter entirely, with good intentions blown away in the blur of everyday life. Meanwhile, the media bombard us with suggestions on how to become healthier—with advice on diets, exercise, social activities, and now also genetic testing. As the exponential and increasingly global spread of obesity and linked chronic diseases suggests, however, much of this advice is falling on deaf ears.

As a result, much of this advice is watered down over time to make it more palatable. Instead of being advised to walk at least thirty minutes a day, for example, we are told we can get by with a few minutes of intensive exercise. And many of us ignore even that advice. The result, as we saw in Chapter 3, is that the world now faces a growing range of Gray—and even Black—Swan outcomes in the form of runaway obesity and linked chronic diseases, among them diabetes.

Exactly the same dilution has happened with the sustainability agenda for governments and business. The need to change the economic system has been understood and argued for decades, largely ineffectively. As the more thoughtful business leaders have promoted greater responsibility among their collaborators and competitors, the focus has shifted from system change to the potential shorter-term benefits for given business organizations: the so-called business case for action. In parallel, we have seen a growing focus on the sort of materiality analyses described earlier: Which of all the potential issues could cost us, financially?

Such approaches can get things moving but tend to favor incremental change rather than the exponential, systemic changes now so urgently needed. To trigger such shifts, we must move well beyond the development of new frameworks and tools, toward new thinking— and, critically, toward new operating systems for our economies.

Imagine the questions that business leaders would ask themselves at each of the five stages of change sketched in the previous chapter. In the Rejection phase, they would be interested in lobbying groups they could join to drive positive system change initiatives—and in resigning from, ideally publicly, those that do not. That would involve a significant shift in their lobbying efforts. Today, huge numbers of lobbyists and influencers are expensively retained to ensure that the interests of their corporate clients are defended, however indefensible some of them may be. As a result, even the most transparent companies tend to clam up when asked about their lobbying and influencing activities.

Consider BP. The *Financial Times* recently reported that the oil giant had lobbied intensively to weaken US rules on methane emissions—even as it cast itself as leading a campaign to cut the release of the potent greenhouse gas.[2] The newspaper reported that documents collated by Unearthed, an arm of Greenpeace, showed "a pattern of behavior related to US methane regulation that jars with BP's calls to cut emissions, and which critics contend will contribute to higher levels of pollution in the future."

Given the combination of market pressures and human nature, it is inevitable that some leaders, companies, and industries get stuck at this defensive stage, largely because they cannot see how they fit into the sort of future their critics are pushing for. They fight on, using fair means and sometimes, the evidence suggests, foul. But as the pressures build, and the evidence becomes more persuasive, leading companies move into the Responsibility, Replication, Resilience, and (increasingly exponential) Regeneration stages.

In the first of these, they are likely to get involved in energetic discussions as to just how far their responsibilities should extend through their value chains. When PUMA, the German sportswear firm, carried out their first Environmental Profit and Loss analysis, they discovered that by far the biggest negative footprints were left by geographically distant "Tier 4" suppliers.[3] For PUMA that included people like leather makers and cattle ranchers in Brazil.[4] So was this their responsibility or not? Was it really a challenge for one brand among many? Or was it perhaps, instead, something for the relevant governments to take in hand? If so, what level of responsibility would a Tier 1 brand have to encourage government action in a different country?

Challenging questions. As the change agenda continues to expand, companies often fight back against emerging issues and movements that threaten their reputation and business models. As we saw with Tetra Pak, even responsibility-oriented companies still lobby politicians and rule makers to defend their current operations—and that is unlikely ever to change completely. To minimize the impact of such lobbying, we must now take action ourselves.

First, the system change sector needs to ensure that all such activities become radically more transparent over time. Second, it must move toward a coherent, converged, and effective model of, and agenda for, change—increasingly endorsed, supported, and practiced by all. There is no shortage of proposed solutions. In fact, there has been a proliferation of business-to-business platforms and related codes, standards, and commitments over the years, a fair few of which I have been involved in creating and developing. Some have taken off, while others stalled. But collectively such efforts are helping to shift the center of gravity of the debate about the roles and responsibilities of business.

Stand back from all this effort, however, and it is possible to detect the outlines of a deeper running paradigm shift. This is taking us toward a wholesale reboot of capitalism and of the ways in which impact, value, and wealth creation are considered, tracked, and rewarded. Still, there are times when I wonder whether we are building a modern-day Tower of Babel. As we worked through the early stages of our Tomorrow's Capitalism Inquiry, the Volans team was repeatedly struck by the multiplicity of initiatives and languages used in this space. Indeed, some business leaders use the very fragmentation of change movements as an alibi for no, or slow, change. Come back when you have sorted yourselves out, they say.

As we scouted around for an evolving approach to system change that held real promise, we kept coming back to the work of the Future-Fit Foundation.[5] In retrospect, it helped considerably that several members of the Volans team and our wider ecosystem have been involved in the work since early on, that the approach was formally built around the triple bottom line, and that we have also worked with a number of the businesses that are now co-evolving the Future-Fit Benchmark.

The deeper we dug into the underlying methodology, the more convinced I became that it has the potential to evolve into a global operating system for business, markets, and, eventually, cities and governments. But in terms of what the future will need, it is still an embryonic answer. There is a yawning gap between where the initiative is, encouraging replication by recruiting new businesses to test and apply the framework, and where it would need to be to deliver a future that was both radically more resilient and increasingly regenerative.

So with those provisos, we now ask two questions: What is the Future-Fit approach? And how can it help us solve the systemic crises we now face? Then, sneakily, there is a third: What would it take to evolve this approach to the point where it was an operating code not simply for businesses and their supply chains but for all markets, cities, and national and international government agencies?

WHAT IT MEANS TO BE FUTURE FIT

Our global economy is failing us in three critical ways, and we must work out how to tackle them together if we are to get things back on track. That is the Future-Fit Foundation's starting point. First, and foremost, they say, we are "disrupting and degrading Earth's natural processes, upon which we as a species and all other life depend." As the global population grows, the climate emergency will press in ever harder on our economies and societies.

Second, the basic needs of billions of people around the world are very far from being met, while the gaps between the haves and have-nots have been growing in ways not seen for a long time. The United Nations' Sustainable Development Goals are certainly an impressive and comprehensive wish list in terms of what needs to be done, but without a very different level of business involvement the results are likely to be disappointing—and, for some, inflammatory.

Third, as the United Nations itself has come to recognize, while governments and public sector agencies can set all the goals and targets they want, only business has the power to address these critical challenges at the necessary pace and scale. With the bulk of business activity stuck in incremental gear, and with today's markets often actively disincentivizing timely and effective action, we are still heading toward Black Swan breakdowns—rather than Green Swan breakthroughs.

A different approach is needed. "As the engines of our global economy," the Future-Fit team concludes, "companies must be encouraged and equipped to tackle these systemic issues."[6] But how do we get a crucial mass of companies on the right track? A critical early step is to rethink how we define and create long-term business value and wealth. The ongoing process by which this is being achieved is sketched in Figure 4.

Rather than being separate areas for consideration, as in the first of the three images below, or being overlapped as in the second, the pursuit of true "system value" requires a different mind-set—where business serves society and where both are contained within, are dependent on, and help to protect and regenerate the wider natural environment.

"To mobilize business in pursuit of future-fitness," the Future-Fit team advises, "we must empower all market actors to recognize and reward the right kinds of action. This starts with understanding that companies don't exist in a vacuum: business can only thrive if society prospers, which in turn demands that we safeguard Earth's life-support systems." The implication: Over time, in an increasingly uncertain world, "focusing on system value will become ever-more critical to business success."

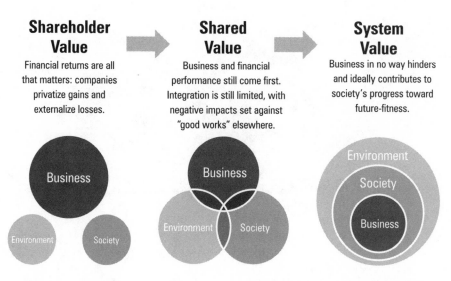

Figure 4: The Long Road to System Value
Source: Future-Fit Foundation

In this future, every company "must be willing to disrupt the status quo—or wait to be disrupted. Markets are already changing in new and unexpected ways. Threats to existing business models—from new entrants, substitutes, advocacy groups or supply chain disruptions—will only continue to rise as societal expectations shift and environmental pressures grow. The companies that thrive tomorrow—and will be celebrated for doing so—will be those that do most to respond to these disruptive market forces today."

The force fields at work are sketched in Figure 5, augmenting Michael Porter's "five forces." The idea here is that competitive rivalry, whether at the economy, industry, or organizational level, is powerfully shaped by four other factors: the threat of new market entrants and substitute products and services, and the power of both customers and suppliers. In the Future-Fit model, however, rather than being handled as a separate set of challenges, they are set within societal expectations and broader environmental constraints.

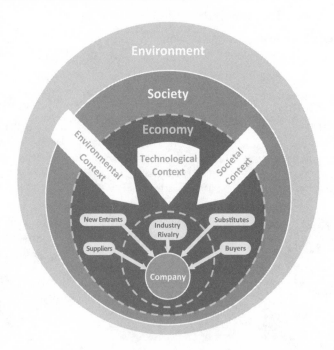

Figure 5: Force Fields, Overlapped with Michael Porter's Five Forces
Source: Future-Fit Foundation

SO WHERE DID ALL THIS BEGIN?

Shortly after we launched SustainAbility in 1987, a Swedish doctor called Karl-Henrik Robèrt launched the Natural Step movement in Sweden. At the time our Green Consumer movement was taking off, so I spent much of my life on the road, speaking at events and advising companies. At several events, particularly in Scandinavia, Robèrt would put in an appearance, but then he would literally run off after speaking—so intense was the pressure on his own time.

Since 1989, the Natural Step movement has worked with thousands of corporations, municipalities, academic institutions, and not-for-profit organizations. In the process, it has demonstrated that a strategic shift toward sustainability can lead to new opportunities, reduced costs, and dramatically reduced ecological and social impacts. By 2018, it had twelve offices, with associates and strategic partners in over fifty countries.

The movement's message remains clear, science based, and rooted in Robèrt's conviction—stemming from his background as a cancer doctor—that diagnosis of complex problems demands a system perspective. It prescribes the following outcomes.

In a sustainable society, nature is not subject to systematically increasing the following:

1. Concentrations of substances from the earth's crust (such as fossil CO_2, heavy metals, and minerals)
2. Concentrations of substances produced by society (such as antibiotics and endocrine disruptors)
3. Degradation by physical means (such as deforestation and draining of groundwater tables)
4. And in that society there are no structural obstacles to people's health, influence, competence, impartiality, and meaning.[7]

Over the last few years, the Future-Fit Foundation has built on the Natural Step's work, collaborating with a range of academic experts—including Robèrt himself—to co-evolve what it refers to as the eight properties of a future-fit society. These are plotted in Figure 6.

GETTING TO BREAKEVEN

Note, however, that this diagram does not yet spotlight the business role in delivering systemic change. This is where the "Future-Fit Business Benchmark" comes in. It translates the sort of systems science developed by the Natural Step community into practical tools, starting with a clear definition of the "extra-financial break-even point," a critical concept that all companies must now strive to reach.

The idea is to create businesses, markets, and economies that are simultaneously environmentally restorative, socially just, and economically inclusive. The term *extra-financial* means those forms of impact and value that are not captured in current financial accounting, which mainly still operates on the basis of a single, financial bottom line. Extra-financial accounting moves us into the area of ethical, social, environmental, and governance accounting and reporting. The ultimate goal is to achieve new, more integrated forms of accounting.

Energy is renewable and available to all	*Water* is responsibly sourced and available to all	*Waste* does not exist

Natural resources are managed to safeguard communities, animals, and ecosystems	The environment is free from *pollution*

People have the capacity and opportunity to lead *fulfilling lives*	Our *physical presence* protects the health of ecosystems and communities

Social norms, global governance and economic growth **drive** the pursuit of future-fitness

Figure 6: Eight Properties of a Future-Fit Society
Source: Future-Fit Foundation

The idea of the "break-even point" comes directly from the financial world. The original term signals that a company's revenues and expenses have balanced out during a specific accounting period.[8]

It implies that the firm did not lose anything but equally did not earn anything either. By extension, the term *extra-financial breakeven* refers to the point where the negative and positive impacts of a business are balanced.

Whereas breaking even would be seen as a failure in most mature businesses, in the sustainability field it would be a major breakthrough—the first, critical step toward a truly responsible, resilient, and regenerative strategy and, over time, economy. The underlying logic shaping the Future-Fit approach is illustrated in Figure 7, with the four boxes explaining key lessons learned during—and about—the process of moving toward greater fitness for the future.

What does this mean in practice? How does the process look in a company that is moving from left to right in Figure 7? The best way to find out is to take a look. A good place to start is the Danish healthcare company Novo Nordisk.[9] This takes us back into the world of the triple bottom line, despite the product recall I announced in 2018. To address any uncertainty this may stimulate, let me tentatively allow that the triple bottom line remains useful, indeed central, as long as it enables and spurs the push toward global system change—and is set in the context of what we might call the three Rs: Responsibility, Resilience, and Regeneration.

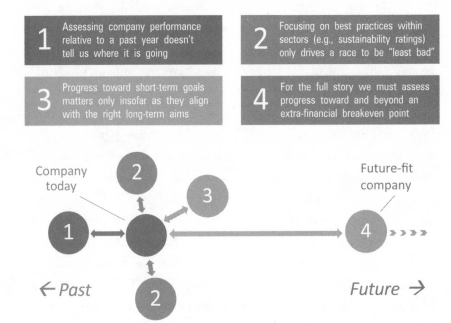

Figure 7: Toward the Future-Fit Company
Source: Future-Fit Foundation

THE NOVO NORDISK WAY

Our Green Consumer work in the late 1980s and early 1990s[10] had a significant impact on Novo Nordisk's industrial enzymes business, with enzymes used in a wide range of products, including household detergents. Our challenge focused on potential skin sensitization issues historically associated with the use of the company enzymes in so-called biological detergents. That turned out to be old news, but other critics were also concerned about the company's use of genetic engineering, a highly contentious technology at the time.

Rather than moving into Rejection mode, however, Novo Nordisk's then president, Mads Øvlisen, took the then extraordinary step of inviting his critics—us—in to speak to anyone we wanted across the business. When we duly reported back, with three main recommendations, the company promptly adopted them all. Even more significantly, it later became the first major company in the world to re-charter itself around the triple bottom line. This happened in 2004, when Novo Nordisk spun out its enzymes business as Novozymes, which also embraced the triple bottom line from the outset. Over time, the company's progress did not go unnoticed.

Still, when I first saw the cover of the November 2015 edition of *Harvard Business Review* (*HBR*), I thought it was probably the weirdest ever published by the once-staid magazine. The featured CEO had a great yellow sticky note smacked onto his face, with the right-hand top edge slightly peeled back. An arrow pointed at his neck and asked, "Who is it?" As it happens, I knew the answer, having first met Lars Rebien Sørensen shortly after he took over as CEO of Novo Nordisk.

As fate would have it, he was hosting a dinner in New York, early in 2002, just around the corner from where the emergency services were still clearing the rubble of the World Trade Center after the 9/11 attacks had upended America and much of the rest of the world.

After the magazine had published its profile, I asked *HBR* editor-in-chief Adi Ignatius why his design team had stuck the sticky on the image of Sørensen, who had just shot to the top of the magazine's ranking of CEOs.[11] Ignatius explained that, despite his extraordinary track record, Sørensen was a virtual unknown outside Denmark.

But why had Sørensen rocketed up the rankings in such an extraordinary way? I wondered. He had dislodged Amazon's Jeff Bezos, who tumbled to the eighty-seventh slot. Ignatius's answer for my query was simple: *HBR* had decided to change its ranking system, with 20% of the final score now allocated to environmental, social, and governance factors. A fascinating example of how the system change agenda is going to upset existing pecking orders. As far as I know, this was the first time that a mainstream CEO ranking had been headed by a business leader who explicitly attributed his company's success to its adoption of the triple bottom line.

Ignatius explained the process in more detail in an article alongside the 2015 rankings:

How did this mild-mannered, bespectacled executive land
in the #1 spot on our list? It's partly due to his company's
(darkly) fortuitous decision years ago to focus almost exclu-
sively on diabetes treatment. The runaway global growth of
the disease has driven up the company's sales and stock price.

But his standing also reflects Novo Nordisk's deep
engagement with social and environmental issues, which
now factor in to our calculations. "Corporate social responsibility is nothing but maximizing the value of your company over a long period," says Sørensen, who has been with
the company for 33 years. "In the long term, social and
environmental issues become financial issues."

Ask chief executives why their companies are performing
so well, and they'll typically credit a brilliant strategy coupled with hard-nosed, diligent execution. But when you ask
Lars Sørensen of Novo Nordisk what forces propelled him
to the top of HBR's 2015 ranking of the best-performing
CEOs in the world, he cites something very different: luck.
Based in Copenhagen, Novo Nordisk was founded in the
1920s to make insulin, then a newly discovered drug. In the
years since, demand for diabetes treatments has exploded;
today close to 400 million people suffer from the disease.
The company now controls nearly half of the market for
insulin products—which are second only to oncology drugs
as the fastest-growing category of pharmaceuticals. The firm
also has branched into growth hormones, hormone replacement therapies, and drugs to treat hemophilia.

In effect, the company had been successfully digging its own gold-
mine, treating a disease that has been growing exponentially around
the world. So something that Sørensen said in his *HBR* interview must
have had at least some of his company's investors sitting bolt upright in
their Aeron chairs, spluttering in disbelief:

HBR: What happens to your business if diabetes is eventually cured?

LRS: After I became CEO, in 2000, I predicted we would cure diabetes in 15 years. We're still 15 years away. But that is the big goal. I tell my employees, "If we wind up curing diabetes, and it destroys a big part of our business, we can be proud, and you can get a job anywhere. We'll have worked on the greatest social service of any pharmaceutical company, and that would be a phenomenal thing."

This is a radically different way of thinking about a need: Solve it if you can, even at the cost of your current business. True wealth creation in the health-care sector, you could say, lies in promoting health and well-being, not manufacturing and selling medicines to cure disease. Important clues to why the company thinks this way were revealed in Sørensen's answer to four subsequent questions:

HBR: Why do you measure results using a triple bottom line?

LRS: Our philosophy is that corporate social responsibility is nothing but maximizing the value of your company over a long period of time, because in the long term, social and environmental issues become financial issues. There is really no hocus-pocus about this. And Novo Nordisk is part-owned by a Danish foundation that obliges us to maximize the value of the company for the long term.

HBR: How do social and environmental issues become financial issues over time?

LRS: If we keep polluting, stricter regulations will be imposed, and energy consumption will become more costly. The same thing applies on the social side. If we don't treat employees well, if we don't behave as good corporate citizens in our local communities, and if we don't provide

inexpensive products for poorer countries, governments will
impose regulations on us that will end up being very costly.

**HBR: Some people believe it's impossible to measure
corporate social responsibility and that it's a mistake to
try to quantify such behaviors.**

LRS: The public is divided about that. There are individuals
trying to push this agenda, and very helpful academics, such
as Michael Porter with his idea of shared value, are trying to
develop measurements and make them more credible.

**HBR: Why don't more companies manage for the long
term?**

LRS: They feel shareholder pressure to create short-term
value, as opposed to strengthening the long-term sustainability of the company. Shareholders can move their capital
around with a flick of a finger, yet in pharmaceutical research
it can take more than 20 years to develop a new product.

As so often happens, the success story did not last forever, at least
for Sørensen. His luck turned. Following unfavorable developments in
the US insulin market, Novo Nordisk got into troubled waters and he
was out. But having kept a close eye on the company since, I believe
it is clear that the triple bottom line approach has largely ridden out
the disruptions. Listen to the company's next CEO, Lars Fruergaard
Jørgensen, speaking in 2019:

> We have a clear ambition to be a sustainable business, and
> our actions in 2018 have significantly strengthened our
> platform for sustainable growth. We are simplifying our
> way of working to become more robust and agile in the face
> of new challenges. And we continue to create long-term
> value for patients and shareholders by driving innovation
> in-house and, notably, in collaboration with new external
> partners. Throughout, we have done all this in a financially,

environmentally and socially responsible way, reaffirming our commitment to the Triple Bottom Line principle that drives our approach to business.[12]

When I visited Novo Nordisk while writing this chapter, I talked all of this through with Susanne Stormer, vice president of corporate sustainability. She underscored three key aspects of the "Novo Nordisk Way," drawing on their work with the Future-Fit team.

First, she said, a successful company delivers value to the world, offering innovative solutions to unmet needs. Second, it must do so in a responsible way—with views on what is responsible inevitably shifting over time. Third, it needs to anticipate and seize the relevant market opportunities.

Over time, the once-contentious use of genetic engineering by companies like Novo Nordisk, in their case for producing both enzymes and pharmaceuticals, gradually made its way into the largely taken-for-granted mainstream. But now the pot is being given another lively stir.

A CLEAR DESTINATION IS A RELIEF

The thing about technology, as Future-Fit CEO and co-founder Geoff Kendall would later tell me, is that "big change can accrue from a large number of tiny decisions. We know of several companies that are using the Future-Fit method to improve their R&D decisions, for example, to assess in a holistic way whether a possible new material would make their products 'better' or 'worse.' What we've found is that many companies already have some way of telling whether a particular technology decision will be better or worse from an environmental point of view, but this usually takes the form of a home-grown spreadsheet that some well-meaning employee (who has often since left) cooked up using some long-forgotten criteria, and which everyone continues to use unquestioningly.

"This could seem depressing," he continued, "but I find it a cause for optimism: We can change direction if we can just tweak all of those spreadsheets which companies already have, which is much easier than getting people to adopt completely new behaviours in the first place." He added, "I see this as kind of equivalent to the martial arts approach of using your opponent's own body weight to achieve what you want, rather than trying to stop and then move him!"[13]

When I asked what had worked well, Kendall noted that participating companies had discovered that "a clear destination is a relief, not a burden." He explained, "It's been encouraging to hear numerous business leaders say that they much prefer having something concrete to work toward, what we might call necessary practice, even if it feels impossibly far away—rather than getting frustrated by aiming for goalposts which move every year, as when they pursue best practice."

Stretch goals stimulate our imaginations. "Absolute versus incremental goals catalyze breakthrough thinking," Kendall stressed. "The Future-Fit mindset gets people thinking differently, very much in line with what they say about having a '10X' goal rather than a 1% or even 10% goal. I talk about this in terms of the familiar moonshot analogy: We didn't get to the Moon by setting out to climb Everest and putting off thinking about the next step until we got to the summit. As an example, one company we're working with has now come up with a multi-stranded plan to completely eliminate all of its product packaging waste within fifteen years. It is not ready to go public with that yet, but that is a real moonshot."

At a time when corporate social responsibility, or CSR, is increasingly undervalued, he advises, CSR teams can reposition themselves as expert collaborators, not just as data consumers as part of their reporting activities. The Future-Fit Foundation's action guides provide twenty to thirty pages of specific guidance on how to pursue and assess progress toward each "break-even" goal. This is far more detail than a CSR team would ever need, but that is because these guides are designed for issue-specific experts on water, human rights, procurement, and so on, elsewhere in the business.

"Typically the CSR team will engage key people in the business about Future-Fit at a conceptual level," Kendall says. "Then those people will say, 'OK, I get it in theory—but what does it mean in practice?' Then the CSR team can hand over the relevant action guide, or guides."

Kendall adds, "What we've heard is that the conversation can completely change at this point. In many cases, the CSR folk have told us that this is the first time their colleagues see them as offering something useful, rather than just asking for information, which will end up in an annual report few people will read. One individual said that it's like being able to hand someone a fire extinguisher, rather than just repeatedly nudging them to pay attention to the fire!

"As one CSR head told me, after doing this his team had a better view than anyone in the business of the systemic risks that the company might be vulnerable to, because they had spotted a number of critical data gaps. Think of this formula: *data gaps = information blind spots = business vulnerabilities*. That particular CSR head got his CEO to sign off on pursuing future-fitness simply by sharing with him what those gaps were and why they mattered."

DON'T TELL ANYONE!

Great, but what has not worked so well, at least to date? "Getting businesses to speak up about their use of the Benchmark is hard," Kendall replied. "A few companies initially recoiled at the idea of setting a goal that they don't know how to reach. It seems that people often struggle to embrace a 'mental time horizon' that goes beyond their budgeting cycle. This appears to be quite a visceral reaction, particularly in engineering-focused companies, where the idea of over-promising is anathema. That said, the problem seems to be more about what people are prepared to say publicly, rather than what they are prepared to do quietly. We've heard from quite a number of companies that have started using the Benchmark but have sent out an internal instruction, 'Don't tell anyone,' because their current performance looks so bad. Hopefully this will change when companies see others who are prepared to speak up!"

What about the financial market reaction? "Investors love the idea," Kendall answered, "but all but the most progressive don't want to have to think about it very much: We've done a lot of work to help investors understand how to look at their portfolios through a Future-Fit lens, and those who actively engage with companies find the approach and tools very helpful. But the reality for most mainstream investors is that they have neither the bandwidth nor the appetite and expertise to think about extra-financial performance in anything but the most simplistic terms. They may be *very* keen to have our data, but they want it spoon-fed to them."

Then he went deeper: "You can see why the world ended up with the Dow Jones Sustainability Indexes[14] and similar schemes, when such investors have for years been saying, 'Just give me a number to say how sustainable every company is.' I've come to realize that 'Coverage is King' when it comes to data for investors. Many would rather have some kind of low-quality data for the world's top ten thousand companies than have excellent data for just one thousand companies. This is nuts, but unfortunately it's the way the system works right now—with massive spreadsheets attempting to rank everyone by combining a wide range of data points in complex but often arbitrary ways."

"That's why," Kendall continued, "we've ended up with organizations like MSCI and Sustainalytics, which provide hundreds of metrics for thousands of companies, but with most of them lacking any kind of comparability because the data have been obtained by manually 'scraping' the values from GRI[15] reports and dumping them into a big database. Since different companies interpret the GRI guidance in different ways, and since the scraping process is prone to human error, the resulting data are nowhere near as comparable or meaningful as they may look when they appear on a Bloomberg terminal."

MAKING MARKETS FUTURE-FIT

So how might the Future-Fit approach work at the level of an entire market? "I could speak volumes on this one," Kendall replied, "but here are two key points: We're starting to actively recognize and guide efforts to shift market dynamics. We improved our guidance relating to shifting markets, which fall under the umbrella heading of *Social norms, Global governance*, and *Economic growth*. There are four so-called 'Positive Pursuits' in this group, relating to governance, infrastructure, market mechanisms, and social norms. These are exactly where I think the link is strongest between Future-Fit and your Tomorrow's Capitalism Inquiry. It is these four areas of activity which contribute to shifting markets so that Future-Fit outcomes *become the norm* rather than the exception."

To my mind, this Positive Pursuits element of the Future-Fit approach is what potentially takes it way beyond the work of others in the field. Kendall went on to say, "Our nascent Future-Fit ecosystem is effectively a market in its own right: Our 'Accredited Partners' and 'Certified Professional' programs are for services and solutions providers looking to make money from helping companies and investors become Future-Fit. It's wonderful to hear that companies we have never even heard of are now seeing enough value in what we do that they are paying consultants to find out how to apply it!"

Finally, what about cities and governments? This will obviously be a big part of any future where all of this properly embeds at the system level. "We haven't yet done anything," Kendall lamented, "but I would *love* to get our City Benchmark built. We know how to do it. It's just a question of finding the time and resources to ensure that we can do it without losing focus on promoting the wider adoption of the Business Benchmark."

The same was true at the time with governments. "We haven't done much here yet, but the need for regulations that incentivize Future-Fit outcomes is obvious. I am mulling over whether to put together a Future-Fit primer specifically for policy makers. One of our

Development Council members brought up the point that companies aiming to become Future-Fit face a tension, in that if they commit to the right ambitions and bold actions to get there, including things like carbon neutrality, then the very fact that they are investing ahead of regulation means that their less progressive peers may be more cost-competitive in the short term. So the leaders are effectively placing a bet that regulation will catch up—and soon—so that their early steps will translate into a business benefit. Otherwise they will be at a commercial disadvantage, which could actually end up impeding their ability to thrive and serve as continuing champions for the cause."

And the answer? According to Kendall, it would be "for these leading companies to be screaming from the rooftops for that new regulation to come in quickly, so that their bet is more likely to pay off. I think this was a key moment for many people. They suddenly saw that making public Future-Fit commitments, and lobbying for regulation to support them, could actually be in their best interests, not just in the interest of society more broadly." Whether or not we succeed in cracking the Green Swan genetic code, new political and commercial pecking orders will be established, a subject we turn to now.

PART III

NEW PECKING ORDERS

Winners and Losers

CHAPTER 6

INCUBATING UGLY DUCKLINGS

Industrial Evolutions

lack Swan futures will hurt many people, while benefiting fewer and fewer—although, inevitably, some people will make a lot of money from doing the wrong thing. Green Swan futures, by contrast, will benefit growing numbers, while inevitably damaging the interests of some of those most invested in the old order. To coin a phrase, you can't make tomorrow's economic omelets without cracking at least somebody's eggs today. So ask yourself: Will you win or lose as the coming disruptions take hold? Will you, your family, your organization, or, indeed, your pension plan prove to be future fit through a decade where the realities of living in the Anthropocene hit home ever more powerfully?

Hard to say, you may conclude, but think of it this way: The fate of your organization and of the wider economy now depends on the speed with which we conceive and incubate new generations of Ugly Ducklings, creating the political, policy, legal, market, and sociocultural conditions that allow Green Swan solutions to flourish. Recall our working definition:

A Green Swan is a profound market shift—generally catalyzed by some combination of Gray and Black Swan challenges and changing paradigms, values, mind-sets, politics,
government policies, technologies, business models, and
other key factors—that delivers exponential progress in
terms of economic, social, and environmental forms of
wealth creation. At worst, a Green Swan achieves this outcome in two dimensions while holding the third steady.[1]
There may be a period of adjustment where one or more
dimensions underperform, but the aim is an integrated
breakthrough in all three dimensions.

Technology is partway through this listing of Green Swan characteristics, but will be make-or-break. In the next decade we will have all
the technology we need, or the potential to develop it in short order.
It is easy to understand, even agree with, those who argue that technical fixes are not the cure-all for the systemic crises that now confront
us. Nothing is. High on any sensible list would be transforming the
way we think, the way we do politics, and the ways in which markets
value things currently dismissed as "nonfinancial," "extra-financial," or
"externalities." But technology still comes thundering in close behind,
a necessary condition for success across all other areas.

Alongside the seemingly inexorable growth in human population
numbers, and our accelerating move into ever-larger cities, probably
our defining technology to date, the rapid evolution of the most
powerful spectrum of new technologies in human history guaran-
tees exponential shifts that test us—and our market and political
systems—to the limit. So how can we better understand and manage
the Black, Gray, or Green Swan implications of these new technologies, together with the novel applications of existing technologies?
How can we keep track of the multifarious ways in which new technologies are hybridizing to create totally new benefits and totally
new challenges?

How do you feel about facial recognition, for example? Users of smartphones, myself included, may like how our phones now recognize our faces, rather than demanding complicated passwords or fidgety fingerprints. The technology may be invisible and unintelligible, but it feels comfortable, personal. Imagine sweeping through airports in a fraction of the usual time, surrounded by customized information as invisible cameras, sensors, and databases work out who we are and whether or not we deserve access—or arrest. This possibility is increasingly reality, welcomed by many but feared by some of those who know most about the potential for misuse and abuse.

Growing concerns are now being expressed about the potential unintended consequences—and ethics—of this emerging set of industrial revolutions. The prevailing "move fast and break things" philosophy in Silicon Valley has proved problematic as new technologies undermine fundamental things like democracy. The shuttering of Google's much-vaunted Advanced Technology External Advisory Council almost as soon as it was formed was a worrying sign that such companies cannot be trusted to do this coherently on their own.[2] This is a real problem, given that facial recognition is an object lesson both in how rapidly new technologies can sweep through our societies and how, in the process, they create consequences unforeseen by those who spawned them.

Think of China, determined to dominate the market for related technologies by the 2030s. One Chinese facial recognition start-up, YITU Technology, can already identify an unknown person from a database of some two billion people within seconds.[3] Put on your Green Swan glasses and it is possible to imagine a future where our interactions with all sorts of technologies become increasingly seamless, frictionless, and personalized. But then switch to your Black Swan glasses and the risks associated with the country's rapidly evolving surveillance state become painfully obvious.

Such dynamics were front-of-stage and front-of-mind when Chris Anderson interviewed Twitter CEO Jack Dorsey at the TED 2019 conference. The context was that the social media platform was being accused of spreading lies and hate—and, in the process, of undermining democracy itself. You could almost imagine Anderson, who runs TED, aching to tell Dorsey to replace Twitter's blue bird symbol with a Black Swan.

As *Wired* magazine reported, the exchange left those onstage—and in the room—deeply agitated, frustrated, and increasingly angry.[4]

TURN THE FUCKING WHEEL!

Dorsey, whom *Wired* described as taking the stage in his "signature black hoodie and jeans, unkempt facial hair, and black beanie," quickly managed to get under Anderson's skin. After twenty minutes of back-and-forth, Anderson erupted. "We're on this great voyage with you on the *Twittanic*," he told Dorsey. "There are people in steerage who are saying, 'We are worried about the iceberg ahead!' And you say, 'That is a good point' and 'Our boat hasn't been built to handle it,' and we're waiting, and you are showing this extraordinary calm and we're all worried but outside saying, 'Jack, turn the fucking wheel!'"[5]

Throughout, Dorsey listened like the yogi he apparently aspires to be. "It's democracy at stake!" exploded Anderson. "It's our culture at stake! It's our world at stake! You're doing a brilliant job of listening, Jack, but can you actually dial up the urgency and move on this stuff?" That anger suggests a growing awareness of the Black and Gray Swan potentials of our fast-evolving electronic habitats.

The day before Dorsey appeared at TED, interestingly, a well-known journalist had issued a challenge to all the "gods of Silicon Valley," listing them—Mark Zuckerberg, Sheryl Sandberg, Sergey Brin, Larry Page, and, yes, Jack Dorsey. Carole Cadwalladr was the brilliant journalist who broke the story about the role of Cambridge Analytica in distorting the UK vote on Brexit.[6] Here is what she had to say: "This technology you have invented has been amazing, but now it is a crime scene. My question to you is, is this what you want? Is this how you want history to remember you? As the handmaidens to authoritarianism all across the world? You set out to connect people and the same technology is now driving us apart."

She summarized her speech in an article in a British newspaper, *The Observer*: "As things stood, I didn't think it was possible to have free and fair elections ever again. That liberal democracy was broken. And they had broken it."

Every scientific and industrial revolution brings its own issues and concerns, as people like the original Luddites knew to their cost. But what feels different this time around is that an extraordinary spectrum of unprecedented powerful technologies is advancing on a historically unprecedented front and unprecedented pace. The consequences are profound, systemic, historic—and those in the know argue that the process is still in its early stages. Indeed, the next couple of decades will likely see the introduction of more disruptive technology than at any previous time in our evolution as a species.

So how can we learn from what is already happening and head off or cope with the inevitable unintended consequences? Technology champions like Peter Diamandis—co-founder of the XPRIZE Foundation and Singularity University—have long argued that technology will create what he calls "a world of abundance." The planet, he argues, has lots of resources—water, energy, and so on—but we are hampered because we cannot access them efficiently. Happily, he says, "technology is a resource-liberating force." Used wisely, it could help us solve our most pressing resource constraints.[7]

The operative word here, mine, not his, is *wisely*. Central to the exponential and abundance mind-sets, technology remains the subject of intense suspicion in the activist world, and understandably so, with most activists able to spool off a growing list of unwise applications of emerging technologies.

Too many change agents, meanwhile, remain distracted by the task of driving incremental improvements in existing and incumbent technologies, ranging from gasoline-powered automobiles to energy- and chemical-intensive air-conditioning systems. All-important work, but we must now move well beyond that. We must engage and shape the thinking of those who will transform our future with such things as artificial intelligence, the internet of everything, autonomous vehicles, synthetic biology, and, some insist, geoengineering.

Do not misunderstand me: This rapid evolution of technologies is exciting and has the potential to tackle many of the central challenges we face in this century, if properly used. In terms of potential upsides, I know from personal experience that a radically better future is already here, or taking shape fast.

Consider one example I came across on a recent visit to Israel. So great is the pressure for water there, with the Dead Sea now truly dying because of water starvation, that investor interest is surging in aeroponics—a technology that involves growing plants in mist or even air, rather than soil or water. To give a sense of the potential, one company is now growing fifty times more plants per meter, and in the process using twenty times less water than traditional agriculture. A breakthrough technology, whichever way you look at it, and we spotlight more below. But how quickly will such applications scale? And, history suggests, for every upside there is generally a downside, even if it may not always be equal and opposite.

THROTTLED BY THE MIDGLEY SYNDROME

Trying to spot potential downsides to emerging technologies, and blind spots in the minds of those developing them, I have for years asked a single question of pioneers I have met in the high-tech world, whether in London, Tel Aviv, or Silicon Valley. The question is, Have you ever heard of Thomas Midgley Jr.? Almost routinely, the answer has been no.

At which point I have explained that there is no great shame in such ignorance. Midgley was at his peak back in the 1920s and 1930s. Yes, he was a brilliant chemist and engineer; yes, he worked with a couple of the corporate giants of the era, General Motors and DuPont; and, yes, he was awarded over one hundred patents. But this, you might conclude, was a long time ago, in a world far, far away.

But the reason I have asked that question so doggedly is this. Midgley came up with leaded gasoline, for example. At the time this was a genuine breakthrough in anti-knock technology, and therefore a key contribution to fuel efficiency for vehicles. An early Green Swan in the making. But it was a breakthrough that proved to have immense unforeseen consequences in terms of the unintended, unsuspected damage to young people's nervous systems. A Green Swan sprouting black feathers, even wings, before turning as dark as the night.

Later, Midgley went on to synthesize early Freons, a form of chlorofluorocarbons (CFCs), chemicals that had a number of significant advantages, including in terms of safety. But they went on to tear a hole in the stratospheric ozone layer. In fact, Midgley has been described as *the single organism in Earth's history that has inflicted the most damage on the planet*. A true creature, indeed a creator, of the Anthropocene. The unintentional patron saint of Black Swans, you might say.

So we really should have heard of him, particularly people working on tomorrow's breakthrough innovations. Surely he, and the devastating lessons learned from his life, should now feature alongside the works of such people as Berners-Lee, Dyson, Edison, Gates, Musk, Venter, or Zuckerberg in the syllabuses of all business schools and university technology departments?

Finally, as a third demonstration of how even the most brilliant of minds can unintentionally trigger unfortunate consequences, I generally conclude the story by noting Midgley's subsequent development of an automatic bed, using ropes and pulleys, to get him in and out of bed after he sadly contracted polio. In 1944, the bed strangled him.

At this point a wave of nervous laughter usually runs through the audience, though my point is deadly serious. At least some—and probably most—of the technologies we are now developing with such enthusiasm and dedication will end up strangling key elements of our future. Not that you would guess it from talking to most people at the cutting edge of technology. For most of the time, inventors and innovators see the future through the proverbial rose-tinted spectacles.

I recall sitting alongside internet pioneer Vint Cerf at a Gallup-hosted dinner when someone asked him why his generation hadn't foreseen the problems we are now struggling with as hackers, cyber-bandits, and secret services test the internet to its limit? His answer was that, at the time, he and his colleagues were fighting so hard to get the internet to stand on its own feet they could hardly imagine a world where it would be so advanced that it could generate such nightmare scenarios.

Sometimes such myopia is a matter of ignorance or an inability to think around corners. But often it represents an act of will, necessary to keep the show on the road, to persuade funders to invest and employees to stay and keep on keeping on. Whatever the innovation, they are told, it is going to change the world for the better.

The Midgley story, however, suggests that the ways in which such people change the world will very much depend on how Black and Green Swan dynamics come into play in our economies, societies, and, crucially, our politics. It also suggests that we should look tomorrow's gift horses very carefully in the mouth. Before we consider how that might best be done, though, it is worth underscoring just how unusual the current moment is in technology's evolution.

RIDING HYPE CYCLES

I have long been fascinated by technology, writing many books about it. I edited a newsletter, *Biotechnology Bulletin*, for fifteen years, enabling me to visit almost a hundred firms involved in genetic engineering in Europe, Japan, and North America during the peak of the first biotechnology boom. If I learned any one thing over that time, it is that new technologies trigger feeding frenzies that typically follow a standard arc like that visualized in the famous Gartner Hype Cycle. This, Gartner tells us, evolves through five main stages:

1. **Innovation Trigger:** At this point we see some form of breakthrough in a key technology, accompanied by one or more initial product launches, sparking growing media and public interest. Early adopters talk up the potential benefits for their businesses and organizations. I recall arriving on the doorstep of one biotechnology firm whose CEO (Martin Apple of IPRI) had promised that his industry would create, in effect, the equivalent of "pork chops on trees." Colorful language, no question, but some will no doubt have taken him literally. Even so, on the day I showed up on the doorstep to meet him, his company filed for bankruptcy.

2. **Peak of Inflated Expectations:** After a period of intensifying interest, speculation, and early-stage investment, we often see rapidly inflating expectations of what a given technology can achieve in the short term. This is often spurred by increasingly breathless media coverage of the gathering tempo of technology and company failures—in contrast to the rapid breakthrough successes expected by employees, customers, and investors.

3. **Trough of Disillusionment:** Now come the hard times. As early expectations of breakthrough success are dashed, the wider world loses interest. For those businesses that are venture capital funded, we often see second or third rounds of funding to keep the show on the road, with investors imposing ever-tougher conditions on the innovators, owners, and management. By 2018, for example, Blockchain had peaked, following in the wake of enthusiasm about such things as the "Connected Home" and "Mixed Reality," and was descending into the Trough. Investors typically become more cautious at this point in the cycle. Inevitably, many firms and, indeed, some technologies, never make it out of the hole. Others do, however, going on to change the world.

4. **Slope of Enlightenment:** Although no longer routinely in the media headlines, leading-edge players continue to evolve the technology, or variants of it. This takes time, effort, stamina, and, often, shedloads of money. This is where the goats are separated from the sheep, breakthrough leaders from the also-rans. And—if we are up to the task—this is also where potential Green Swans are separated out from possible Gray and Black Swans.

5. **Plateau of Productivity:** By now surviving technologies have settled down a bit, their benefits demonstrated. It is increasingly obvious to the wider world whether a given technology is likely to be trapped in niche markets or whether it is heading for mass adoption. Back in the day, the internet moved to mass adoption, whatever early critics might have suggested as reasons why it could never scale. In doing so, it created a wide spectrum of niche markets for new products and services. Designed in the right way, Green Swan technologies can perform the same magic. One striking example is the remarkable, exponential fall in the cost of energy generated by solar and wind farms.

A DROP-DOWN MENU OF DISRUPTION

Perhaps the best-known recent review of where we are in terms of technology came in the form of the World Economic Forum's (WEF's) report, *The Fourth Industrial Revolution.*[8] This upbeat assessment concluded the following:

> We stand on the brink of a technological revolution that will fundamentally alter the way we live, work, and relate to one another. In its scale, scope, and complexity, the transformation will be unlike anything humankind has experienced before. We do not yet know just how it will

unfold, but one thing is clear: the response to it must be integrated and comprehensive, involving all stakeholders of the global polity, from the public and private sectors to academia and civil society.

The First Industrial Revolution used water and steam power to mechanize production. The Second used electric power to create mass production. The Third used electronics and information technology to automate production. Now a Fourth Industrial Revolution is building on the Third, the digital revolution that has been occurring since the middle of the last century. It is characterized by a fusion of technologies that is blurring the lines between the physical, digital, and biological spheres.

There are three reasons why today's transformations represent not merely a prolongation of the Third Industrial Revolution but rather the arrival of a Fourth and distinct one: the velocity, scope, and systems impact. The speed of current breakthroughs has no historical precedent. When compared with previous industrial revolutions, the Fourth is evolving at an exponential rather than a linear pace. Moreover, it is disrupting almost every industry in every country.

That last point about the shift from linear to exponential trajectories, scaling, and pace is crucial. WEF's Center for the Fourth Industrial Revolution has since zeroed in on a growing number of disruptive technologies, all showing exponential dynamics, with key ones shown below as a drop-down menu in the same order WEF listed them and using the same labeling.[9] The summaries, however, are mine, adding in additional commentary linking back to the theme of Green Swans:

- **Artificial Intelligence and Machine Learning:** The impacts of AI and machine learning are now popping up all around, in homes, businesses, and political processes. On the entertainment front, we see sci-fi films like *A.I.*, *Minority Report*, and *I, Robot*. In the form of robots, says WEF, AI "will soon be driving our cars, stocking our warehouses and caring for the young and elderly." As far as potential Green Swans are concerned, "rapid advances in machine learning hold the promise of solving some of the most pressing issues facing society." But both Gray and Black Swan challenges will erupt, including shocking job losses, scandalously unethical use of data, and pernicious embedded blind spots reflecting blind spots in the minds and experience of those designing such systems. We already see growing concerns about wrongful exclusion and arrest, privacy, cars that are happy to run over black people, and the surveillance state.

- **The Internet of Things, Robotics, and Smart Cities:** There are now more connected devices in the world than there are people. Collectively dubbed the Internet of Things (IoT), they range "from smart building technologies that monitor and manage energy usage, to connected vehicles that help anticipate and avoid potential collision." The number of IoT devices is projected to exceed 20 billion by 2022, owing both to "continued technological advances and the plummeting costs of computing, storage and connectivity." As a result, Gray and Black Swan challenges will proliferate, particularly linked to technologies eventually embedded in our bodies. Already there are controversies about data ownership, accuracy, and privacy protection. And in an increasingly interconnected world where "electric grids, public infrastructure, vehicles, homes and workplaces are capable of being accessed and controlled remotely, the vulnerability to cyber-attacks and the potential for these security breaches to cause serious harm are unprecedented."

- **Blockchain and Distributed Ledger Technology:** This one is now shuddering down from the Peak of Inflated Expectations. This set of technologies has caused intense excitement because it potentially enables the decentralized and secure storage and transfer of information. As WEF notes, it "has already proven itself to be a powerful tracking and transaction tool. It can minimize friction, reduce corruption, increase trust and empower users." The challenge "is to unlock this potential in a way that ensures inclusion, safety, interoperability and scale." The ability to control corruption is very welcome, but human ingenuity is such that it presumably cannot be long before such technologies are also used to make corrupt practices even stealthier.

- **Autonomous and Urban Mobility:** As urbanization intensifies, WEF argues that we urgently need new mobility solutions, "while also minimizing increasingly complex social, economic, and environmental challenges. Autonomous vehicles have the potential to improve road safety, decrease pollution levels, reduce congestion and increase traffic efficiency. However, this transition involves a disruptive industry shift bound to reshape public and private transportation." Collaboration is now needed across industries, sectors, and geographies to identify the best strategies for promoting the wider adoption of autonomous mobility solutions in a "safe, clean, and inclusive manner." One question here will be whether private applications of such technologies will undermine—or complement—public mobility solutions, which tend to be more inclusive and energy efficient.

- **Drones and Tomorrow's Airspace:** Unmanned aircraft, or drones, WEF reports, are "democratizing the sky. Each day, participants in the drone ecosystem are discovering new uses for this transformative technology, from delivering packages and lifesaving medicines to airborne taxis and photographing the world." Among the areas WEF has been investigating are new paradigms for drone regulation, drone delivery for remote populations, policies for drone-derived data, reimagining aircraft certification, and protocols for medical delivery. Meanwhile, the growing use of drones by people like terrorists and drug traffickers ought to unsettle those who see them as an unqualified blessing. The drone attacks that knocked out around half of Saudi Arabia's crude oil production late in 2019 turned a different mirror on the technology.[10]

- **Precision Medicine:** Another potential blockbuster, offering the opportunity to "tailor diagnosis and treatment of disease to a specific person or population, improving outcomes and potentially lowering costs." WEF's areas of focus here include "generating evidence of precision medicine's effectiveness; data-sharing and related infrastructure; integrating a precision medicine approach into clinical practice; new approaches to regulation, pricing and reimbursement for diagnostics and treatment; and patient and public engagement." How long, though, before this actively or passively shapes new forms of discrimination in societies already suffering from acute wealth divides?

- **Digital Trade:** Whether in the form of America's Amazon, China's Alibaba, or Japan's Rakuten, global e-commerce now generates trillions of dollars annually in economic activity and is growing exponentially. However, WEF insists, "trade policy must evolve to empower new forms of digital commerce and cross-border data flows, addressing such challenges such as outdated regulations, fragmented governance and strict data localization policies." Some sensitive issues that have surfaced here include the avoidance of tax, conditions of employment, and the hollowing out of conventional shopping centers.

- **Fourth Industrial Revolution for the Earth:** This is probably the biggest potential Green Swan of all the areas WEF covered, at least in its listing. It explains, "Increasingly urgent global environmental challenges—such as climate change, loss of biodiversity and ocean health—also need fresh solutions. This project aims to build and test governance frameworks to realize the benefits of technology for the environment and society, including understanding the environmental impact of new technologies, while mitigating harm arising from deployment."

The way in which unintended consequences can impact the evolution of such technologies is strikingly evidenced by what has happened
with one part of the Blockchain world, the cyber-currency Bitcoin. The
Chinese government actually published a notice adding Bitcoin to a list
of industries that could be shut down.[11] With China, there are always
other reasons for such decisions and announcements, but the argument
made is that the amount of energy consumed by the industry, in which
the currency is created by "mining" activities involving computers solving ever more complicated puzzles, contributes to pollution and wastes
valuable resources.

Every new technology creates unexpected problems, but if I had to
pick three or four personal priorities from the WEF list, I would take
AI and the Fourth Industrial Revolution for the Earth—and then I
would add several not on the list: among them the renewable energy
and smart grids nexus, the replacement of animal farming by precision
biology and fermentation, and synthetic biology. The latter was the
subject of a wonderfully insightful survey by Oliver Morton, published
by *The Economist*.[12]

New tools like Crispr are helping to radically accelerate genetic
engineering.[13] "Every now and then," noted *Wired* magazine, "nature
politely taps us on the shoulder and hands over a world-changing gift.
A mold spore wafts through the open window of a laboratory, and lo,
we have penicillin. A military radar array melts a chocolate bar in an
engineer's pocket, and voilà, it's humanity's first microwave oven. The
discovery of the gene-editing technology known as Crispr was just such
a fluke [. . .]The results have been revolutionary. Crispr is fast, cheap,
and shockingly simple to operate."[14]

As *Wired* continued, Crispr "is gradually giving us the power to alter
not only our own genetic destiny, but also that of the entire planet—to
eradicate illness, develop new crops and livestock, even resurrect extinct
species." Spielberg territory, you might conclude.

A moment when the *Wired* team were brought up sharp was
when they came across work designed to tackle the critical shortages

of transplant organs—hearts, kidneys, lungs, and so on—by growing them inside pigs. One of the *Wired* team then asked a yuck-factor-driven question: "What if scientists inadvertently created a pig able to intellectualize its own suffering, one with a sense of moral injustice?" she asked. "Even if you could accept killing a farm animal to harvest its organs—which many animal welfare activists don't—surely it would be monstrous to kill one with humanlike intelligence?"

That's even before we get to things like gene drives, a key part of gene editing. The idea here is that Crispr is used to drive a harmful DNA mutation into a pest population. Normal biology dictates that such a gene would be passed on to around 50% of any offspring, whereas gene drives push the probability closer to 100%. In one experiment, researchers showed that it was possible to "crash" caged populations of the malarial mosquito *Anopheles gambiae* in just seven to eleven generations.[15]

So what happens if and when this particular type of mosquito disappears from the wild? One researcher behind the work said that there were only "a few billion" of these particular mosquitos alive in Africa at any one time. More to the point, he argued that "it is not a 'keystone species' in the ecosystem. Its ecology is closely associated with human settlements and no predator relies on it for food." But the sheer power of such technologies, for good and ill, surely dictates that we put them through increasingly rigorous testing before they are used, and ensure continuous monitoring once they have been? One suggestive idea is that all significant technologies, including new algorithms, should be subjected to FDA-style trials like those applied to new drugs.[16]

Work such as that carried out by WEF is helpful, of course, but even their longish list of disruptive technologies is only scratching the surface. It misses a wide range of other technologies that are bubbling under, or actively brimming over into today's world. With the development of many of these technologies now radically decentralized, and with biohackers working in garages with little or no government supervision, something more is needed to ensure that Gray and Black Swan risks are minimized and Green Swan opportunities optimized.

Good intent will not be enough to ward off the inevitable dangers and crises. Indeed, it is worth remembering that each of the Black Swans covered in Chapter 3 began as some form of Green Swan, a technology that at the time was seen to offer significant advantages over what had gone before. Plastics were lighter and more flexible, among other things replacing ivory from increasingly endangered species. CFCs were safer for humans than the chemicals they replaced. Antibiotics offered semi-miraculous recoveries, while modern diets were a welcome relief from past privations, and space technology allowed us to see Earth from a totally different angle.

It took time and much scaling before Green Swan products like CFCs or antibiotics began to sprout black feathers—and, in some cases, began to transform into different animals entirely. AI could well breed Green Swans, but already there are some striking black feathers. We learn, for example, that training a single AI model can emit as much carbon as five cars would through their entire lifetimes.[17] So, short of developing some sort of time machine to shuttle back and forth between today's world and the future, how can we get ahead of the curve, in effect looking back into today's world from the perspective of the future?

The WEF team will no doubt say they are already doing everything necessary, that they are linked to many of the leading people and organizations in the field, but perhaps something less exclusive and less tied to corporate interests might be more helpful? If so, where should we be looking for precedents and emerging models?

GREEN OR BLACK?

It has been almost a quarter of a century since Newt Gingrich sacrificed one of the most inspirational and educational of twentieth-century institutions—the US Office of Technology Assessment, or OTA—on the altar of federal budget cuts. A sad day.[18] If we are to weed out potential Black and Gray Swans from future rounds of Ugly Ducklings, and accurately identify those with real Green Swan potential, then we will need something very much like the OTA, albeit this time ideally operating on a global basis.

Founded in 1972, the OTA ran for twenty-three influential years, employing a staff of about two hundred, two-thirds of them professional researchers. Of these, over 88% had advanced degrees, mainly in economics, engineering, and the physical, life, and social sciences. They did heavy-duty investigative work on emerging technologies and, as a tiny sidebar, had a profound impact on my own thinking and work.

At a time when we see an acrimonious civil war between America's political parties, it is worth recalling that the agency's board was genuinely bipartisan. It comprised six senators and six representatives, with equal representation from both parties. The chairmanship and vice chairmanship alternated between the Senate and House in succeeding Congresses. Plus there was an advisory council of ten eminent folk from industry, academia, and elsewhere outside the federal government.

Exemplary, perhaps, but why was the OTA so important? And why might we now need something similar at the global level? Let's begin with an archived Charlie Rose interview with Carl Sagan, dating back to 1996. Sagan, an astronomer and science popularizer who was hugely influential in his day, asked, "Who is making all the decisions about science and technology that are going to determine the type of future that our children are going to live in? Just some members of Congress? But there's no more than a handful of members of Congress with any background in science at all."[19]

Great and unsettling questions, even today. Congresses, Parliaments, and similar bodies around the world are still far from adequately equipped to probe the implications of new science and technology. You could argue that China has one of the few national governments where many leaders have relevant higher degrees, but complicating factors are at work there—not least the conspicuous lack of the democratic principles that were hardwired into the OTA.

In any event, Sagan was fingering a worrying gap in governance that the agency later worked hard to address. Unease about the dark sides of new technology had been powerfully expressed by critics such as Rachel Carson, who wrote books like *Silent Spring*, and the consumer activist Ralph Nader. Launched around the time of the 1972 UN environment conference in Stockholm, the OTA eventually would carry out some 750 studies on various aspects of science and technology, ranging across such areas as energy, environment, health, and national security.

So where would you turn these days to find such deep insight into emerging science and technology? Tough, although one answer would be what is now called the Institute for Transformative Technologies (ITT), at the Lawrence Berkeley National Lab in California.[20] It was created in 2012, under the acronym LIGTT (pronounced "light"), to leverage the lab's capabilities—including 3,500 scientists and engineers, $800 million in annual R & D expenditures, hundreds of patents, and dozens of facilities for experimentation, simulation, testing, and fabrication—to develop and deploy breakthrough technologies for the rapidly emerging field of sustainable development.

"Through the history of international development," LIGTT noted in a study of fifty high-potential technologies, "a small number of breakthrough technologies have had transformative impact: the polio vaccine; the new seed varieties which launched the Asian Green Revolution; anti-retroviral drugs which appear to have rendered HIV/AIDS a chronic and manageable disease; and more recently, the M-PESA mobile payments platform."[21] But it cautioned, "Such major breakthroughs are rare. The truth is that far too much of the effort is focused on incremental technologies which—despite compelling narratives, significant funding, and considerable media hype—fail to reach any reasonable scale or impact."

Among LIGTT's fifty (actually fifty-one) breakthrough technologies spotlighted, several rapidly caught my eye. They included a "utility-in-a-box," to help remote areas plug into renewable energy; innovative water desalination processes; and the use of drones to monitor large-scale human rights violations. A key part of the work involved determining the likely dependence of each potential breakthrough on such things as policy reforms, infrastructure development, education and human capital development, behavior change, access to user finance, innovative business models, and new technologies.

For each technology, LIGTT asked the following: Are there any quick wins? Which breakthroughs have the most difficult path to impact? Which of these are commercially attractive for profit-seeking businesses, and which are important public goods without commercial prospects? What are the most appropriate funding mechanisms for these breakthroughs? How can various governments, funders, and other institutions shape their agendas to enable the realization of these breakthroughs?

Fascinating, essential work, but the task is expanding all the time as new technologies crowd into the public arena. Among next-generation technologies we have been watching are 3-D printing, AI, big (and little) data, drones, autonomous and electric cars, food technology (including synthetic meat and fish), fusion power, genomic medicine, geoengineering, the Internet of Things, mini-satellites, nanotechnology, new materials and sensors, smart buildings and infrastructures, soil carbon capture, synthetic biology, and vertical farming.

As the OTA would have been quick to point out, such technologies will cross-pollinate in unexpected ways. Rather than simply observing such trends from the sidelines, the system change community must now proactively shape the next round of industrial revolutions.

In the big scheme of things, the cost of an international OTA (or IOTA, perhaps) would be miniscule. But the benefits of probing and helping to shape tomorrow's technologies could be off-the-scale valuable. How about investing just a small fraction of the billions currently devoted to subsidizing fossil fuels?

Some approaches could be much simpler than having a global version of the old OTA cranking out technology assessments and helping society prioritize where to spend its scarce resources for maximum effect. When I Googled unintended consequences, for example, I stumbled across an organization based in our own building, London's Somerset House.[22] Doteveryone notes that "technology has introduced us to new knowledge, wonder and ingenuity. It has made our lives easier, faster, and more fun." Then came the *but*. "But at the same time, many of the social harms of digital technologies built with a move fast and break things ethos—from its impact on social interactions to the results of national elections and large-scale hacks—are now becoming apparent."

Then a more positive *but*. "But there are a lot of exciting opportunities to do better." Doteveryone has developed an event format that allows innovators to think about impact and potential unintended consequences, early and often. The aim is to answer three questions. First, in relation to any innovation, what are the intended and possible unintended consequences? Second, what are the positive aspects that we need to focus on? And, third, what are the not-so-positive aspects we want to mitigate?

Crucially, any such network or institution would need to ask questions about how those positive aspects of new technologies are not simply best studied but also best supported. There is a growing number of competing frameworks to guide such thinking, effort, and investment, including the Future-Fit Benchmark and, at a larger scale, the seventeen United Nations' Sustainable Development Goals. But my brain more readily embraces the shorter list of twelve developed by Singularity University (Panel 2), all designed to help shape exponential solutions.

PANEL 2: GREEN SWANS IN ABUNDANCE

So what sorts of habitats—or market opportunity spaces—are Green Swans most likely to emerge and flourish in? How do we best create futures with Green Swan characteristics? I like the global grand challenges approach developed by Singularity University (SU). They believe "that leveraging the convergence of exponential technologies will set us on the path to solve our global grand challenges and shift from an era of scarcity to abundance." They have prioritized twelve global grand challenges (GGCs). In addressing each, they aim to "solve for" three goals: (1) ensuring basic needs are met for all people, (2) sustaining and improving the quality of life, and (3) mitigating future risks. This approach certainly has the virtue of simplicity.

The challenges are "interrelated and interdependent," they say, and some of the feedback loops can act as virtuous cycles. "For example, as we solve for the water challenge, we are also helping to address the health challenge. As we make progress against the learning challenge, we also help address the prosperity challenge." The grand challenges then cluster under two headings, "Resource Needs" and "Societal Needs," in effect the environmental and socioeconomic dimensions of the triple bottom line agenda:

- **Resource Needs:** These include *Energy* (ensuring "ample, accessible, and sustainable energy for the needs of humanity"), *Environment* (ensuring "sustainable and equitable stewardship of Earth's ecosystems for optimal functioning both globally and locally"), *Food* (ensuring "consumption of sufficient, safe, and nutritious food to maintain healthy and active lives for all people at all times"), *Shelter* (ensuring "secure, safe, and sustainable shelter for residence, recreation, and industry for all people at all times"), *Space* (ensuring "safe and equitable use, and stewardship of, space resources and technologies for the benefit of humanity and our future as a multi-planetary species"), and *Water* (ensuring "ample and safe water for consumption, sanitation, industry, and recreation for all people at all times").

- **Societal Needs:** These include *Disaster Resilience* (ensuring "effective and efficient disaster risk reduction, emergency response, and rehabilitation that saves lives and livelihoods, minimizes economic loss, and builds resilience both globally and locally"), *Governance* (ensuring "equitable participation of all people in formal and societal governance that is in accordance with principles of justice and individual rights, free from discrimination and identity-based prejudices, and able to meet the needs of an exponentially changing world"), *Health* (ensuring "optimal physical and mental health, including access to cost-effective prevention, early diagnosis, and personalized therapy for individuals and communities"), *Learning* (ensuring "access to information and experiences that build knowledge and skills for all people at all stages of their lives for personal fulfillment and benefit to society"), *Prosperity* (equitable "access to economic and other opportunities for self-fulfillment where all people are free from poverty and able to thrive"), and *Security* (ensuring "safety of all people from physical and psychological harm, including in virtual worlds; and protection of physical, financial, digital systems").

What we need next is a set of exponential blueprints, showing how Green Swan solutions can evolve and flourish in each area. Work is already well advanced at SU and is publicly accessible.[23] A significant step forward came with the launch of the Exponential Climate Action Roadmap[24] at 2018's Global Climate Action Summit in San Francisco. Interviewed about the ambitions informing the Roadmap, co-author Owen Gaffney explained as follows:

> It is actually a deep dive into what needs to be done by 2030. Greenhouse gas emissions need to peak by 2020 and fall very rapidly—as a rule of thumb emissions should halve every decade, that is the kind of ballpark figure we are now contending with. The roadmap will outline the 30 scalable solutions that have the potential to put the world in that ballpark.
>
> Technology alone will not solve the climate challenge so the roadmap focuses on policy and behavioral change to accelerate existing technology diffusion. We need to talk about diet, lowering meat consumption, food waste, reforestation and building efficiencies—at global scales. One new aspect of this roadmap is that it explores how existing general technology platforms, for example search engines, social media and eCommerce—which increasingly influence the behavior of 3+ billion people—can contribute to behavioral change.

This is exactly the sort of thinking and approach that can help overcome the Gray and Black Swan challenges summarized in the GGCs—and unleash the creative energies, government backing, and private sector funding that we now need to create new generations of Green Swan solutions. At the heart of the process must be what Mariana Mazzucato dubs the "Entrepreneurial State," fixing market failures and actively shaping markets to ensure the right outcomes.[25] Her argument is that often the private sector only finds the courage to invest after an entrepreneurial state has de-risked the future.

CHAPTER 7

GREEN SWANS TAKE OFF

Exponential Progress Is Possible

The deeper you dig into Green Swan dynamics, the more you see that their evolution reflects both push and pull. They are pushed along by public and political reactions to the failings of the old order, and pulled along by our evolving sense of what the future might want us to do and, over time, be prepared to "pay for," for example through investments made on its behalf today.

On the push side of the equation, it is encouraging to see growing numbers of ordinary citizens waking up to the nature and scale of the challenges we face. "I think I am growing up at last," was, for me, the most memorable line in a filmed interview with an eighty-two-year-old Extinction Rebellion, or XR, protestor in Britain. Explaining why he had become one of the oldest XR activists during that group's first round of protests in 2019, he encouraged other "elders" to wake up and take action.[1] As a retired probation officer he said that he had huge personal respect for the law, but had concluded that the pursuit of money above all else was leading our species—and our world—into a literal dead end.

Activist Phil Kingston commented that he had woken up relatively recently, as many other people are now doing. In the process, they can face the same incomprehension that previous generations of change-makers experienced. People, even family members, often reject and deny. And the closer we get to the inflection point, beyond which the system changes forever, the more those vested in the old system feel impelled to resist.

Indeed, something I have long admired about long-distance activists is that they take this pushback for granted, accepting it as part and parcel of being one of those who "push the human race forward."[2] But, however much we may expect to encounter different views, it can be disconcerting, even shocking sometimes, to grasp how differently other people understand the future—if they think about and understand it at all.

FUTURE SHOCKS

Here is a very personal case in point. I was having an animated discussion, back in the 1980s, with a colleague who was at least twice my age—a conversation that has often resurfaced in memory. He was David Layton,[3] an extraordinary man who had founded a highly successful industrial relations company, Incomes Data Services (IDS), and then gone on to found Environmental Data Services (ENDS) in 1978, with environmental pioneer Max Nicholson as managing editor and myself as founding editor. Not long afterward, drawing on the work we had done to date, I wrote a report on the future, arguing that information would be the new oil.

That may seem obvious now, but some found it far-fetched back then. In fact David Layton disagreed, profoundly. He argued, in his charming, considered, and wonderfully wise way, that this was a logical impossibility. Only energy, materials, labor, and finance could play this lifeblood role in our economies. From today's perspective, he was right as far as the argument went, but wrong in relation to the increasingly central role of data, information, and intelligence. It is clear that he was channeling the then prevailing worldview.

This should have come as no surprise to me. He had worked for a couple of decades for Britain's National Coal Board, the government body that controlled the production of what we now see as the dark, satanic fuel that powered the country's Industrial Revolution. Along the way, coal caused seemingly endless unintended consequences. They ranged from mining disasters that ripped the hearts out of communities to slower, but often much more damaging, particulate pollution, acid rain, and global warming.

At the time, coal was seen as nature's energy gift to the British Isles. For those running them, our economies were not fueled by data but by fossil energy dug from open-pit and deep mines—and from the oil and natural gas increasingly pouring out of North Sea fields. Once again, our species was tapping into Earth's seemingly inexhaustible fossil resources.

So why has this mild-mannered exchange so haunted me over the years? One reason is that David was a highly intelligent man, whom I admired immensely. More than that, he had had the vision to bankroll ENDS, a pioneering platform designed to wake industry up to the growing environmental challenge. The key thing, though, was that this was the moment where I truly woke up to the fact that one of the people I admired most was operating in one paradigm while I was stepping into another.

I had read about such things, of course. Indeed, as already mentioned, I used to say that the book that most influenced my young mind was Thomas Kuhn's *The Structure of Scientific Revolutions*, which I had read at school in my early teens.[4] This long-ago conversation made paradigm shifting personal. At what point, I wondered, would I suffer from the same fate, finding myself trapped in a fading reality while new realities bubbled up all around—in younger minds than mine?

If you knew where to look, even back then, the future was already doing precisely that. Bubbling up. That is what our ENDS team was investigating and reporting on. On the energy front, the world had already experienced two major oil shocks, spurring significant changes in the fuel mix. More importantly still, the idea that there might be planetary limits to economic growth was gaining currency, with work like that of the Club of Rome's Limits to Growth team later evolving into the work of the Planetary Boundaries and Great Acceleration initiatives.

New information technologies were thrusting into our lives. As I traveled around the world, I carted around early portable—or "luggable"—computers. As I tapped away at their keyboards, it struck me that earlier generations would have ruled out the very possibility of such immense computing power packed into such relatively small and relatively inexpensive devices. Yet by today's standards those machines now look positively Stone Age, while the internet was still years away.

As new hardware—and, critically, new forms of software—rippled through the economy, we saw a strange process of metamorphosis playing out. The world of data went into overdrive. *Wake Me Up When the Data Is Over*, as one book put it,[5] but of course it never was. Indeed, data production has followed an exponential curve ever since.[6] As a result, digitalization is now seen as one of the most disruptive forces of all time.

The real inflection point, as already signaled, came with the launch of the internet. The number of internet users worldwide has skyrocketed since the birth of the World Wide Web in 1990, when the world's first website went live at CERN. The number of internet users increased to 44 million in 1995, then almost tenfold to 413 million by 2000. By 2019, there were 4.39 billion internet users, an increase of 366 million (9%) versus January 2018.

Energy remains critically important, of course, but way more value is now created by collecting and analyzing data than by burning coal, oil, natural gas, or uranium. And now we have those oceans of data, new technologies are evolving to feed on them, so we increasingly hear of big data, machine learning, and artificial intelligence.

Partly as a result, we live in extraordinary—and exponentially disrupted—times. "For we who are living at this moment," as Roberto Calasso put it in his provocative book *The Unnamable Present*, "the most exact and most acute sensation is one of not knowing where we are treading from day to day. The ground is brittle, lines blur, materials fray, prospects waver. Then we realize more clearly than before that we are living in the 'unnamable present.'"[7]

Unnamable it may be, but the present contains many pockets of the future, if you know where to look for them, all potential stepping-stones to a transformed world. But transformed in what ways? And to whose benefit? The exponential forces that can take us up can also take us down, as we saw with the wicked and super wicked problems covered earlier.

LOSING CONTROL

So how can we ensure that the coming transformations push us in the right direction, rather than pulling us down into exponential vor-texes with increasingly Black Swan characteristics? Someone who had a profound influence on my thinking in this area, and with whom I had an impromptu breakfast in Reykjavik back in 1977, was R. Buckminster Fuller. "Bucky," as his many fans called him, noted that the key thing about our planet, which he may have been the first to dub "Spaceship Earth," is that we took over the controls only to find there was no operating manual.

As a result, we often find out that things we have been doing to improve our lives are destroying the health—and even the futures—of other people and other species. Think of the extraordinary pushback against industrial chemistry catalyzed by the incomparably brave and influential Rachel Carson. Her book *Silent Spring* ranks alongside *The Structure of Scientific Revolutions* (also published in 1962) in terms of its impact on me and many of my generation.[8] Pilloried by chemical corporations that refused to accept the grim reality her book portrayed, Carson died relatively young but is now an immortal, effectively a patron saint of the global environmental movement.

Such things were in the back of my mind as I raced to finish this book, and then I heard of the crash of a Boeing aircraft in Ethiopia. As it happens, Boeing had played a significant part in my family's story, with cousins working with the company, the eldest of whom was Mr.

Boeing's personal lawyer for many years. It was one of those brands you trusted, literally, with your life. But what caught the world's attention was that this crash was the second of its type involving Boeing's commercially successful 737 Max 8 aircraft.

I have never been afraid of flying, though I have certainly had frightening moments in flight. But reading the transcripts of the last words of the doomed crew certainly gives one pause. Here is how the BBC described the last moments of the Ethiopian Airlines crew: "As alarms sounded in their cockpit, the captain and first officer struggled to regain control of their stricken aircraft. They were far too close to the ground, and needed to gain altitude. Yet when Capt. Yared Getachew tried to guide the nose of the Boeing 737 upwards, an electronic system forced it down."[9]

And so it went on, with the team pulling their controls this way and that, switching the electronic systems on and off, but with the automatic systems promptly overriding their best efforts every time they seemed to be on the point of turning things around. Soon all that was left was a smoking crater.

Boeing initially denied any connection between the crashes of Lion Air flight 610 and Ethiopian Airlines flight 302, but the evidence increasingly pointed to systemic defects in the aircraft's anti-stall software. This was designed to point the plane downward to counterbalance the 737 Max 8's heavy, forward-mounted engines.[10] Confounding the expectations of the designers, of the crew of the doomed flights, and of the regulators whose job it is to make sure such things do not happen, it turned out that in certain conditions the software made fatal nosedives virtually inevitable. Software, you might conclude, with strong Black Swan characteristics.

So, I wondered, what if the way we have wired the global economy also now makes it virtually inevitable that we will drive our civilization into the ground? Turning it into a new fossil layer? What if our entire economic operating system has similar Black Swan characteristics? And the more I read about Boeing's serial and cultural failures, the less confident I became that our species could both take over the planet's controls in the Anthropocene and make a success of it all.

The parallels between this aerospace company and our species are stark. Boeing, analysts noted after the second crash, suffered from a very human condition, hubris, blinding it to a lurking danger.[11] There were many reasons for the failures, which later inquiries will no doubt pick over for years to come. But key among them was an arrogant confidence that the company's prior commercial success and safety record more or less guaranteed success. "It could not believe it had blundered so badly in trying to avoid harm," as John Gapper commented in the *Financial Times*.

Our species has built many great civilizations, but so far it has failed to learn the hard lessons from the fact that every single one eventually crashed. An excellent, jarring guide to this phenomenon is Jared Diamond's 2005 book, *Collapse: How Societies Choose to Fail or Succeed*.[12] His latest book, *Upheaval*, is a fascinating account of how nations can lose control, for many different reasons. Subtitled "How Nations Cope with Crisis and Change," it investigates how six countries have survived defining catastrophes, from the West's forcible opening up of Japan's markets through the Soviet invasion of Finland to the brutal Pinochet regime in Chile. Diamond identifies some of the ways in which the recoveries have begun, but provocatively asks whether the United States is now squandering its natural advantages and launching itself on the path toward catastrophe.[13]

In microcosm, the Boeing crashes echo factors now driving so-called advanced economies toward ruin—or, on the upside, regeneration. Take the growing wealth divides and, at the corporate level, executive compensation. How shocking it now seems that the board of Boeing gave their then-chief executive Dennis Muilenberg a 27% pay raise for 2018 for his success in speeding sales of the profoundly flawed 737 Max 8.[14] Similarly, we are generously rewarding our elites, or allowing them to reward themselves, for turning our civilization into a slow-moving, but now accelerating, cataclysm.

There was more to the story, too, which can be seen as a parable for our broader political and governance failures. As economist Irwin Stelzer archly noted in an article titled "Why We Need to Rescue Capitalism," Boeing's governance was deeply flawed. Boeing CEO Dennis Muilenberg, Stelzer observed, "is supervised by and reports to board chairman Dennis Muilenberg."

Then there was the wider, systemic failure in the aviation industry's regulation in President Trump's increasingly deregulated America. As columnist Will Hutton summed up the situation, "America First nationalism, indulgent free market economics, Republican libertarianism, and a political system in hock to corporate lobbying has just contributed to killing 356 innocent people."[15] The unintended consequences of ideologies can be profound. Neoliberalism, it turns out, can be fatal for airline passengers and societies alike.

Hutton's recommendation to ensure the future safety of the aircraft was provocative. The authorities, he suggested, should insist that Trump and his transportation secretary, whose main qualification for office appeared to be that she was the partner of the Republican leader of the Senate, "go on the first 300 test flights when the Max 8 goes back into service."

Whether we are trying to keep aircraft in the air or working to maintain the health of our economies, societies, and wider environment, it pays to be critically aware of the assumptions we and others make along the way. Indeed, one fundamental mistake Boeing seems to have made was to assume that the anti-stall software would rarely, if ever, be activated. As the investigators dug deeper, they discovered that this belief was dangerously misguided. It depended on a single "angle-of-attack" sensor, which failed early on in both fatal flights.

Similarly, we failed to discover the growing Antarctic ozone hole for years because we had programmed the computers analyzing the data from the Nimbus 7 satellite overflying the icy continent to ignore data showing the hole, which was assumed to be outside the bounds of possibility.

Back to Boeing. It was also discovered that when the company delivered the plane to customers in 2017, it had assumed that a key cockpit warning light, designed to notify pilots of malfunctions with this critical sensor, was a standard feature in all the new jets. Not true. In effect, it turned out to be a premium add-on.[16] People had to pay extra to survive.

This still-unfolding story underscores not only the critical importance of market regulations and rules in shaping corporate behavior but also the increasingly radical influence of software in shaping the successes and failures of our capitalist economies. Indeed, some observers were soon pointing out the parallel risks in relation to autonomous road vehicles.

To ensure our assumptions, our flawed technologies, and market myopia do not crash our civilization, we need very different values and priorities. Plus different dashboards, with instruments showing a much wider array of economic, social, governance, and environmental information. Despite the deadly glitches in Boeing's software, we must rapidly develop and deploy new forms of machine learning and artificial intelligence able to avoid such disasters. Yes there will be glitches, some catastrophic, but the complexity of our rapidly evolving economies and societies is moving beyond the capacity of the unassisted human mind to understand, let alone control.

REINVENTING EVERYTHING

So what must we now do to head off such risks and solve the global challenges confronting us? One obvious—if challenging—answer is that we must now reinvent ourselves, our organizations, and our economies if our societies and the wider environment are to survive and, longer term, thrive.

One interesting learning opportunity in this area came when I spoke at a conference in a forest outside Brussels, hosted by the global business association Amfori.[17] Promoting open and sustainable trade,

Amfori brings together over two thousand retailers, importers, brands, and associations from more than forty countries, with a combined turnover of more than one trillion euros. It recently went through a profound refresh of its purpose and membership offerings, embracing sustainability at the very core of its business model. At its "Unleashing Opportunity" event in the summer of 2019, I found myself speaking alongside the extraordinary Nadya Zhexembayeva.[18] Dubbed "the Reinvention Guru," she aims to turn everyone in business into "chief reinvention officers." Her motto is "Reinvent Yourself. Reinvent Your Company. Reinvent Your World."

I learned a great deal that day, not least about storytelling. She spoke of what she called "the Titanic Syndrome," defining it as follows: *A corporate disease in which organizations facing disruption create their own downfall through arrogance, excessive attachment to the past, or an inability to recognize the new and emerging reality.* As someone who had a step-great-grandfather involved in creating the doomed liner, I thought I knew much of the sorry saga, but she promptly told three stories I did not know.

First, the story of how no one had issued the lookouts in the ship's crow's nest with binoculars. The man who held the key to the binocular cabinet had left before the ship sailed, taking the all-important key with him—and no one had the wit or nerve to take an axe to the spanking new cabinet.

Second, the story of how other ships nearby had been sending the *Titanic* radio messages warning of ice ahead, but had been aggressively told to get off the air. Why? Because the doomed ship's radio operators had to send messages for its all-important first-class passengers. In the aftermath, an investigation showed that those urgent messages were instructions to ensure that there were flowers at grand lunches in New York and the like.

And the third story spotlighted the man at the helm. Not the captain but the quartermaster, Robert Hichens, who had built a reputation for avoiding catastrophic collisions. Ironically, it later transpired that if he had held the ship's original course, rather than obeying the infamous "hard a-starboard" order, the ship might have remained afloat. The subsequent behavior of Hichens in Lifeboat 6 also echoes the thinking of some nations as the impacts of climate chaos ravage a growing number of communities around the world. He refused to pick up other survivors until an American socialite, the "Unsinkable" Molly Brown, threatened to throw him overboard.

So what moral did Zhexembayeva extract from all of this? The one she shared that day was that the sheer pace of change now demands that each of us, and every organization, go through a process of profound reinvention—not once a century, not even once a decade, but every three and a half years. As someone who has done that intuitively for decades, I strongly resonated with her advice.

But what about people who work for big, established, incumbent organizations—and who do not yet enjoy the title of chief reinvention officer? What is the purpose of all this reinvention, of that injunction to "Reinvent Your World"? For me, it has to be integrated responsibility, resilience, and regeneration across multiple dimensions of value.

In short order, we must regenerate ourselves, our teams and organizations, our communities and societies, and our economies. All of this in the service of regenerating the natural world, where the melting of the planet's icecaps prefigures events that could cost us many, many orders of magnitude more than the *Titanic* cost in lives and treasure.

THE REGENERATION GAME

Fine, but how can we bend the curve toward futures with pronounced Green Swan characteristics? Authors and other creatives are often encouraged to keep their powder dry. Told to keep the content of their upcoming article, book, or film under wraps before they hit the newsstands, bookshelves, or screens. Wise counsel, but, for better or worse, I have taken a different road. This has involved sharing—and testing—content earlier than would once have seemed sensible. And this is what

I did with the Green Swans agenda. As I developed the book, I blogged about it, spoke about it, and even hosted a major event to give the agenda space and oxygen.[19]

The event was a celebration of the first Green Swan Day, hosted at one of the world's outstanding regeneration projects, the Barnes Wetland Centre opened in 2000. In headlines, four huge obsolete water reservoirs that once supplied London were transformed into a huge wetland ecosystem that has become an international staging post for a myriad of wildfowl, including swans. The site is close both to my home and to my heart.

One key participant was Nick Haan, who chairs the faculty for Singularity University's "Global Grand Challenges" work.[20] He noted that our global challenges are going exponential, necessitating that our solutions must do the same. Much of the corporate sector may be lumbering along in incremental gear, but the market winners will be those who can deliver exponentially greater value across the triple bottom line. Those who help create tomorrow's market miracles. Emerging technologies are already driving business models and markets in related directions, so it is only a matter of time before our mind-sets and cultures follow suit.

The Green Swan Day event began life as my seventieth birthday party but then took off in a different direction.[21] With real-life swans cruising past outside the windows, we convened over one hundred people from around the world, from government, business, and the financial markets, alongside leaders from the citizen sector.

In terms of the bigger picture, World Wildlife Fund UK CEO Tanya Steele reviewed the findings of her organization's Living Planet Index. This measures the state of global biological diversity, based on population trends among vertebrate species. It does this in much the same way that a stock market index might track the value of a set of shares or a retail price index might track the cost of a basket of consumer goods. Cutting to the chase, the Living Planet Report 2018 revealed that a subset of 16,704 populations of 4,005 species had declined by 60% in abundance between 1970 and 2014.[22] The position was—is—worst in freshwater systems and tropical realms. Freshwater populations declined by an average of 83%, while tropical realms declined by between 23% and 89%, with the Neotropical (89%) and Indo-Pacific (64%) realms showing the steepest falls.

We heard of an even worse collapse in populations of the European eel, from Andrew Kerr, chairman of the Sustainable Eel Group. One key problem is that eels are migratory fish, yet an estimated 1.3 million obstructions in Europe alone hinder their journeys. Millions of eels are killed each year during their migration. Each female eel may carry around three million eggs, so the potential for life snuffed out with each dead eel is enormous.

Hydropower is seen as one of the greenest sources of energy, but 21,000 of the 25,000 hydroelectric power plants and pumping stations across Europe are small hydropower plants. These produce less than 1% of Europe's total electricity, yet block 21,000 migration pathways and access to upstream habitats for trout, salmon, eels, and other migratory fish. The implication is our frequent failure to think systemically can have a huge negative impact, even in industries considered to be among the most sustainable.

CHANGING SYSTEMS

A few weeks after that first Green Swan Day, I was involved in an away-day session with the board and executive committee of the Lloyds Banking Group, whose history tracks back to 1765. Like most such sessions, it was subject to a nondisclosure agreement, but it breaks no confidences to say that one of the key themes that emerged was the intergenerational transfer of wealth. I made the point that, if we take into account the unintended consequences of current forms of wealth creation, we must also now take into account the unintentional cascading of intergenerational debt via climate breakdown and similar trends, something most banks have yet to properly consider in their carefully honed and polished statements of purpose.

During a breakout session, Lloyds chairman Lord (Norman) Blackwell quizzed me on what I meant by system change. During my presentation I had explained that the change agenda was expanding its focus from triple bottom line accounting and reporting to the market, social, and political drivers and constraints that shape corporate behavior. I went on to say that after the recall of the triple bottom line I had increasingly been thinking of expanding the spotlight to embrace economic, social, and environmental systems.

In this spirit, I replied by highlighting the three target areas for the 2020s change agenda outlined below: transforming capitalism, democracy, and the sustainability agenda. Moving toward a conclusion, we will now briefly summarize the challenges—and opportunities—in each of these areas before considering the implications for leaders and leadership.

One thing is clear, however, and that is that effective systemic change can only come where there are extended timescales in investment and in politics. In what follows, we will refer to the time horizons introduced in Panel 1 (pages 38–39), with Horizon 1 stretching through the "Teens" and ending in December 2020, Horizon 2 embracing 2021–2030, and Horizon 3 extending from 2031–2100, the last seventy-year timescale being equivalent to my lifetime to date.

1. Capitalism with Green Swan characteristics

Some of the biggest design failures of modern capitalism have already been discussed. No wonder, then, that many people initially encouraged me not to talk of capitalism in the book—and to drop the word from the branding of our Tomorrow's Capitalism Inquiry. I have begged to differ, in that most people have at least some sense of what is meant by the word, and it is fascinating that this form of wealth creation is now under challenge even from high-profile capitalists.

If we are to transform capitalism, a key task must be to transform economics. As already declared, I gave up the discipline after a year at university in 1968, concluding that it had little useful to say about the pressing social and environmental issues of the day. So I was fascinated recently to come across these words from the late Nobel laureate Gary Becker about his own reactions to economics when he was at college: "I began to lose interest in economics [. . .] because it did not seem to deal with important social problems. I contemplated transferring to sociology, but found that subject too difficult."[23] As it happens, I did transfer to sociology and got my first degree in that subject. Interestingly, Becker went on to apply the tools of economics to social issues related to addiction, discrimination, education, and marriage.

Another of my favorite economists, Nikolai Kondratiev, was shot in 1938 because he told Stalin that capitalism, at the time flat on its face during the Great Depression, would recover and come back even stronger than before the crash. Brave, right, but suicidal. Stalin preferred to think that capitalism was down and would stay down. Not true then and, I suspect, very unlikely to be true now.

Kondratiev's work was picked up by Austrian economist Joseph Schumpeter, another huge influence on my thinking, and more recently by Carlota Perez, ditto.[24] As Perez herself would argue, stories like that of Thomas Midgley Jr., told on pages 171–173, are powerful reminders that new technologies periodically disrupt our economies—and are likely to do so in the coming decades, in the process creating whole new generations of challenges alongside the undoubted benefits.

Another Nobel laureate for economics, George Akerlof, concludes that a key design fault in the discipline is that it has favored "hard" research over "soft," numbers over narrative, causation over correlation. From this perspective, physics is hard, sociology soft. But if economists are to be helpful in reining in Black Swan trajectories and blazing Green Swan pathways, they must work out how to embrace the "too difficult" worlds of environmental and social impact, and linked forms of valuation.

Interestingly, Akerlof concludes that hard approaches favor silos, whereas the generalism needed to achieve successful cross-pollination and synthesis is too often seen as soft. Two other Nobel laureates who have blazed a trail to better syntheses are psychologist Daniel Kahneman and the late Elinor Ostrom, a political scientist who blew traditional assumptions about the use of scarce resources out of the proverbial water.

Ostrom's Nobel profile explained her work as follows: "It was long unanimously held among economists that natural resources that were collectively used by their users would be over-exploited and destroyed in the long-term. She disproved this idea by conducting field studies on how people in small, local communities manage shared natural resources, such as pastures, fishing waters, and forests. She demonstrated that when natural resources are jointly used by their users, over time rules are established for how these are to be cared for and used in a way that is both economically and ecologically sustainable."[25]

Critical, and highly provocative, work. Among other economists who have been doing great work in this space is Joseph Stiglitz, another Nobel laureate for economics. Here is how he frames the implications of our intensifying climate emergency: "Advocates of the Green New Deal say there is great urgency in dealing with the climate crisis and highlight the scale and scope of what is required to combat it. They are right. They use the term 'New Deal' to evoke the massive response by Franklin Delano Roosevelt and the United States government to the Great Depression. An even better analogy would be the country's mobilization to fight World War II."[26]

Stiglitz goes on to say, "The war on the climate emergency, if correctly waged, would actually be good for the economy—just as the second world war set the stage for America's golden economic era, with the fastest rate of growth in its history amidst shared prosperity. The Green New Deal would stimulate demand, ensuring that all available resources were used; and the transition to the green economy would likely usher in a new boom. Trump's focus on the industries of the past, like coal, is strangling the much more sensible move to wind and solar power. More jobs by far will be created in renewable energy than will be lost in coal." Jobs and careers.

Meanwhile, it is very encouraging to see women pushing into the field, among them Kate Raworth and Mariana Mazzucato. The former is renowned for her work on "Doughnut Economics." Raworth explains her approach: "Humanity's 21st century challenge is to meet the needs of all within the means of the planet. In other words, to ensure that no one falls short on life's essentials (from food and housing to healthcare and political voice), while ensuring that collectively we do not overshoot our pressure on Earth's life-supporting systems, on which we fundamentally depend—such as a stable climate, fertile soils, and a protective ozone layer. The Doughnut of social and planetary boundaries is a playfully serious approach to framing that challenge, and it acts as a compass for human progress this century."[27]

As I worked to finish *Green Swans*, as already mentioned, I had the great pleasure of debating Mariana Mazzucato at UCL.[28] The idea was that I would assert that only the private sector could deliver the sort of breakthrough innovation now needed, while she would counter that only the public sector could shape markets in the right way. Not surprisingly, we began the session in furious agreement, concluding that both were essential and neither could do without the other. Other thinkers who have stimulated our own thinking include Marjorie Kelly, with her brilliant book *The Divine Right of Capital*,[29] and Paul Collier with *The Future of Capitalism*.[30] Kelly noted that she has been "fascinated by the way an idea becomes antique, intrigued that a concept once considered ordinary can later seem absurd." One such idea she flagged, way back in 2001, was shareholder primacy. The Business Roundtable announcement referred to earlier suggests that the tide is at last turning.

To shift from Black Swan to Green Swan trajectories, we must drop or evolve many such business and investment concepts, currently taken for granted but on the cusp of becoming absurd. In the early stages of the Tomorrow's Capitalism Inquiry, for example, I had a profoundly helpful exchange with Steve Waygood, chief responsible investment officer at Aviva Investors, on "discounted cash flow," known in the trade as DCF. Here is some of what he told me:[31]

I see DCF as a super wicked problem with profoundly negative real world consequences. Our financial services system
should serve society and the real economy. But very few policy makers, politicians or civil society representatives understand how the many different financial services institutions
work together to finance the world we live in today and will
retire into tomorrow. In the absence of appropriate over-
sight, society and the real economy serve financial interests,
rather than the other way around.

This is dangerous for a range of reasons, particularly
because of the short termism inherent within market valuation techniques. DCF valuation is important because it
underpins every fundamental analysis in the global market
today. But DCF ignores social capital as it is external to the
corporate profit and loss statement. DCF ignores future
generations with its discount rates. And it assumes away the
need to preserve natural capital by assuming all investments
can grow infinitely with its Terminal Value.

We are left with millions of professional investors managing trillions of assets on our behalf, all of which largely ignore
the one planet boundary condition. Until, that is, we are
forced to think about them by governments correcting the
market failures, properly pricing natural and social capital and
ensuring corporations pay the full price for the goods and services they consume. This is why fiscal measures such as carbon
taxes, market mechanisms like emissions trading schemes,
and standards and regulations are vital to sustainable development. They help ensure that the market price reflects the full
social and environmental costs, which drives corporate valuation. The valuation of every company helps it to compete: a
higher market price means a lower cost of capital; which is a
competitive advantage. Sustainable companies should be able
to raise capital more cheaply than unsustainable ones.

There was more. "Given how important this is," Waygood said, "and that all students aspire to become savers and investors, why isn't sustainable finance and financial citizenship part of the national curriculum? Too often, the result is that we are left criticizing corporate sustainability platitudes without realizing that a fundamental part of the problem is all of us: How do we vote, spend, save, and invest as individuals? And that doesn't just mean how we vote in local and national elections: How many of us with pensions have bothered to check whether shareholder votes cast on our behalf at the annual general meetings of the companies we own reflect values we agree with?"

Waygood concluded, "People are ignored unless they cost or spend money. The interests of future generations are literally discounted. The planet is regarded as a free resource and a limitless litter bin. In short, we have a giant Ponzi scheme for the planet—taking from the future in favor [of] some of those alive today. However, with over $300 trillion in the global capital market, capital markets have the potential to solve the [UN Sustainable Development Goals] many times over. We do not lack capital. We lack imagination, compassion, and equality of opportunity. So it is time to declare war on these market failures and cure capitalism by restoring conscientiousness at its core."[32]

There are a number of signs that financial markets are waking up, like so many Rip Van Winkles. An early—and always wide-awake—Volans advisory council member has been professor Robert G. Eccles, originally of Harvard Business School and then the Saïd Business School, Oxford University. In a major article in the *Harvard Business Review*, Bob and his co-author Svetlana Klimenko reported the following:[33]

Most corporate leaders understand that businesses have a key role to play in tackling urgent challenges such as climate change. But many of them also believe that pursuing a sustainability agenda runs counter to the wishes of their shareholders. Sure, some heads of large investment firms say they care about sustainability, but in practice, investors, portfolio managers, and sell-side analysts rarely engage corporate executives on environmental, social, and governance (ESG) issues. The impression among business leaders is that ESG just hasn't gone mainstream in the investment community.

That perception is outdated. We recently interviewed 70 senior executives at 43 global institutional investing firms, including the world's three biggest asset managers (BlackRock, Vanguard, and State Street) and giant asset owners such as the California Public Employees' Retirement System (CalPERS), the California State Teachers' Retirement System (CalSTRS), and the government pension funds of Japan, Sweden, and the Netherlands. We know of no other research effort that involved so many senior leaders at so many of the largest investment firms. We found that ESG was almost universally top of mind for these executives.

The sustainable investing sector now manages assets worth around $30 trillion, according to the Global Sustainable Investment Group.[34] And among the financial world people taking part in our first Green Swan Day were Mark Campanale, of the Carbon Tracker Initiative,[35] and professor Nick Robins, who co-led UN Environment's Inquiry into a Sustainable Finance System.[36] The work of such people is helping to reboot capitalism, although they acknowledge that the political dimension is too often ignored. Which brings us to the second meta-challenge we face, to transform Democracy so it is fit for the future as we move toward Horizons 2 and 3.

2. Democracy with Green Swan characteristics

To survive and thrive, capitalism must be embedded in healthy ecosystems, healthy societies, and, critically, healthy political systems. That is not what we have today, although the Green wave in the 2019 EU elections suggests that all is far from lost. Still, addicted to the daily news cycle, many of us struggle to raise our eyes to the future.[37] The sociologist Elise Boulding put it this way: "If one is mentally out of breath all the time from dealing with the present, there is no energy left for imagining the future."

As a result, some people see China's push into clean technology as evidence that democracy's growing myopia can only be countered by more rigidly run surveillance states. I disagree, strongly. Over time, despite its messiness, democracy is the best way to handle complex long-term challenges, but current forms are in urgent need of seismic shocks and a radical overhaul. The first are guaranteed, the second all to play for.

The design failures now afflicting a growing number of modern democracies could hardly be more painfully clear. I was returning from the Ivory Coast when I heard the news about Brexit, an ill-informed, indeed externally corrupted vote that tipped the so-called Mother of Parliaments into an existential meltdown. Populist leaders have now grabbed the reins in countries as diverse as Brazil, Britain, the Philippines, Russia, Turkey, and the United States. At times it is as if these governments have ingested a potent psychoactive drug that promotes narcissism and paranoia, radically shrinking both planning timescales and the range of people actually served, whatever the promises and campaign rhetoric may have been.

Very few governments and policy makers are now able to seriously project out into Horizons 2 and 3, having been pretty much glued to the spot in Horizon 1. This is a major headache at a time when so many of our grand challenges require intergenerational thinking, priorities, and investment. One bright spot in this gloomy landscape, however, is New Zealand's efforts to build intergenerational well-being—including improved approaches to issues like mental health and child poverty—into strategic planning and reporting at all government agencies.[38]

That said, our assumption, as sketched in Figure 1 (page 4), is that we are in a historical U-bend, with very different forms of capitalism and democracy likely to emerge in surprisingly short timescales. For a while, we must rely increasingly on the longer-term thinking of many corporate leaders, paradoxical though that may seem, given that many people see them as unable to think beyond the next quarter.

Certainly, the pressures on business are set to drive a radical awakening as we move toward Horizon 2. As Aviva's Steve Waygood put it to me, "One might reasonably ask when will big business realize that sustainability is a business imperative and that it needs to drive genuine change? It will be when big business realizes that its long-term survival is threatened by unsustainable business practices. As an insurer, many of the issues outlined in the United Nations' Sustainable Development Goals, such as climate change and antimicrobial resistance—represent existential risks to [Aviva's] sector. The market will only help to safeguard our future and promote genuinely sustainable corporate activity when prices and valuations reflect the true costs to society and the environment. Politicians, policy makers and NGOs need to welcome all the fantastic developments in sustainable finance while also realizing that they are nowhere near enough."[39]

Alongside business leaders, attention is also now turning to cities—and to city mayors in particular. Democratically elected for the most part, they are much closer to local politics than are most presidents and prime ministers. As it happens, I trained as a city planner and things now seem to be coming full circle, with cities increasingly central to our work. This reflects global reality, with 55% of the world's population now living in urban areas, a proportion forecast to increase to 68% by 2050. Projections show that urbanization combined with the overall growth of the world's population could add another 2.5 billion people to urban areas by 2050, with close to 90% of this increase taking place in Asia and Africa.

On the flip side, some cities have experienced population declines in recent years. Most of them are located in the low-fertility countries of Asia and Europe where overall population sizes are stagnant or declining. Economic contraction and natural disasters have also contributed to population losses in some places. A few cities in Japan and the Republic of Korea (for example, Nagasaki and Busan) experienced population decline between 2000 and 2018. Several cities in Eastern European countries, such as Poland, Romania, the Russian Federation, and Ukraine, have also lost population since 2000. In addition to low fertility, emigration has contributed to the lower population size in some of these places.

But the city is where democracy started and where it must now largely be reinvented for the twenty-first century. One interesting place to look for signals of where politics and policy may be headed is Apolitical, an online platform that aggregates best practice from around the world and makes it easily available to public servants.[40]

The Apolitical team explains, "Whether we like or dislike government, love it or despair of it, most of us can agree that government plays a pivotal role in solving wicked problems—from the refugee crisis and the strain of urbanization to climate change, cyber security and adapting to a world where an algorithm somewhere is chasing your job. And innovative solutions often already exist. Around the world, the hundreds and thousands of men and women working in government are tackling similar problems. Often the solutions they find can be shared. But with public servants working under tight time pressure and often in silos, good ideas often remain confined to a country or a sector. This leads to duplication of effort, wasted taxpayer money and poorer services for citizens."

As an example of what can be done to tilt the landscape in favor of sustainability, ask yourself why you see so many electric cars in Norway. Again, a key part of the answer is government policy. In Norway you can drive in the bus lane, park for free, and get a 25% tax break when you buy an electric car.[41]

At the Lloyds meeting already mentioned, I spoke alongside professor David Soskice of LSE, someone I knew of but had never met. He helped me get my brain around the vital links between capitalism and democracy. His latest book, co-written with Harvard professor Torben Iversen, is called *Democracy and Prosperity* and subtitled "Reinventing Capitalism through a Turbulent Century."[42] Their thesis is simple to state: "In contrast to the widely held view that democracy and the advanced nation-state are in crisis, weakened by globalization and undermined by global capitalism, in turn explaining rising inequality and mounting populism, advanced democracies are resilient, and their enduring historical relationship with capitalism has been mutually beneficial."[43]

For all the chaos and upheaval over the past century—major wars, economic crises, massive social change, and technological revolutions—Iversen and Soskice show how democratic states "continuously reinvent their economies through massive public investment in research and education, by imposing competitive product markets and cooperation in the workplace, and by securing macroeconomic discipline as the preconditions for innovation and the promotion of the advanced sectors of the economy. Critically, this investment has generated vast numbers of well-paying jobs for the middle classes and their children, focusing the aims of aspirational families, and in turn providing electoral support for parties. Gains at the top have also been shared with the middle (though not the bottom) through a large welfare state."

Contrary to the prevailing wisdom on globalization, they conclude, advanced capitalism is neither footloose nor unconstrained. It thrives under democracy precisely because it cannot easily subvert it—although in America the increasingly problematic power of campaign finance is corroding the system from within. Still, populism, inequality, and poverty are among the great scourges of our time, are failures of democracy, and must be solved by democracy.

As UK Government minister Nick Hurd put it during the first Green Swan Day, we now need a manifesto—or manifestos—for the regeneration of our economies, societies, and the biosphere. And for the regeneration of our politics. As minister for London, he said, "We have the brains, we have the money and now we have the sense of urgency in relation to the climate emergency." If not now, as they say, when? And if not us, who? That is a fundamentally political question that each of us must now answer in our own way, but the right way.

3. Sustainability with Green Swan characteristics

Black Swans happen because we fail to think things through properly. Green Swans, in contrast, happen because we succeed in doing so. As I look back, my recall of the triple bottom line was an intuitive version of what Zen Buddhists call a *kōan*. This is a question, challenge, or paradox designed to disrupt business-as-usual—or, in this case, change-as-usual. Used at the right time, in the right way, such provocations can force us to rethink and, when truly effective, to move toward some form of enlightenment.

The further we dig into the relationships between capitalism and democracy, the more sustainability looks like the natural bridge between the two, focusing as it does on intergenerational equity and balanced, inclusive, and environmentally sustainable value creation and distribution over extended timescales. My decision to attempt the recall, even as a *kōan*, stemmed from my sense that the triple bottom line operating system I had helped create has an intrinsic weakness when used by people, however well intentioned, subject to incentive systems that powerfully focus on short-term Horizon 1 targets.

Of course I am delighted to see growing numbers of businesses embracing this mind-set, whether by becoming B Corporations or producing integrated reports covering all three dimensions of value creation—or destruction. Take the case of Apple, a company whose products I have used since the very first Macs, with *Green Swans* typed on one of the latest MacBooks. But that did not stop me on November 15, 2013, from asking Apple design guru Sir Jony Ive a challenging question about the working conditions at the company's Chinese suppliers, particularly Foxconn. This was during a session at a Generation Investment Management event, with former American vice-president

Al Gore in the chair. Ive became quite agitated, insisting there were no problems and that he had even slept in the worker dormitories at Foxconn: I left thinking there was more to this than met the eye.

How interesting, then, to see the media commentary around Ive's announcement that he was leaving Apple. This marked a shifting in expectations of brands like Apple, as the *Financial Times* explained in a full-page article. Noting that it was no longer good enough for products to be beautiful and easy to use, the piece stressed, "The priorities of many consumers are changing. A new generation of environmentally conscious consumers may no longer fetishize a MacBook's aluminum body or see the latest iPhone as less of a status symbol than their predecessors."[44]

The newspaper noted that it is impossible to change the batteries in Apple's AirPods, its tiny wireless headphones, because the components are glued together to keep their volume as small as possible. The leading edge of the design profession senses that it must rethink its role. "The whole product durability issue is absolutely key here with our students," RCA vice chancellor Paul Thompson was quoted as saying. Ironically, the RCA is the art and design university where Ive served as chancellor. Thompson continued, "People want social purpose and they want to work with the circular economy—locally grown and sourced products, not shipping things backwards and forwards across the oceans."

Growing numbers of major companies are now taking the plunge and working on transformation strategies that would have seemed out of the question even a few years ago. Elon Musk, for example, has so spooked competitors that an array of auto companies is now speeding to catch up with Tesla. BMW expects profits from its electric vehicles to match those from traditional cars by 2025.[45] VW plans to roll out seventy fully electric models.[46] Shell aims to become the world's biggest electricity company as the world plugs into green power.[47] Companies like Denmark's Ørsted, formerly a big player in the coal-fired power market, which has transformed itself into a green energy giant.[48]

In essence, Ørsted has switched from a Black Swan energy pathway to a progressively more Green Swan alternative. It may have suffered some pretty spectacular reverses along the way, but its recent share price performance has been spectacular.

Or take Umicore, a company that two decades ago was an old-school smelting company, but today is a leading-edge player in the circular economy, having transformed itself into an "urban miner," recycling waste metals.[49] In some cases, too, it may not be the company that survives but the underlying business model, spreading to other companies and other sectors. Consider Uber's dynamic pricing model, which is likely to spread from companies like Uber to very different sectors.

The impact of such changes will be profound, particularly in countries like Germany, whose national business model depends on the automotive sector. Its high-end engineering skills may become less relevant as the role of software and imported batteries grows.[50] Elsewhere, we could see "fire sales" of carbon intensive assets as the risks of stranded assets in the fossil fuels sector grow, destabilizing the financial system, warned Bank of Canada governor Stephen Polos.[51]

So, whether they are designing cars or economic and political systems, tomorrow's designers will need to take sustainability considerations into account to a far greater degree than in the past. In the process, they will need very different perspectives on Horizons 2 and 3, with an emphasis on resilience, regeneration, and, the very essence of sustainability, intergenerational equity.

They will need new icons, models, and gurus. One I have long admired in the regeneration space, and who also spoke at our first Green Swan Day event, is Sir Tim Smit of the Eden Project. When the Eden Project team say that sustainability is at the heart of everything they do, they mean it—and have done their level best to make it part of the Eden reality.

The project restored a massive china clay pit. It pumped over £1.5 billion into the regional economy. And, having been expected to attract perhaps 750,000 visitors, by its tenth birthday in 2010 it had attracted 13 million people. By the time of this writing, that number was over

20 million.[52] And the irrepressible Smit beavers on, launching a new company in 2017 to develop new Eden projects around the world, including in China.

Back in the economic mainstream, meanwhile, today's global challenges are so far beyond our collective experience that they demand a radically different kind of engagement from senior leadership teams in the private sector. Most dramatically, the threats that the climate emergency poses to business, markets, and, indeed, capitalism are still peculiarly hard for most top teams to spot, let alone act on.

Our brains evolved to respond reflexively to immediate threats but ignore or downplay systemic crises that creep up on us. Such market dynamics behave like vortexes—a whirlwind in the air, or a whirlpool in water. When a vortex is just beginning to form, it is virtually invisible unless you have extremely good peripheral vision and happen to know what you are looking for. At this stage, things move at a deceptively slow pace. But even the best-designed vessels—or ventures—can find themselves drawn inexorably into the danger zone. Then, suddenly, you reach a point of no return.

Such slow—but ultimately exponential—dynamics characterize what I think of as the carbon vortex.[53] Recall the three major hurricanes photographed from space in the autumn of 2017 in a single, unparalleled NASA image. Think, too, of reports that carbon dioxide emissions, instead of declining, have been growing, in part because much economic growth in China is still fueled by coal.

But as the carbon vortex gains momentum, there is also evidence of an equal and opposite vortex pulling us toward breakthrough innovation and a more sustainable future. Remember the Norwegian Sovereign Wealth Fund's landmark commitment to run down its coal industry holdings. Or Siemens explaining that the major job cuts planned for its gas turbine business have been partly triggered by the renewable energy boom. GE, which decided to double down on coal, despite its much vaunted "Ecomagination" platform, is now caught in the same market riptides, forced to eliminate thousands of jobs from its power division.

It is clear that much of the world is at a market inflection point, where issues once seen as peripheral are surging into the mainstream. As Generation Investment Management put it in *The Transformation of Growth*, their 2017 white paper, "The Sustainability Revolution appears to have the scale of the Industrial Revolution and the Agricultural Revolution—and the speed of the Information Revolution. Compared to these three previous revolutions, the Sustainability Revolution is likely to be the most significant event in economic history."[54]

Emerging technology will certainly challenge us in new and profound ways. AI will eliminate or squeeze a huge number of jobs and careers, leading some to question whether when Silicon Valley and the financial centers of cities like London, New York, and Tokyo are fully robotized, they might move anywhere in the world where there was (a critical new strategic advantage) a sufficient supply of clean energy.

Then there is another emerging area of science, technology, and enterprise that quite literally has the power to transform life on Earth. It was not spotlighted in the World Economic Forum (WEF) listing mentioned in Chapter 6, at least when accessed, but it has the potential to drive more change in the world than many other technologies put together. This is synthetic biology.

As someone who has followed the biotechnology industry fairly closely for decades, I have seen a fair few much-vaunted ideas make their way through the hype cycle minefield. Some were blasted to pieces, and others ended up crippled on the sidelines. But there is something about this new synthesis of biology, engineering, and data that reminds me of information technology in the early days. The focus then was on information, data, and intelligence, whereas with synthetic biology it is on the fundamental reprogramming of life itself to bend it to human needs.

In what is sometimes dubbed "the century of biology," a Black Swan scenario would see synthetic biologists help evolve weapons Hitler or Putin could only have dreamed of, catalyzing catastrophes that would keep future generations of Spielbergs supplied with disaster movie scripts. In a Green Swan scenario, by contrast, the world could move onto more sustainable trajectories in areas like food, nutrition, health, and, linking back to WEF's Fourth Industrial Revolution for Earth, environmental restoration.

We spotlight some ways in which all of us can now help drive this process forward in Chapter 8. Looking back, I have spent forty-five years working on the change agenda, co-founding four social businesses, serving on over seventy boards and advisory boards, speaking at over one thousand major events, and writing, to this point, twenty books. But I genuinely feel that I am only just getting started. My sense is that the next ten to fifteen years will be by far the most exciting, challenging, and dangerous in my working life.[55]

A key part of the challenge will be to bridge between the generations. At the Green Swan Day event, Tim Smit celebrated the combination of the internet, which enables everyone in the world to have a voice, and the rise of the "smartest generation that has yet lived."[56] The five principles of exponential leadership outlined next are all based on things we have been experimenting with. There have been ups and downs, of course. Several things I have been involved in have failed, including the Social Stock Exchange. On the other hand, several have gone ballistic, including the extraordinarily successful EcoVadis, a supply chain management company that has gone from perhaps a dozen employees in Paris when I first got involved to more than six hundred today, operating from a dozen offices worldwide.

The five principles outlined in the next chapter are no guarantee of success, but they do seem to be working for us. I hope that at least some of them will work for you. If not, as Tim Smit concluded, "The octopuses are waiting to take over from us."

CHAPTER 8

EXPONENTIAL MIGRATIONS

Tomorrow's Capitalism Takes Shape

E verywhere you look, there are signs of so-called "global weirding."[1] One of my favorite cities, Seattle, up to its eyeballs in nature, has been forced to build clean-air shelters for people choking on smoke billowing from forest fires way down south in California, and also now way north in British Columbia, Canada.[2] As I drafted this chapter, an area of rotting seaweed the size of Jamaica, more than 550 kilometers (roughly 342 miles) long, was approaching the coast of Mexico.[3] France had recorded its highest-ever temperature, at 45.9°C (114.6°F). And snow falling in remote Arctic and Alpine regions had been found to contain unexpectedly high levels of microscopic plastic particles.[4]

People are increasingly worried. A 2019 Ipsos study of more than 18,000 adults from twenty-seven countries around the world confirmed that dissatisfaction with the system and traditional politics is high almost everywhere. Globally, seven in ten (70%) agreed that their economy is rigged in favor of the rich and powerful (little change at up one point from 2016), with a majority saying this in every single country except for Sweden (50%).[5]

Most of us avert our eyes, close our minds. We assume that the natural order will reassert itself, somehow—just as we assume that populism, trade wars, and deglobalization will sort themselves out, somehow. But eleventh hour escapes seem increasingly unlikely. Instead, we seem to be forcing ourselves into the biggest civilizational migration in history, where we have no option but to shift our economies and our businesses technologically, geographically, politically, and culturally.

Too often, we perceive our political institutions, economic structures, social practices, and cultural values as permanent, like the laws of nature. Not so. "Can you imagine what nation-states would be like without three branches of government?" asks Dominic Hofstetter. "Transportation without cars? Commerce without corporations? Education without schools?" One thing now seems blindingly clear: Many institutional arrangements and structures we take for granted today, like it or not, will be transformed out of recognition tomorrow.[6] And we should welcome that fact.

Swans have long migrated, we humans too. Some of us, including Amazon's Jeff Bezos and Tesla's Elon Musk, even yearn to see a human migration into space.[7] Fine, though robots might be better equipped. But others, more firmly anchored to Earth, are working toward a very different migration, a decades-long shift from pathways forcing us into Black Swan territory to ones enabling futures with enhanced Green Swan characteristics.

Viewed in this way, much of the recent political confusion and enraged populism can be seen as an existential swan song, a lament for the certainties of older, ailing forms of capitalism, democracy, and, yes, sustainability. This should come as no great surprise, given that this is what happens when economies and societies find themselves heading into the sort of U-bend spotlighted in Figure 1 (page 4).

And if any city is a model for where Black Swan trajectories could take us, perhaps it is Jakarta, Indonesia's rapidly sinking capital. In a double whammy, Jakarta is pumping so much water from underground that, combined with rising sea levels, perhaps as much as 95% of its area could be underwater by 2050.[8] The response? Indonesia has announced plans to move its capital to a new site in Borneo.[9]

So imagine two simple scenarios, one symbolized by Black Swans, a we-all-live-in-Jakarta world, the other by Green Swans.[10] In the first scenario, we are caught up in a series of downward-spiraling vortexes, the sort of wicked and super wicked problems spotlighted in Chapters 2 and 3. Our political and economic systems struggle to cope but are overwhelmed and ultimately sucked under. Some parts of our planet's future will be like that, whatever we do.

Disappointingly, perhaps, whatever enthusiasts may believe, the Green Swan scenario will not take us to utopia, or anything remotely like it. We are too human for that, and our planet is too far gone to allow for quick remedies. Still, this scenario does at least offer pathways to a world where future generations have a real and growing chance to achieve lives worth living. For that to happen, though, and for capitalism to survive in any recognizable form, market-based forms of value creation must evolve mightily. They must be redesigned from the ground up to value and promote the conditions for life, not just human life but all life—and not just life today but all life "for all time."

Impossible, you may think, at least viewed from today's reality. But our pan-generational task is to help make a Green Swan future appear—and then become—inevitable. This final chapter focuses on five core principles that can help make what seems impossible today pretty much inevitable tomorrow.

Politics may seem to have attracted a generation of breakers not makers, grim portents of a Black Swan future, but you could equally well see them as symptoms of accelerating processes of creative destruction. Processes helping to break down old orders to clear the ground for the new. Whatever they may intend, and narcissism seems to be a key factor, the "breakers," unwittingly, may be playing the role of slime molds in forests, breaking down the old to liberate space and nutrients for the new.

That, at least, is how I see it, and a distinctly personal thread has run through this book. Now I will pull it slightly closer to the surface. What follows is intended as advice for leaders in all sectors, but also has strong elements of a personal change manifesto. A Swanifesto, perhaps, in the spirit of "Doctor heal thyself."

To this end, as already mentioned, we convened the world's first Green Swan Day in a venue overlooking a huge area of regenerated wetlands on the outskirts of London. In what follows, I draw heavily on thinking shared there by leading champions of transformational change.

The overarching question is: How do we succeed in repurposing capitalism through the 2020s? A decade that Nick Haan, who chairs Singularity University's Grand Challenges program, stressed will be "exponential times." How, in summary, can we avoid being sucked into the top left-hand ("Breakdown") quadrant in the Breakthrough Compass (Figure 2, page 35), writhing with Black and Gray Swans, and shift ourselves, our organizations, and our economies into the top right-hand ("Breakthrough") corner, the uplifting domain of Green Swans?

One Graying Swan that has haunted me for some time is the aging trend in many parts of the world. People over sixty-five are now the fastest-growing segment of the global population, with the number of people who are eighty or older likely to triple by 2050.[11] The implications for public health care, pensions, and social protection for the elderly are profound. But think, too, of the political impact of increasingly conservative old people unwilling to take the risks—or to vote for others who plan to do so—needed to pursue Green Swan outcomes.

Already we see such trends hitting poor regions in East Germany, fueling a sense of abandonment and spurring the growth of far right parties.[12] Japan is predicted to lose the equivalent of a midsized city each year for the foreseeable future as its rate of population decline accelerates.[13] Some even now warn that instead of increasing exponentially, the global population could decline alarmingly over time. A recent book in this vein is Darrell Bricker and John Ibbitson's *Empty*

Planet: The Shock of Global Population Decline.[14] This could take a Gray Swan and turn it Black or, if things went nature's way, Green.

But who said this was going to be easy? In the spirit of "Do what I do, not what I say," here are five principles we have been testing out at Volans. To confirm they are rooted in real-world experience, and indicate where to find more information, I quote some of those most directly involved. Their ambition, appetite for change, and stamina have inspired us mightily.

1. BE A LEADER, NOT AN ALGORITHM

Long before the internet, I surfed the first wave of personal computers through the 1980s, experiencing firsthand what some now see as the single most significant revolution in human technology since the invention of the wheel.[15]

It is now commonplace to say things like, "The computational power in the cheapest mass-produced smartphone is exponentially more powerful than anything that existed in the early days of computing. The software that powered the Apollo mission that put a man on the moon was about as sophisticated as an app on your phone is today. All of it powered by algorithms that harness the incredible power of modern processors to accomplish the seemingly impossible."

Commonplace, but with immense implications for all of us, and for all life on Earth. Once again, language is a guide to possible futures. One Italian leader recently accused his rival of being an algorithm, not a leader.[16] But, as often happens, as the term *algorithm* has gone mainstream, it has come to be understood—and misunderstood—in new ways.

To set the scene, an algorithm is a series of steps taken to solve a specific, discrete problem. From Google's search engine to the management of rush hours on city roads and subway systems, our world is increasingly directed and run by algorithms. Paradoxically, however, the more this becomes the case, the more urgently truly human leadership will be needed.

The political implications of all these algorithms have been explored by Jamie Susskind in his book *Future Politics*.[17] His conclusion: "We are not yet ready—intellectually, philosophically, or morally—for the world we are creating." Politics in the future, he says, will be quite unlike politics in the past. And the same now holds true for economics.

Capitalism's master discipline, economics, now crawls with algorithms, including formulae for valuing things and for measuring progress against current definitions of wealth creation. Recall again the not-always-helpful impact of economist Milton Friedman, discussed in Chapter 1. Whether well understood or badly misunderstood, he powerfully influenced generations of business leaders, investors, and even regulators.

The net result is that capitalist algorithms have increasingly driven yawning wealth divides and helped wipe something like 60% off the Living Planet Index, a measure of the vitality of Earth's biosphere calculated by the World Wildlife Fund (WWF).[18] "We are the first generation to know we are destroying our planet and the last one that can do anything about it," WWF UK CEO Tanya Steele told our Green Swan Day audience.

Since the New Economy period, we have seen what we might inelegantly call the exponential algorithmicization of our economies. Indeed, leading CEOs like Apple's Tim Cook have spotlighted the dysfunctions of many of today's algorithms—and of those who code them. Giving a commencement address at Stanford, he warned his Silicon Valley compatriots, "If you have built a chaos factory, you can't dodge responsibility for the chaos."[19]

Some of these problems can be solved fairly quickly, but others—including the implications of the burgeoning surveillance state—represent intergenerational challenges. Which brings us back to that comment about the last generation able to do very much about the state of our planet. The heart of the sustainability agenda has always been intergenerational equity.[20] Indeed, much of my own work has been driven by a growing sense that we need stronger, longer, and wider bridges across our generational divides.

Occasionally, inevitably, this bridge-building urge has got me into trouble, as when I helped persuade twenty-plus CEOs and business leaders to sign a letter to *The Times* newspaper supporting the agenda advanced by Extinction Rebellion, known as XR.[21] At the time, XR's peaceful occupation of iconic sites like Trafalgar Square and Waterloo Bridge, just outside our London office, had begun to spark pushback from retail businesses impacted by the blockades.

By way of background, here is our letter in full:

> Sir, Contrary to belief, there is business support for the Extinction Rebellion (XR) agenda. The multi-million-pound costs that the Extinction Rebellion protests have imposed on business are regrettable, as is the inconvenience to Londoners. But future costs imposed on our economies by the climate emergency will be many orders of magnitude greater.
>
> Hard pressure drives change, but even the most committed businesses will need time to respond. We welcome the news that Extinction Rebellion is evolving a new platform, "XR Business," to engage business leaders, investors and advisers. To drive things forward, the idea is to convene a meeting of XR activists and experts with business leaders and influencers.
>
> Most businesses were not designed in the context of the developing climate emergency. Hence we must urgently redesign entire industries and businesses, using science-based targets.
>
> To kick start the process, businesses should make a declaration that we face a climate emergency and organise a session at a full board meeting to consider the case for urgent action. We will encourage the senior management teams of which we are part to do likewise.

We had been invited to submit the letter by XR itself, but its pub-lication—although well received by most people—created something of a firestorm within the movement itself. Activists in countries like France and Germany were outraged that XR seemed to be getting into bed with capitalists, fearing co-option. The notion that there might be an "XR Business" platform, an idea that came from within the move-ment, poured fuel on the flames. Things eventually calmed down, to a degree, but it was intriguing to see the business reaction meanwhile.

In short order, I had emails from one CEO demanding to know why I was going political, while others wanted to know whether they could invite the activists in and how they might declare a "climate emergency," a key XR demand. Soon, the tempo picked up dramati-cally. A few weeks later, I was in Barcelona chairing a discussion session with four young activists, all schoolgirls, two from XR and two from Greta Thunberg's Fridays For Future movement. All girls, several were understandably nervous about going on stage in front of a big audi-ence, but they hit the proverbial ball out of the park.

So I was fascinated shortly afterward to see a discussion between Thunberg, a one-person Green Swan,[22] and Representative Alexandria Ocasio-Cortez, the American politician who lit up the presidential debates by calling for a Green New Deal. Often known as "AOC," the latter was in no doubt that leadership is tough. As she said, "To be a leader is to come first, to set the agenda. But what people don't real-ize is that leadership is also enormously difficult [. . .] Leadership is about taking decisions when you don't know 100% what the outcome is going to be."[23]

Thunberg's response was spot-on: "I know so many people who feel hopeless, and they ask me, 'What should I do?' And I say: 'Act. Do something.'"

So where can we look for breakthrough leadership and action at the country level these days? One option is tiny Costa Rica, determined to become the world's first carbon neutral country.[24] The fly in the oint-ment, as *The New York Times* cautioned, is that things might go seriously awry if the rest of the world went carbon neutral too quickly—since the country's economy is highly dependent on tourists flying in, trailing huge carbon footprints behind them.

One thing is clear, meanwhile: Whether we focus on citizens, corporations, cities, or countries, it is time for us all to become activists ourselves—or to actively support those with the courage to do so. Chris Davis, chief sustainability officer at The Body Shop International, insisted on Green Swan Day that business leaders must now become activists, however uncomfortable they may find it. They must stand up, speak out, and, above all, he insisted, take risks. Interestingly, having been owned by the French cosmetics company L'Oréal for ten years, which severely suppressed its appetite for social innovation, The Body Shop had now been acquired by Brazil's Natura, a widely recognized champion of change—and a B Corporation to boot. As a result, the internal pressure for change and activism had ramped up dramatically.

Another recent corporate example saw thousands of Amazon employees launch a climate rebellion against their own CEO, Jeff Bezos.[25] Their argument was that climate change is an existential threat, Amazon has the resources and scale to help address the challenge, but the company's efforts are still too small and slow, and—perhaps worst of all—the company still donates to climate-action-delaying legislators.[26] But be warned, such uprisings do not always work out well for the activists. After the so-called Googler Uprising, many activists left the company, often citing management pressure.[27]

The role of the professional media in all of this should not be underestimated, both in providing fact-checked information and countering false facts—as when Brazil's president Jair Bolsonaro accused environmentalists of torching Amazonia to make him look bad.[28] Alarmingly, in an age of populism, journalists are increasingly being aggressively silenced in countries like China.[29]

So how many of us are willing to stand up for democracy like the protestors in Hong Kong? We will all pay for the resulting lack of transparency and accountability. Periods of appeasement rarely end well. And as we agitate, we should also remember that most people want their near-term needs met before they are willing to think about the longer-term future for other people or species. It is a rare politician who can bridge between these realms. Again, it is time to build bridges, not wreck them.

As AOC described her political platform, "This movement for Congress is about education and healthcare; it's about housing, jobs, justice and civil rights. It's about preparing for the future of our environment, energy and infrastructure. It's about championing the dignity of our neighbors. And it's about getting money out of politics."[30]

Being an activist, as XR insists, means telling the truth, to others and to ourselves. That is why Thunberg's extraordinary clarity, urgency, and brutal honesty were so effective. As she told a group of leaders at a WEF event in Davos, "Adults keep saying we owe it to the young people to give them hope. But I don't want your hope, I don't want you to be hopeful. I want you to panic, I want you to feel the fear I feel every day. And then I want you to act, I want you to act as you would in a crisis. I want you to act as if the house was on fire, because it is."[31]

When OPEC declared Thunberg and other young climate activists the "greatest threat" to the fossil fuels industry, her tweeted response caught the emerging spirit exactly: "Our biggest compliment yet."[32]

Inevitably, such trends are spurring a growing number of people in the sustainable business and investment sectors to challenge their own thinking. Duncan Austin, whom I first met when he worked with Generation Investment Management, has recently accused the sustainable business movement not so much of *greenwash* but of *greenwish*, saying that the movement embraces "the earnest hope that well-intentioned efforts to make the world more sustainable are much closer to achieving the necessary change than they are."[33]

As we now move even deeper into the U-bend, leaders must simultaneously play into the worlds of both breakdown and breakthrough, of Black Swans and Green—radically different realities but both rooted in exponential dynamics. This can be a real brainache. As already noted, writer F. Scott Fitzgerald concluded that it takes an extraordinary brain to operate effectively while holding two contradictory ideas in tension at the same time.

Similarly, in his book *Good to Great*,[34] Jim Collins spotlighted the "Stockdale Paradox." James Stockdale, a high-ranking American officer, was taken prisoner during the Vietnam War, held for seven years, and horrifically tortured.[35] With no reason to expect he would survive, he held on by embracing both the harshness of his situation and maintaining a degree of optimism. As Stockdale himself later explained, "You must never confuse faith that you will prevail in the end—which you can never afford to lose—with the discipline to confront the most brutal facts of your current reality, whatever they might be." In simple terms, it now makes sense to hope for and work energetically over extended periods of time toward Green Swan outcomes, while acknowledging and preparing for wicked and even super wicked outcomes, those looming Gray and Black Swans.

Transformation is easy to talk about but way tougher to deliver. Which is why it has so often followed searing experiences like depressions and wars. Happily, in the wake of the "contained depression" of the last decade, we see growing interest in transformative system change. But it will be much easier for business leaders to deliver if the political, policy, and financial environments powerfully incentivize the right behaviors. Happily, green bonds have been one useful step in this direction, catching the eye of corporate finance and treasury departments because the lending rates are typically lower for companies that can demonstrate good sustainability performance.[36]

Recently we have also been helping WBCSD, the World Business Council for Sustainable Development, with its refresh of its Vision 2050 project, first launched in 2010.[37] Due to launch late in 2020, the project again focuses on the transformation agenda. As project director Julian Hill-Landolt told me, "We're splitting the work up into five main buckets: understanding systems transformation, updating the original pathway, creating a picture of the 2020–2030 operating environment for business, exploring the barriers and enablers of transformation, and regionalizing our global recommendations for key geographies."[38] The sort of language used, once again, points to where key parts of the change agenda are headed.

2. TAKE THE ANTHROPOCENIC ROUTE

Like it or not, we find ourselves in the Anthropocene epoch, whether we entered it seventy years ago, as many scientists now assume, or hundreds of years ago, as discussed in Chapter 2. The implications can be distilled using a metaphor from the world of IT. When our computers or other electronic devices are corrupted or congested, we reboot them. That is now what we must do with capitalism, democracy, and the much more recent sustainability agenda.

That will happen most rapidly where two things happen: first, the new order bubbles up from the bottom, from the edges of the system, and second, where the overarching paradigm shifts. We briefly explored the "Kuhn Cycle" in Chapter 4. Thomas Kuhn's book *The Structure of Scientific Revolutions* may feel a bit tired when encountered these days, but it was revolutionary back in the 1960s when I first read it. I sense that we are now moving toward the late stages of the next paradigm shift, a process that will have transformative impact on how most of us think, prioritize, and act.

Someone who has had a profound influence on my own worldview is James Lovelock.[39] The man who came up with the Gaia theory and invented one of the last century's most vital pieces of technology, the electron capture detector.[40] This helped uncover the impact of synthetic insecticides that led to Rachel Carson's book *Silent Spring* and to the discovery of the impact of CFCs on the stratospheric ozone layer. So it was beyond an honor, just after *Green Swans* had gone to the publishers for final editing, to attend his centennial birthday party.

Various elements of Lovelock's thinking may have been disputed over the years, but I believe that he will ultimately be to earth system science what Darwin has been for life science. Indeed, his provocative thinking is exactly what we need to begin to get our brains around tomorrow's Swans, Black, Gray, and Green.

In that spirit, he sees the Anthropocene now being overtaken by what he dubs the "Novacene." He argues that the Anthropocene is already coming to an end after just 300 years.[41] In the Novacene, which he concludes is already beginning, new beings will emerge from existing artificial intelligence systems.[42] They will think ten thousand times faster than we do and will regard humans as we regard plants, as desperately slow creatures. Already we hear that AI can solve Rubik's Cube quicker than we can click our fingers, with no advance knowledge of how the puzzle works.[43] And even that may seem like child's play for future AI systems.

Still, Lovelock believes, this need not be the cruel, violent machine takeover of the planet imagined by many sci-fi writers and filmmakers. Instead, these hyperintelligent beings will be as dependent on the health of the planet as we are. They, too, will need the planetary cooling systems of "Gaia"—of all life acting in concert to sustain living conditions on Earth—to defend them from the increasing heat of the sun. And since Gaia depends on organic life, we can hope to be partners in the planet management project.

Having worked on a book called *The Gaia Atlas of Planet Management* back in the 1980s, I have long been interested in this theme. It probably tracks back to the various editions of *The Whole Earth Catalog*, which I read assiduously between 1968 and 1972.[44] Imagine my joy, then, to find myself sitting next to *Whole Earth Catalog* founder Stewart Brand at the Lovelock centennial event, and across the table from his wife Ryan Phelan, who runs an organization called Revive & Restore.[45]

I learned that her team had been using the triple bottom line to evaluate their work on saving the horseshoe crab from exploitation by the pharmaceutical industry. Between 500,000 and 750,000 crabs are bled every year as part of product safety testing for drugs, even though there is a safe, effective, and cheaper alternative made with recombinant DNA.[46]

Happily, Ryan immediately saw the value of the 3R, Responsibility-Resilience-Regeneration, framework. Her appeal to companies like Eli Lilly has been based both on responsibility and cost reduction, she noted, while making the switch would lead to more resilient supply chains and estuarial ecosystems—and radically reducing the harvest of crabs would help regenerate an extraordinary species, which is around 450 million years old.[47] Of the crabs bled, somewhere between 5 and 30% are thought to die.[48] Happily, Eli Lilly has pledged to cut its use of the active ingredient extracted in this way by 90% in the next few years.

Intriguingly, too, Ryan has been working on the restoration of the woolly mammoth, a project I had come across via Project Drawdown, launched by our mutual friend Paul Hawken. The idea is to bring back versions of this extinct mammal to reclaim and protect vast areas of the Arctic tundra, stopping the thawing of the permafrost and ensuring that as reflective snow replaces forests that absorb solar energy, the planet's albedo effect would be boosted, slowing global warming.[49]

But while such thinking may appeal to out-of-the-box folk, how can we persuade those who fear they will lose their jobs as we accelerate the shift from today's degenerative economies to tomorrow's regenerative ones? The Industrial Revolution showed that a generation had to lose their jobs to create the "great enrichment" for others.[50] New generations of Luddites will be back in force, no doubt, and with dramatically greater powers of disruption.

And how, in the midst of all this, can we pull in mainstream businesspeople and investors? One greed-can-be-good approach is to point to almost inevitable multitrillion-a-year market opportunities by 2030.[51] The key: meeting the United Nations' Sustainable Development Goals.[52] This was the point made by Jeremy Oppenheim, senior partner at McKinsey spinout SYSTEMIQ, at our Green Swan Day event. He noted that the goals, a set of 17 stretch goals and 169 related targets championed by the United Nations, are hugely ambitious. But in a report called *Better Business, Better World*,[53] the Business & Sustainable Development Commission, which Oppenheim led, concluded that meeting the goals in just four out of sixty sectors (food and agriculture, cities, energy and materials, and health and well-being) could open up market opportunities worth up to $12 trillion a year by 2030.

In a parallel initiative, the latest round of the Green Transition Scoreboard, operated by Hazel Henderson's Ethical Markets,[54] has concluded that there had been a cumulative investment of $10.39 trillion in things like clean energy, green construction, and plant-protein food between 2009 and 2019.[55] One telling indicator of the shift was the public listing of Beyond Meat, whose shares skyrocketed 135% shortly after the listing, even though the meat alternatives company warned that it may never make a profit.[56]

In one of my favorite new sectors, producers of plant-based meat, chicken, egg, and fish substitutes are working toward true Green Swans—and maybe, with alternative fish products, what we might call "Blue Swans." In addition to Beyond Meat, other firms to watch include BlueNalu (which grows fish products using fish cells fermented in bioreactors), Good Catch (working on plant-based tuna alternatives, a hugely overfished species), Impossible Foods (known for its plant-based hamburgers, but also now exploring fish alternatives), Just, Inc. (whose founder, Josh Tetrick, told me he had been inspired by the triple bottom line), New Crop Capital (an investor in the sector), New Wave Foods (which makes vegan shrimp alternatives from seaweed and soya protein), and Ocean Hugger (which turns tomatoes into raw tuna-like slices, and eggplants into eel alternatives).[57]

For the necessary market breakthroughs to happen in good time and good order, though, we must move way beyond incremental change, way beyond "change-as-usual." Incrementalism has its uses, clearly, but it is worrying to see even committed business leaders treating the UN goals as an incremental change agenda. Their apparent assumption is this: If we just do a little bit more of what we have been doing, a little bit faster and a little bit better, we can deliver many—if not most—of the goals by the target date of 2030. Not so.

Indeed, the spotlight is now expanding to include business and economic models, the essence of how wealth is created. For tomorrow's capitalism to work, business models must become exponentially more social, lean, integrated, and circular, as we concluded in our own report to the Business & Sustainable Development Commission.[58] Our collective challenge is to ensure that emerging technologies meet difficult-to-reach societal goals, while being "lean" across scarce forms of capital, integrated from the point of use right out to the edges of the atmosphere and biosphere, and, crucially, part of an increasingly circular economy.

3. UNCLOG YOUR OWN U-BEND

All of this must be done as the global economy enters what I once dubbed its "Chrysalis Economy" moment, as explained in the Introduction, with an old order melting down and new ones racing to self-assemble themselves in the midst of growing chaos.[59]

A key skill in what comes next will be to think and act systemically, as SYSTEMIQ's Jeremy Oppenheim insisted on Green Swan Day. When we look at the entire system, he said, a "strange magic" can happen: "Suddenly you see opportunities everywhere—and they are potentially exponential."

That was the spirit in which we set up Volans in 2008, to bridge between the Ugly Duckling worlds of social enterprise, impact investors, and B Corporations on the one hand, and, on the other, mainstream business and finance. Next we began to engage exponential innovators, then young climate activists. But, however hard you try to build such bridges, there is a limit to what you can do with individual innovators and enterprises if the wider system fails to incentivize relevant change.

Which shifts the spotlight to the possibility of creating Global New Deals, most particularly Green New Deals. If handled right, the result could eventually be the sort of global economic boom seen in the wake of the Second World War. This is a metaphor and reality that the legendary Lester R. Brown championed for years in his Plan B work, which is well worth revisiting.[60]

Meanwhile Carlota Perez, who investigates the sort of long-wave economic cycles I first studied at university and who has powerfully influenced my own thinking, has this to say about New Deals: "I see the Green New Deal (GND) bill presented by [Rep. Alexandria] Ocasio-Cortez and [Sen. Ed] Markey to the House of Representatives as the first draft of a blueprint for bringing the U.S.—and the countries that might follow—into a boom similar to the one achieved after WWII. It turns the environmental problem into a solution for the social challenges facing America—and the world. It does so by giving a 'smart' and green direction to innovation and investment that can bring employment, profits, and growth, at the same time as providing a set of guidelines for government policy to aim at increasing social wellbeing."[61]

Listening to Perez, the latter stages of the U-bend snap into focus. She continues, "My historical research shows that, at first, technological revolutions bring decades of 'creative destruction,' with income-polarizing bubble prosperities. When the bubbles collapse, the reality of the rich getting richer while the poor get poorer is fully revealed and the victims of the transformation become easy prey to extremists, as in the 1930s and now."

She concludes, "Getting out of the doldrums requires feasible win-win policies to be established to reverse the social polarization at the same time as opening the way for profitable investment and innovation. That is how—and when—golden ages occur. During the Great Depression, after the previous mass production revolution bubble crashed in 1929, Roosevelt proposed many measures that were, at the time, received with outrage by the business and political worlds. He was accused of both fascism and communism for trying to set up the very policies that later brought the greatest boom in history. I don't doubt that the bill presented by Ocasio-Cortez will be met with equal ferocity. But they are wrong, and she is right."

The thing about extraordinary times is that they call forth extraordinary leaders. I am not sure if it was Churchill who first said that, but whoever it was it rings true today. Currently we see extraordinary politicians, simply in the sense that they are breaking with political precedents by throwing their rattles out of their national cradles, but once there is enough chaos the opportunity for new, future-fit leaders to break through can grow significantly.

Think again of that steep slope up and out of the U-bend. Remember, too, that exponential dynamics mean that some of those new growth opportunities will present themselves like distant thermals to a glider pilot. Having tried gliding as a teenager, finding it both vertiginous and stomach-churning, I know the turbulence that accompanies both rapid aerial climbs and rapid economic growth can be disorientating. But if we once know that new types of growth are coming, then a key part of our challenge is to find the leverage points to turn a critical mass of today's Ugly Ducklings and early-stage Green Swans into tomorrow's apparent market miracles.

We should be fully aware, however, that much of this will be intensely political. Among other things, if capitalism is to be restored to anything like vibrant good health, we must get back to trust-busting. America's FAANG companies are the most obvious targets.[62] That is why the work of people like EU trustbuster Margrethe Vestager is so crucial, both within the region and as a model for others to follow. And it is also why the work of economists like Mariana Mazzucato and Kate Raworth is so central in creating the systemic conditions within which Green Swan innovation is massively more likely to happen and succeed.

4. RIDE A GREEN SWAN

Swans, Black, Gray, Green, or even Blue, are exponential life-forms, or at least exponential forms of wealth creation or destruction. While we may be increasingly expert in how social media memes go viral or on how a virus like Ebola spreads through human populations, most of us remain sorely behind the curve when it comes to the ability to design and drive exponential positive change.

So where should we look for at least an inkling on how this might best be done? Where would you turn to learn how to make the impossible inevitable? In my home country, I have turned to people like the Eden Project's Sir Tim Smit, spotlighted in Chapter 7—and a standout speaker on that first Green Swan Day. Not that there are many people like him. Yet.

Elsewhere, America has long been an inspiration, with California up there in lights. I first went to the Golden State early in the 1970s, returning regularly since. Then in 2016, early on in our Project Breakthrough initiative with the United Nations' Global Compact,[63] I zoomed around Silicon Valley and Los Angeles with two colleagues in search of clues as to how to drive exponential—breakthrough—change.

Out at Mountain View, Google territory, we visited Singularity University (SU). There they were energetically discussing a concept used by military planners to capture an increasingly unpredictable and dynamic world. VUCA refers to an environment of nonstop volatility, uncertainty, complexity, and ambiguity.[64]

Why, the SU folk were asking, "do so many of us—individually and collectively—fail to imagine, let alone anticipate, the massive and disruptive changes that are unfolding? Driven by fast moving technologies and globalization, the pace of change is accelerating, our brains are struggling to keep up, and surprise, discomfort, and unrest are the result. This is no anomaly. VUCA isn't going away. Change promises to speed up, not slow down. To thrive in a world where 'change is the only constant,' leaders need to replace old thinking with a new framework."

Exponential change calls for exponential leaders, and for SU that means four things. First, exponential leaders need the skills of the **Futurist**, "imagining new possibilities boldly and optimistically—and understanding they are quite likely to arise sooner than expected." They need to "get comfortable asking open-ended questions about unspoken assumptions to see new possibilities. They need to be curious about the future and blend imaginative practices of strategic foresight, futures backcasting, science fiction design and scenario planning into traditional business planning."

Second, they must act as **Innovators**, "discovering new ideas through creative ideation and rigorous experimentation. These days, great product ideas can come from a single tweet or a surprising customer interaction and be tested with a working prototype in less than 24 hours. Yet, many businesses still focus primarily on getting existing products to market faster while reducing costs and increasing margins." Rigorous innovators, we are told, iterate over and over "to uncover opportunities obscured by the fog of uncertainty."

Third, as innovation accelerates, leaders must understand which technologies will most directly impact their industry and which will disrupt adjacent industries. This means that all of us, to a degree, must become **Technologists.** The latest technology "can digitize, manipulate and replace physical products and services, challenging the status quo of many existing companies. The best way to understand technological change is not to read about it," we are told, "but to experience it first-hand by learning to code, building or manipulating a simple robot, trying new products and services that go beyond what's familiar or comfortable, and seeking the resources of innovation and experimentation."

In parallel, and crucially, exponential leaders must grapple with the ethical, moral, and social implications of the technologies they are evolving. Which brings us to the fourth skill set, that of the **Humanitarian**. Here we are advised, "Exponential leaders use the skills and behaviors of futurist, innovator and technologist to improve the lives of the people they touch, and society as a whole. They aim to do well by doing good—not as a separate set of 'corporate social responsibility' activities, but as part of the integrated company mission."

A key part of this will involve sidestepping the Midgley Syndrome outlined in Chapter 6, ensuring that tomorrow's capitalism avoids causing systemic crises like those spotlighted in Figure 8 (see Annex, page 254), including "Insectageddon,"[65] involving the catastrophic undermining of insect populations, and "The Great Hack," the latter a Netflix branding of the hacking of the 2016 US presidential elections.[66]

Business cannot solve such challenges on its own. Political, cultural, and behavioral changes are also needed. But as far as the business contribution goes, it is clear that new forms of incorporation are needed. B Corporations, as SU (which is one) reminds us, are for-profit companies certified to meet rigorous standards of social and environmental performance, accountability, and transparency.

Having long been involved in the B Corp world, with two of the companies I co-founded becoming the first and second B Corps certified in the United Kingdom, I know how powerful this approach can be. At their best, B Corp leaders combine these four roles—of futurist, innovator, technologist, and humanitarian. They know that these four dimensions of learning make it easier to "imagine, create, capture and scale hidden value in an increasingly complex and dynamic world."

But cities are also now a rapidly growing focus of attention. They are increasingly seen as the places where humanity's greatest challenges impact the most people, from inequality, migration, and climate change—and where some of the most powerful solutions will come from.[67] As a result, they too suffer from the forces of creative destruction. However, cities like Pittsburgh, once known as "Steel City," are showing how urban transformations can succeed, with the new economy built around technologies like autonomous vehicles, AI, and renewable energy.

At the same time, too, we see a new breed of urban scientist, among them Geoffrey West of the Santa Fe Institute, demonstrating how we can exploit new forms of system thinking to great sustainability effect across what some call the "World City."[68] West explained his team's early findings, "With every doubling of city size, whether from 20,000 to 40,000 people or 2M to 4M people, socioeconomic quantities—the good, the bad, and the ugly—increase by approximately 15% per person with a concomitant 15% savings on all city infrastructure-related costs."[69] Understanding these new laws of life, growth, and death in organisms, cities, and companies will be critical in managing tomorrow's urban Swans, Black and Green.

Meanwhile, whatever damage the Trump era may prove to have done to America, the country remains a beacon in the exponential world. On the same trip where we visited SU for the first time, we also visited Google's X facility. This, by their own account, is a diverse group of inventors and entrepreneurs who build and launch technologies to improve the lives of millions, even billions, of people. Their goal is "to produce a 10x impact on the world's most intractable problems, not just 10% improvements."[70]

"X is perhaps the only enterprise on the planet where regular investigation into the absurd is not just permitted but encouraged, and even required," reported *The Atlantic* magazine. "X has quietly looked into space elevators and cold fusion. It has tried, and abandoned, projects to design hoverboards with magnetic levitation and to make affordable fuel from seawater. It has tried—and succeeded, in varying measures— to build self-driving cars, make drones that deliver aerodynamic packages, and design contact lenses that measure glucose levels in a diabetic person's tears."[71]

I recently met up again with X's Sarah Hunter, this time in London. She was responsible for X's public policy team, helping governments and policy makers around the world understand new technologies and their impacts. She noted both that X is now embracing the sort of challenges flagged by the Sustainable Development Goals as the very core of its mission, while the World Economic Forum is also now actively integrating its own sustainability and "Fourth Industrial Revolution" programs. Powerful signals of the paradigm shift now underway.

Once you start thinking in this way, both the world and our future look quite different. Here are two quick examples from our own work. One involved reviewing a fascinating new report for RethinkX, based in London and Silicon Valley, exploring the future of agriculture and food into the 2030s.[72] The report's subtitle gives a flavor of its dramatic message:

"The Second Domestication of Plants and Animals, the Disruption of the Cow and the Collapse of Industrial Livestock Farming."

In the old order, authors Jamie Arbib and Tony Seba note, we grew a cow or steer and bloodily, messily, and inhumanely broke it down into its component parts. Now precision biology and precision fermentation mean that we can produce any of those components much more efficiently for a radically lower, and constantly decreasing, cost. By 2035, if trends go as they expect, the number of cattle in traditional American farming could fall by as much as 90%.

Unimaginable for many of us, even if the date were set at 2040 or 2050. But when I discuss the need to disrupt the current sustainability agenda and mind-set, this is the sort of trajectory I have in mind. As RethinkX sums up the prospect: "By 2030, demand for cow products will have fallen by 70%. Before we reach this point, the U.S. cattle industry will be effectively bankrupt. By 2035, demand for cow products will have shrunk by 80% to 90%. Other livestock markets such as chicken, pig, and fish will follow a similar trajectory. There will be enormous destruction of value for those involved in rearing animals and processing them, and for all the industries that support and supply the sector (fertilizers, machinery, veterinary services, and more). We estimate this will total more than $100bn. At the same time, there will be huge opportunities for the producers of modern foods and materials." So will we ride and shape this wave of disruption, or allow it to surprise and overwhelm us?

The second example can be more rapidly summarized, even if it will take generations to play through. While evolving *Green Swans*, I was contacted by the former chief scientist of the XPRIZE Foundation, Paul Bunje. We had known each other since that same 2016 tour of Silicon Valley and LA. Indeed, in its wake we had invited him to join the Volans board. Now, it turned out, he was returning the favor. He had left the XPRIZE Foundation to launch Conservation X Labs.[73] Their immodest yet vital ambition: to reverse extinction.

It's time for us all to hitch rides on tomorrow's Green Swans, so how could I say no? As Conservation X Labs explains, "We are in the middle of a period of extraordinary change: a sixth mass extinction, the first in earth's history driven by the actions of a single species. Conservation, as we know it, is not succeeding fast enough. Conservation X Labs applies technology, entrepreneurship, and open innovation to source, develop, and scale critical solutions to the underlying drivers of human-induced extinction, whether in conservation or other fields. Humans have driven the sixth mass extinction. Humans have the power to reverse it." And only we humans.

5. JOIN THE GREEN SWAN ROADSHOW

It's time to prepare for the coming boom in more responsible, more resilient, and, ultimately, increasingly regenerative capitalism. Easy to say, but in the capitalist world, like it or not, the rubber really hits the road when it comes to raising capital for a given activity. For anyone unfamiliar with the deep workings of finance, and most of us are, a "roadshow" is a series of presentations (or "pitches") made to investors and financial analysts in various locations, en route to an initial public offering (IPO).

Typically, the pitches are made by the underwriting firm backing the offer of shares and, critically, by the top management team of the business going public. Some such activities, as with renewable energy or electric vehicles, clearly link to emerging Green Swan stories. Others, for example those involving new coal mines or coal-fired power stations, are increasingly seen as part of Black Swan stories and can expect to be punished as a result.

Take thermal coal, whose days are clearly numbered. According to an Institute for Energy Economics and Financial Analysis report,[74] more than one hundred leading global financial institutions have already pulled the plug on funding the sector, squeezing investments and making the operating environment way more challenging. This "progressive strangulation" is denying coal companies access to capital markets for possible expansions, mergers, or acquisitions, as well as cutting off avenues for insurance, or making it more expensive.

Other industries are being impacted too. Take oil tankers, which risk losing almost a third of their value when the shift to green energy gains real momentum.[75] Today's $160 billion tanker market would see a rising tide of stranded assets, with few other cargos available to fully replace fossil fuels. All of this was predicted. One interviewee for our Green Swan Day film was Mark Campanale, a co-founder of the Carbon Tracker Initiative. He conceived of the "unburnable carbon" capital markets thesis, outlined in his 2011 report, *Unburnable Carbon—Are the World's Financial Markets Carrying a Carbon Bubble?*[76] His answer: They are.

While some investors fret about stranded assets, tougher souls look for "cockroach stocks," businesses that can survive no matter what happens![77] But our best hope lies in the pioneers pushing the change agenda upstream into the deep recesses of the financial markets from which so many Black nightmares and Green Swan dreams will flow.

Another financial pioneer present and interviewed on Green Swan Day was Nick Robins. From 2014 to 2018 he was co-director of UN Environment's Inquiry into a Sustainable Finance System.[78] He led activities in Brazil, the EU, India, Italy, and the United Kingdom, as well as work focused on investors, insurance, and green banking. The eventual road map to a more sustainable financial system noted, "Historically the financial system has responded to the needs of the time. A global consensus has arisen that sustainable growth will be one of the greatest challenges of the 21st century [. . .] As in previous structural transformations, the financial system will play a major role in this process: the full potential of the financial system needs to be harnessed to serve as an engine in the global economy's transition toward sustainable development."

The inquiry's aim is to encourage "an integrated approach that can be used by all financial sector stakeholders—both public and private—to accelerate the transformation toward a sustainable financial system. This approach can bring policy cohesiveness across ministries, central banks, financial regulators, and private financial sector participants to focus efforts."

It is telling that the ultimate vision is "one of a financial system that integrates sustainability considerations into its operations, including the full costing of positive and negative externalities that sustainability implies, leading to a reorientation of the flow of resources toward more inclusive and sustainable activities." In this future the triple bottom line and similar concepts are no longer add-ons but are increasingly hardwired into the system.

Over time, it must become radically harder to raise funding for initiatives with Black Swan characteristics—and easier to fund-raise for those with Green Swan characteristics. As a recent example of the latter, think of the molecule ZIF-8, seen by some as some sort of holy grail in capturing carbon from the atmosphere.[79] There will be many such excitements—and many disappointments—as the world shifts from Black to Green trajectories. Indeed, an accelerating failure rate could be an inverse indicator of our ultimate chances of breakthrough success. The more failures, the greater the likelihood that real breakthroughs will be achieved.

Inevitably some people, businesses, and economies will be caught between conflicting trajectories. Late in 2019, for example, I keynoted a major conference in Alberta, Canada. Here the money largely comes from the regional oil sands industry, increasingly seen as possibly the ultimate Black Swan of all fossil fuel Black Swans.[80] As a result, Canada and its Alberta oil sands industry are now a test case for how governments and business will respond to the intensifying climate emergency.

Caught between a rock and hard place, Canada wants to boost earnings from the industry, yet also wants to be a global climate champion. Longer term, it must be one or the other. But one key thing the country is doing today is investing furiously in technology, business models, and initiatives that could turn out to have pronounced Green Swan characteristics. Indeed, the conference I spoke at, SPARK 2019, convened many hundreds of leading clean technology innovators with investors to "reimagine carbon." A case of Black Swan money doing Green Swan work?

Too soon to know. But the future of capitalism has more to do with money than with technology, regulation, or standards—even if all three are crucially important. And my concern about the limitations of CSR, shared value, and even current conceptions of the circular economy stems from the respective movements' absolute, and sometimes insufficiently critical, reliance on current forms of capitalism. True, we can expect the accelerating shift to intangible assets and investments to accelerate the transition to lower resource input economic models, but this alone is very unlikely to save us.[81]

So, alongside initiatives designed to redirect investment and, even more fundamentally, to reinvent economics, we need to dedicate a growing effort to exploring how business leaders, entrepreneurs, investors, city mayors, policy makers, and politicians can co-evolve what we might call the "Tomorrow's Capitalism Roadshow." Or the Green Swan Roadshow.

Picture this as a rolling set of presentations pitching a cleaner and more integrated, circular, and socially inclusive economy, helping investors, financial analysts and institutions, government funding sources, and foundations manage down Black Swan risks and grow Green Swan opportunities. Among the questions we need to ask are the following: Who has been pitching such transformations to investors? What works—and what does not? Where pitches have been successful, how do the impacts look across the triple bottom line and over time? How are the relevant returns measured and valued? And what more needs to be done to bring the relevant solutions and markets to scale?

These are now strategic, top team questions. Recall that Chapter 4 opened in the boardroom of the Finnish energy company Neste, which is increasingly embracing renewable energy and playing into the circular economy. One outlet for its biofuels is the private jet company Victor, whose CEO, Clive Jackson, has publicly admitted that his company's planes emit twenty times more carbon per passenger mile than commercial airliners.[82] Victor has been meeting the cost of double-offsetting the emissions, but now Jackson has invited clients to match that amount. The result may be some interesting new conversations taking place literally way over our heads.

We are in the midst of a planetary, multigenerational re-education process. Education, at all levels, is among the best investments our societies make, with extraordinary (if not always predictable) long-term returns. The ultimate Green Swan pursuit, perhaps. Which is why I was intrigued to head across recently to Buckingham Palace, London, for an event organized by the Cambridge Institute for Sustainability Leadership. CISL, as it is generally known, or even "Sizzle," has trained nearly ten thousand executives worldwide. At this, its thirtieth anniversary event, long-standing director Dame Polly Courtice told several hundred leaders the following:

> Nothing short of transformation is required right now to set us on a path to a safe and stable climate, a healthy environment, and fair and prosperous societies. It will now require the corporate sector as a whole to contribute innovative solutions and show strong leadership to let go of the old ways and to create the new. It will require the finance sector rethinking current operating practices and adopting longer term, more forward-thinking strategies. Ultimately it will require closer collaboration between all of these sectors to drive the systemic change needed for a sustainable economy.[83]

A revolution discussed in the very heart of the incumbent order. With Prince Charles in attendance, as a long-standing champion of CISL and sustainability, we debated the future—and the impact of groups like Extinction Rebellion and Fridays For Future on acceptable directions and speeds of change. On my table, participants even toyed with the idea of removing everyone aged over fifty from leadership roles to allow younger, more aware, and more committed people to come through. A South African colleague said that had happened in South Africa after the apartheid regime was toppled.

Provocative, certainly, and another illustration of the seismic shocks now rattling the windows in palaces, ministries, and headquarter offices. When it comes to naming today's Horsemen of the Apocalypse in this moment of populism, bellicosity, trade wars, and possible deglobalization, we are spoiled for choice. But, perhaps self-interestedly, I argued in that table discussion that what we really need is radically improved intergenerational working. And for that to work and succeed over time, we must all reinvent ourselves, not "just" our organizations, economies, and educational systems.

We all need to link to a wider world. Some people may conclude that Elon Musk is on the verge of cracking this problem, with his company Neuralink announcing groundbreaking progress on its "Brain-Computer Interface" technology. The goal is a two gigabit-per-second wireless connection between a human brain and the cloud within a few years.[84] In many ways, however, I suspect this will simply add to the distraction, to the background noise, and to have—and have-not—divides, at least for a while.

Which is why, instead, I find the work of people like Nadya Zhexembayeva so inspiring, particularly her recommendation that—in order to avoid what she calls the "Titanic Syndrome"[85]—we should all now become "chief reinvention officers."[86] True, it is tempting—and very human—to overuse terms like sustainability, disruption, transformation, reinvention, and regeneration, without actually sustaining, disrupting, transforming, reinventing, or regenerating anything. But we must now ensure that tomorrow's capitalism, markets, and businesses —and the relevant politics, governments and public policy frameworks—genuinely serve the interests of all life. This means embracing exponential migrations drawn into the future by positive visions, not just rudely shoved along by global weirding.

For a sense of the challenges and opportunities covered during our first Green Swan Day, take a look at the film *Green Swans* co-produced with Atlas of the Future.[87] Consider what sort of Green Swans—or initiatives with Green Swan characteristics—you want to see evolving through the 2020s and beyond. Let us know your priorities and plans. And help us further evolve our embryonic Swanspotter's Guide (see Annex, pages 254–256).

Given how central energy will be to our economic transition, my personal favorite Green Swan candidate as this book went to press was the proposal from Stanford University showing how 143 countries around the world can take to plug into 100% clean, renewable energy by 2050. The low-cost, stable electricity grid solutions outlined could cut world energy needs by 57%, create over 28 million more jobs than are lost, and reduce energy, health, and climate costs by 91% compared with business-as-usual pathways. The initial investment of $73 trillion worldwide may seem impossible, but our challenge now is to make it seem—then become—inevitable.

Nor is there just one narrow road to this outcome. Lead researcher, Mark Z. Jacobson, explained: "We're just trying to lay out one scenario for 143 countries to give people in these and other countries the confidence that, yes, this is possible. But there are many solutions and many scenarios that could work. You're probably not going to predict exactly what's going to happen, but it's not like you need to find the needle in the haystack. There are lots of needles in this haystack."

Meanwhile, for anyone still wondering whatever happened to the triple bottom line, that recall process was part of my own reinvention process. I am now more than happy that it be used, so long as it operates on three of the five levels outlined in Chapter 4: **Responsibility** (where most current practice clusters), **Resilience** (where too little effort yet focuses), and **Regeneration** (where the spotlight must now shift).

Ultimately, any true Green Swan will help—simultaneously—to regenerate the natural, social, and economic worlds. An existentially taxing, civilizational task. But we have left ourselves no alternative. The upside is that, for the foreseeable future, this will be by far the biggest opportunity for adventure, growth, and evolution in the tightly coupled stories of humankind, capitalism, and our home planet, Earth.

The Author

John Elkington is a writer, thought leader, serial entrepreneur, and, at heart, an environmentalist. Sometimes described as the "Godfather of Sustainability," he has now written or co-authored twenty books, including the million-selling *Green Consumer Guide* series.

At the age of eleven, in 1961, he raised money for the newly formed World Wildlife Fund (WWF), where he has for many years served on the organization's Council of Ambassadors. He went on to dedicate his life to helping influence, inspire, and stretch the thinking of business leaders through informed storytelling and delivering what one client called "constructive discomfort." In this spirit, he coined the term "triple bottom line" in 1994—and followed up in 1995 with the popularization "People, Planet & Profit," terms that have gone into the business lexicon.

Elkington has worked with many scores of corporations, often at board and C-suite level, as well as with the financial community, industry bodies, government, the media, NGOs, academia, innovators, and entrepreneurs. Along the way, he has co-founded four social-purpose businesses since 1978: Environmental Data Services (ENDS, 1978), John Elkington Associates/CounterCurrent (1983), SustainAbility (1987), and Volans Ventures (2008). All four still exist, and the last two were respectively the second and first certified British B Corporations in the United Kingdom.

Over the years, Elkington has also served on over seventy boards and advisory boards, advising companies, nonprofits, and policy-making organizations. He is a visiting professor at the Cranfield School of Management, as well as at Imperial College London and University College London (UCL).

In 2004, *BusinessWeek* described Elkington as "a dean of the corporate responsibility movement for three decades." He has received many awards and honors, including from the United Nations (Global 500 Roll of Honour, 1989). In 2005, he landed a "Social Capitalist of the Year" award from *Fast Company*, and that year he was also awarded a three-year, $1 million field-building grant from the Skoll Foundation for Social Entrepreneurship. In 2011, he was awarded the Spencer Hutchens Jr. Medal by the American Society for Quality (ASQ) for "outstanding leadership, as an advocate for social responsibility, and for bringing about positive social change." In 2014, he was awarded the Recycla/*El Mercurio* International Prize in Chile and in 2015 the Ethical Corporation Lifetime Achievement Award.

He considers the last of these seriously premature, as the next ten to fifteen years, he suggests, are when his—and our collective—mettle will be tested to the limit. Seen in this light, *Green Swans* is a draft manifesto not only for the future of capitalism, democracy, and sustainability, but also for the author, his team, and their wider ecosystem of change agents and market revolutionaries.

Acknowledgments

enerally, I think best in conversation. So a critical element in our offices over the years has been the generations of sofas on which hundreds—indeed now thousands—of conversations have happened. I have also traveled constantly for work since the early 1970s, earning a Gold Card for life from one airline. A sign of shame in these days of Extinction Rebellion and school climate strikes, but also an indication of a life spent carrying versions of the change agenda to places they might not otherwise have reached. Hence my Chief Pollinator job title.

All of which complicates the task of thanking those who have helped evolve the thinking outlined in *Green Swans*. An early attempt at a comprehensive survey of influences can be found on my website.[1] And I have leaned over backwards to credit published sources I have drawn upon here in the references section. So rather than go broad, I will zoom in on those who have helped in evolving this latest book and the linked Green Swan campaign.

As usual, all faults in the published work are mine.

At Volans, my profound thanks go to Louise Kjellerup Roper, our wonderful, shake-it-up executive director, and to Richard Roberts, the inspired and indefatigable lead on the Tomorrow's Capitalism Inquiry. Then, alphabetically, I also thank our team, particularly Yinka Awoyinka, Paul Bunje, Tom Farrand, Amanda Feldman, Jan Gilbert, the late Pamela Hartigan, Richard Johnson, Laura Kibble, Sam Lakha, Charmian Love, Geoff Lye, Jenny Poulter, Kavita Prakash-Mani, Noah Roper, Lorraine Smith, Nathalie Thong, Roxanne Tibbert, and Kate Wolfenden.

Because the book is one output of our Tomorrow's Capitalism Inquiry, I owe a particular debt of gratitude to the organizations supporting the project. Most notably, to Aviva Investors (particularly Steve Waygood), The Body Shop International (David Boynton and Chris Davis), Covestro (Markus Steilemann, Eric Bischof, Stefan Koch, and Burcu Unal), EcoVadis (Sylvain Guyoton, Pierre-François Thaler, and Fred Trinel), the Scottish Environmental Protection Agency (Terry A'Hearn and Lorraine Rahmani), and Unilever (Paul Polman and Jeff Seabright).

My thanks also go to Lise Kingo and Ingvild Sørensen of the UN Global Compact, our partners on Project Breakthrough.[2] Another key strategic partner in this work has been Atlas of the Future, where I thank Lisa Goldapple and Cathy Runciman. And I owe elements of the book's subtitle and our growing embrace of regeneration to the pioneering work of John Fullerton and the Capital Institute.[3] Meanwhile, a book that had a particular impact on my thinking back in 2014 was *Exponential Organizations* by Salim Ismail, with Michael S. Malone and Yuri van Geest.[4]

At Fast Company Press and Greenleaf Book Group, I am indebted to Amanda Hughes, April Murphy, Jen Glynn, Neil Gonzalez, Carrie Jones, Daniel Sandoval, Jeffrey Curry, and their colleagues, both for embracing this book project and for supporting it in so many ways. At *Fast Company* itself, particular thanks go to senior editor Morgan Clendaniel.

I thank pretty much everyone who has worked at SustainAbility since 1987. Although I fought for decades to keep the company independent, its acquisition by ERM early in 2019 injected crucial and timely financing into my Green Swan work, for which I am profoundly grateful.

Thank you, too, Silvio Rebêlo for the Green Swan visual identity, used on the front cover—and Carlo Schifano and Conor Dowse of Twist Creative for their help with the visual side of Green Swan Day, among other things.

In addition to those already mentioned, I thank our wider ecosystem, particularly: Salla Ahonen, Simon Anholt, Jamie Arbib, Duncan Austin, Azeem Azhar (as editor of *Exponential View*), Oli Barrett, Janine Benyus, José Luis Blasco Vazquez, David Blood, Gail Bradbrook, Stewart Brand, Sir Richard Branson, Sarah Brunwin, Tom Burke, Peter Byck, Mark Campanale, Jay Coen Gilbert, Dame Polly

Courtice, Peter Diamandis, Robert (Bob) Eccles, Paul Ekins, Fiona Ellis, Thomas Ermacora, Marie Gad, John Gilbert, James Gomme, Al Gore, David Grayson, Sarah Green Carmichael, Nick Haan, Julia Hailes, Sonja Haut, Paul Hawken, Katie Hill, Julian Hill-Landolt, Dominic Hofstetter, Simo Honkanen, Sarah Hunter, the Rt. Hon. Nick Hurd, MP, Adi Ignatius, Geoff Kendall, Andrew Kerr, Clare Kerr, Colin Le Duc, the late David Layton, Tim Lenton, Jacqueline Lim, Charmian Love, James and Sandy Lovelock, Joel Makower, Joseph Mariathasan, Mariana Mazzucato, Maria Ortiz de Mendivil Schwartz, Tell Münzing, the late Max Nicholson, the late Richard Northcote, Jeremy Oppenheim, Sally Osberg, Carlota Perez, Ryan Phelan, Jørgen Randers, Erik Rasmussen, Beth Rattner, Martin Redfern, Martin Rich, Tom Rippin, Nick Robins, Will and Carla Rosenzweig, Samer Salty, Judy Samuelson, John Sauven, Alan Schwartz, the late Sir Peter Scott, Robyn Scott, Tony Seba, Jeff Skoll, Terri Slavin, Sir Tim Smit, Gavin Starks, Tanya Steele, Laura Storm, Susanne Stormer, Pavan Sukhdev, Mike Tennant, Patrick Thomas, Peter Vanacker, Diana Verde Nieto, Jan-Olaf Willums, Jochen Zeitz, Zheng Jieying, and Nadya Zhexembayeva.

This is a partial listing at best, and the fact that someone is listed here does not necessarily imply that they support all the ideas in the book, though I have drawn on their thinking and work to create it.

Finally, and perhaps most important of all, I thank my family. My parents, Pat and Tim, of course, and my siblings Caroline, Gray, and Tessa, who cared for Pat and Tim as their lives came to a long-drawn-out close. But my biggest debt, by far, is to Elaine—whose wisdom and support I have benefitted from since 1968. She has helped birth twenty of my books to date. Speaking of which, huge love and profound thanks also go to our extraordinary and beloved daughters, Gaia and Hania, and their families, notably Gene, Jake, and Paul.

Thank you all for putting up with the endless peregrinations of a migratory son, brother, husband, father, colleague, friend, father-in-law, and now grandfather. Raised on the move, I have come to value family and friendship more than many. But even I must admit I have spread myself perilously thin at times. Perhaps the 2020s will be different?

Annex

The Swanspotter's Guide 1.0

So how can we spot a Black, Gray, or Green Swan in the making? As I talked to people about the book's theme, this question was often raised. The definitions used here are looser than those used by Nassim Nicholas Taleb in his book *The Black Swan*, as already mentioned, but some working notes on how to identify two types of Swan, Black and Green, can be found in Figure 8.

The entries are meant to be suggestive, not definitive. An invitation to scratch and peck, not to parrot. The sequence runs as follows: Row 1 lists some key characteristics of Black and Green Swans; row 2 highlights some typical impacts; row 3 identifies some areas in which relevant dynamics can be seen in the world of carbon, whose life cycle is increasingly critical to our economies, societies, and planet; and row 4 underscores a number of wider examples.

To be truly worthy of the name, a Green Swan solution must simultaneously solve multidimensional challenges, although the timings of the positive outcomes may be different. Let's take a single example to make the point: urban greenery. Trees, says The Nature Conservancy, are "sustainability power tools."[1] They clean the air, removing particulate matter; they regulate temperatures, counteracting the urban "heat island" effect; they shade streets and damp down background noise. And they are pleasing to look at. Yet in the United States alone, 4 million urban trees die each year, with replanting efforts lagging.

Time for a Green Swan approach. Let's start with the economics. A 2016 study by the US Forest Service found that every dollar spent on planting urban trees then delivered an estimated $5.82 in public benefits.[2] An earlier study found that urban trees remove so much pollution from the air that they trigger signification reductions in public health-care needs. Perhaps it is time for city greening funding to be underwritten from health-care budgets? In this spirit, a few years back, Kaiser Permanente, a large California-based insurer, announced a $2 million investment in public parks in low-income communities.

Perhaps the most striking example of urban greening are the twin towers of Bosco Verticale (or "Vertical Forest"[3]) in Milan, Italy, where the landscape agronomist Laura Gatti has wreathed the towers in trees and trailing greenery.[4] "Living walls" are now popping up in cities around the world. And planting is also central to the growing number of "sponge cities" evolving in China and elsewhere, designed to absorb high tides and storm waters as the climate emergency builds.

Where architects like Frank Lloyd Wright embedded their buildings in nature, in the twenty-first century, nature must be invited to take root in our cities and communities again. In London, where I live, a key step in this direction has been its designation as the world's first National Park City.[5] Now that's a Green Swan worthy of the name.

THE SWANSPOTTER'S GUIDE, 1.0

	BLACK SWANS	GREEN SWANS
1. Characteristics	• Often degenerative • Unplanned (with some exceptions) • Exponential • Largely unforeseen • Vicious cycles, mainly • Undermine resilience, promote fragility • Rob future generations • Increasingly unsustainable	• Regenerative • Planned (with some exceptions) • Exponential • Foreseen, to some degree • Virtuous cycles, mainly • Build resilience, promote "anti-fragility"[6] • Reward future generations • Increasingly sustainable

continued

2. Impacts	• Often drive breakdowns • Produce net negative impacts across TBL • Corrode social capital, via intensifying cycles of blame and shame • Counterintuitively, can trigger positive unintended consequences, including Green Swan solutions	• Spur breakthroughs • Produce net positive impacts across TBL • Generally require robust social capital to achieve—and also help build it • Counterintuitively, can trigger negative unintended consequences, tomorrow's Gray or Black Swans
3. Carbon examples	• Climate weirding, driven by e.g., greenhouse gases, ecosystem destruction, ocean acidification, unpriced externalities, rejection of science, myopia, and selfishness • Icons of Black Swan carbon futures: e.g., Donald Trump, the Koch Brothers[7], ExxonMobil, Jair Bolsonaro, and Vladimir Putin	• Carbon increasingly brought back into technological, economic, and ecological loops via policy incentives and investment in the circular economy, promoting resilience and regeneration • Icons of Green Swan carbon futures: e.g., James Lovelock, Margrethe Vestager, Tesla, Alexandria Ocasio-Cortez (AOC), and Greta Thunberg
4. Other examples	• Outbreak of World War I; "Spanish flu" epidemic, 1918–1920; ecological impact of e.g., DDT; dissolution of the USSR for those living there; 9/11 attacks; the opioid crisis in the US; "The Great Hack"[8]; Brexit; "Insectageddon"[9]; spread of meat-based diets and fossil-powered cars across a growing global population; death of more than 500 million animals in Australian brushfires in 2019	• Impact of "Earthrise" image of our planet; rapid rise of environmentalism; restoration of Loess Plateau, China; rise of renewable energy; electric vehicles; green bonds; Denmark's "Green Transition"; London declared a National Park City; development of plant-based alternatives to eggs, meat, poultry, and fish; Stanford University $73 trillion Green New Deal plan for 143 countries; EU €1 trillion Green Deal

Figure 8: The Swanspotter's Guide, 1.0

Clearly, this is very much a work in progress. We would appreciate any suggestions of possible additions to—or deletions from—these lists. They will feed into our thinking about the Green Swan Awards, see https://volans.com/green-swans-2020/, the first two being won by Sir Tim Smit of the Eden Project and Sacha Dench of Conservation Without Borders. Please send any suggestions, ideally with an explanation and links to further details, to me at john@volans.com.

Endnotes

WELCOME

1. For more on Taleb's books, including *The Black Swan*, see his website: http://www.fooledbyrandomness.com.

2. Nassim Nicholas Taleb, *The Black Swan: The Impact of the Highly Improbable*. New York: Penguin Random House, 2007.

3. https://www.ssga.com/blog/2019/01/gray-swans-for-2019.html

4. Camilla Cavendish, *Extra Time: 10 Lessons for an Ageing World*. New York: HarperCollins Publishers, 2019.

5. https://jembendell.com/about/

6. Andrew Edgecliffe-Johnson, "Capitalism Keeps CEOs Awake at Night," *Financial Times*, April 23, 2019.

7. Ray Dalio, "As most of you know, I'm a capitalist, and even I think capitalism is broken," @RayDalio, April 7, 2019, 1:26 p.m., https://twitter.com/raydalio/status/1114987900201066496.

8. Irwin Stelzer, "Save Capitalism from Capitalists," *The Sunday Times*, April 21, 2019.

9. https://en.wikipedia.org/wiki/Capitalism

10. https://www.theguardian.com/books/2017/sep/28/death-homo-economicus-peter-fleming-review

11. http://theageofconsequences.com

12. Taleb, *The Black Swan*.

13. https://en.wikipedia.org/wiki/Black_swan_theory

14. Stephen Gibbs, "Economy Shrinks by Half under Maduro," *The Times*, May 30, 2019.

15. John Summers, *Black Swan Events*, Institute of Risk Management NW seminar, January 26, 2012. See also: https://www.theirm.org/media/1120524/Popularmisconceptionsaboutblackswanevents-JohnSummers.pdf.

16. https://www.historynet.com/failed-peace-treaty-versailles-1919.htm

17. One exception was John Maynard Keynes. The story is told here: https://www.history.com/this-day-in-history/keynes-predicts-economic-chaos.

18. Jana Randow, "'Green Swan' Climate Event Could Trigger Global Financial Crisis, BIS Warns," *Bloomberg Green*, January 20 2020. See also: https://www.bloomberg.com/news/articles/2020-01-20/-green-swan-event-could-trigger-global-crisis-bis-warns.

19. I am indebted for this part of the definition to Patrick Thomas, when he was CEO of Covestro.

20. *Green Swans: Sketching a Manifesto for Tomorrow's Capitalism*, Volans and Atlas of the Future, September 2019. See also: https://volans.com/greenswans-video.

21. For example: Professor Jem Bendell, "Deep Adaptation: A Map for Navigating Climate Tragedy," *IFLAS Occasional Paper 2*, July 27, 2018.

22. Matt Simon, "Jakarta Is Sinking," *Wired.com*, May 2, 2019.

23. John Elkington and Pamela Hartigan, *The Power of Unreasonable People: How Social Entrepreneurs Create Markets That Change the World*. Cambridge: Harvard Business School Press, 2008. See also: https://hbr.org/product/the-power-of-unreasonable-people-how-social-entrepreneurs-create-markets-that-change-the-world/4060-HBK-ENG.

24. Thanks to the generous support of the Skoll Foundation for Social Entrepreneurship.

25. The opening of this preface draws on my *Harvard Business Review* article, "25 Years Ago I Coined the Phrase 'Triple Bottom Line.' Here's Why It's Time to Rethink It," June 25, 2019. See also: https://hbr.org/2018/06/25-years-ago-i-coined-the-phrase-triple-bottom-line-heres-why-im-giving-up-on-it.

26. For more details, please see here: https://volans.com/project/tomorrows-capitalism-inquiry/.

27. Anand Giridharadas, *Winners Take All: the Elite Charade of Changing the World*. New York: Penguin Random House, 2018.

28. Hannah Kuchler, "Tech Entrepreneurs Attack Opioid Crisis," *Financial Times*, May 27, 2019.

29. Beth Mole, "DEA Tracked Every Opioid Pill Sold in the US. The Data Is Out—And It's Horrifying," Arstechnica.com, July 17, 2019.

30. Hannah Kuchler, "J&J: The Next Target of Anger over America's Opioid Crisis?" *Financial Times*, September 5, 2019. See also: https://www.ft.com/content/c4eddc22-cd86-11e9-99a4-b5ded7a7fe3f.

31. Chris McGreal, *American Overdose: The Opioid Tragedy in Three Acts*. London: Faber & Faber, 2018.

32. Henry Mance, "Anand Giridharadas On the Fallacy of Billionaire Philanthropy," *Financial Times*, February 1, 2019.

33. Rick Wartzman, "America's Top CEOs Say They Are No Longer Putting Shareholders before Everyone Else," *Fast Company*, August 19, 2019. See also: https://www.fastcompany.com/90391743/top-ceo-group-business-roundtable-drops-shareholder-primacy.

34. Irwin Stelzer, "Why We Need to Rescue Capitalism," *The Sunday Times*, May 26, 2019.

35. Marc Benioff, "We Need a New Capitalism," *The New York Times*, October 14, 2019. See also: https://www.nytimes.com/2019/10/14/opinion/benioff-salesforce-capitalism.html.

36. John Elkington with Tom Burke, *The Green Capitalists: Industry's Search for Environmental Excellence*. London: Victor Gollanez, 1987.

INTRODUCTION

1. L. Randall Wray, *Why Minsky Matters: An Introduction to the Work of a Maverick Economist*. Princeton, NJ: Princeton University Press, 2016.

2. Deborah Summers, "No Return to Boom and Bust: What Brown Said When He Was Chancellor," *The Guardian*, September 11, 2008. See also: https://www.theguardian.com/politics/2008/sep/11/gordonbrown.economy.

3. Robert J. Walker, "Beware the 'Grey Swan'," *Huffington Post*, May 15, 2001.

4. Christina Lamb, "Congo's miners dying to feed world's hunger for electric cars," *The Sunday Times*, March 10, 2019.

5. I am indebted to Tom Rippin of OnPurpose for pointing me to Charles Eisenstein and his thinking.

6. https://charleseisenstein.org/essays/in-the-miracle/

7. Here is the original ad: https://www.youtube.com/watch?v=cFEarBzelBs. And the background can be found here: https://en.wikipedia.org/wiki/Think_different.

8. http://thecorporation.com/film/about-film

9. James Gorman, "It Could Be the Age of the Chicken, Geologically," *The New York Times*, December 11, 2018. See also: https://www.nytimes.com/2018/12/11/science/chicken-anthropocene-archaeology.html.

10. Donald D. Hoffman, *The Case against Reality: How Evolution Hid the Truth from Our Eyes*. London: Allen Lane, 2019.

11. *Natural Capital At Risk: The Top 100 Externalities of Business*, Trucost plc, April 2013, https://www.naturalcapitalcoalition.org/wp-content/uploads/2016/07/Trucost-Nat-Cap-at-Risk-Final-Report-web.pdf.

12. Simon Atkinson, "The Optimism Divide," Ipsos, 2018. See also: https://www.ipsosglobaltrends.com/the-optimism-divide/.

13. Jonathan Foley, "Inflection Point," *Medium*, March 10 2018. See also: https://globalecoguy.org/inflection-point-97d81c4ec445.

14. Sadly, but inevitably, he died on February 1, 2019: http://johnelkington.com/2019/05/a-salute-to-tim-elkington/. This book is dedicated to his memory.

15. https://www.stockholmresilience.org/research/planetary-boundaries/planetary-boundaries/about-the-research/the-nine-planetary-boundaries.html

16. http://www.igbp.net/globalchange/greatacceleration.4.1b8ae20512db692f2a680001630.html

17. Simon L. Lewis and Mark A. Maslin, *The Human Planet: How We Created the Anthropocene*. London: Pelican Books, 2018.

18. Verdantix, "Verdantix Forecasts The Global Sustainability Consulting Market Will Exceed $1 Billion In 2019, Far Below Expectations Of The Consulting Industry," February 18, 2015. See also: http://www.verdantix.com/newsroom/press-releases/verdantix-forecasts-the-global-sustainability-consulting-market-will-exceed-1-billion-in-2019-far-below-expectations-of-the-consulting-industry.

19. John Elkington, "Saving the Planet from Ecological Disaster Is a $12 Trillion Opportunity," *Harvard Business Review*, May 4, 2017. See also: https://hbr.org/2017/05/saving-the-planet-from-ecological-disaster-is-a-12-trillion-opportunity.

20. "Triple Bottom Line," *The Economist*, November 17, 2009. See also: https://www.economist.com/news/2009/11/17/triple-bottom-line.

21. John Elkington, "25 Years Ago I Coined the Phrase 'Triple Bottom Line.' Here's Why It's Time to Rethink It," *Harvard Business Review*, June 25, 2018. See also: https://hbr.org/2018/06/25-years-ago-i-coined-the-phrase-triple-bottom-line-heres-why-im-giving-up-on-it.

22. John Elkington, "Saving the Planet from Ecological Disaster Is a $12 Trillion Opportunity," *Harvard Business Review*, May 4, 2017. See also: https://hbr.org/2017/05/saving-the-planet-from-ecological-disaster-is-a-12-trillion-opportunity.

23. https://kk.org/mt-files/books-mt/ooc-mf.pdf; http://kk.org/thetechnium/where-the-linea/

24. https://www.ted.com/talks/peter_diamandis_abundance_is_our_future#t-942829

25. C. Otto Scharmer, *The Essentials of Theory U: Core Principles and Applications*. San Fransisco: Berrett-Koehler Publishers, Inc., 2018.

26. John Elkington, *The Chrysalis Economy: How Citizen CEOs and Corporations Can Fuse Values and Value Creation*. Oxford: Capstone Publishing/John Wiley & Sons, Inc., 2001.

27. https://volans.com/project/tomorrows-capitalism-inquiry/

28. Quote Investigator, *It Always Seems Impossible Until It's Done*, 2016. Among those to whom similar sayings have been attributed are Pliny the Elder, who died in 79 AD. See also: https://quoteinvestigator.com/2016/01/05/done/.

CHAPTER 1

1. https://charleseisenstein.org/about/

2. Again, I am indebted to Tom Rippin of OnPurpose for pointing me to Charles Eisenstein and his thinking.

3. Charles Eisenstein, Pachamama Alliance webcast: http://www.pachamama.org/webcast/charles-eisenstein?_ga=2.90634386.92140876.1565892412-248161406.1565892412.

4. Charles Eisenstein, Pachamama Alliance webcast: http://www.pachamama.org/webcast/charles-eisenstein?_ga=2.90634386.92140876.1565892412-248161406.1565892412.

5. Charles Eisenstein, *The More Beautiful World Our Hearts Know Is Possible*. Berkeley, CA: North Atlantic Books, 2013.

6. Eisenstein, *The More Beautiful World Our Hearts Know Is Possible*.

7. Charles Eisenstein on Twitter @ceisenstein: https://twitter.com/ceisenstein/status/1015928509858971648.

8. Eisenstein, *The More Beautiful World Our Hearts Know Is Possible*.

9. Edward Luce, "Declining US interest in history presents risk to democracy," *Financial Times*, May 3, 2019.

10. https://en.wikipedia.org/wiki/Loess_Plateau

11. Simon Lewis and Mark A. Maslin, *The Human Planet: How We Created The Anthropocene*. New York: Penguin Random House, 2018. See also: https://www.penguin.co.uk/ books/298/298037/the-human-planet/9780241280881.html.

12. Jacopo Prisco, "Illusion of Control: The World Is Full of Buttons That Don't Work," *CNN Style*, September 3, 2018.

13. Nick O'Donohoe, "What is the true business of business?," World Economic Forum, February 25, 2016. See also: https://www.weforum.org/agenda/2016/02/ the-business-of-business-is-what/.

14. This and other quotes and definitions of *Lexicon* from http://lexicon.ft.com/.

15. Ian Shuttleworth, "Where Did Capitalism Go Wrong?," *Financial Times*, July 16, 2018.

16. https://quoteinvestigator.com/2014/12/09/sand/

17. Martin Wolf, "Rethink the Purpose of the Corporation," *Financial Times*, December 12, 2018.

18. https://bcorporation.net/about-b-corps

19. Volans, *Breakthrough Business Models: Exponentially More Social, Lean, Integrated and Circular*, commissioned by the Business and Sustainable Development Commission, September 2016.

20. The term "extra-financial" means those forms of value and impact that are not captured in current financial accounting, which mainly still operates on the basis of a single, financial bottom line.

21. "The Most Dangerous People on the Internet in 2018," *Wired.com*, December 31, 2018.

22. Paul Mozur, "A Genocide Incited on Facebook, With Posts From Myanmar's Military," *The New York Times*, October 15, 2018.

23. John Elkington and Jochen Zeitz, *The Breakthrough Challenge: 10 Ways to Connect Today's Profits with Tomorrow's Bottom Line*. San Fransisco: John Wiley & Sons, Inc., 2014.

24. PUMA's Environmental Profit and Loss Account for the year ended 31 December 2010, PUMA, 2011. See also: https://glasaaward.org/wp-content/uploads/2014/01/EPL080212final. pdf.

25. https://www.clubofrome.org/report/the-limits-to-growth/

26. https://www.stockholmresilience.org/research/planetary-boundaries/planetary-boundaries/ about-the-research/the-nine-planetary-boundaries.html

27. https://timjackson.org.uk/ecological-economics/pwg/

28. https://www.degrowth.info/en/what-is-degrowth/

29. *Better Business, Better World*, Business and Sustainable Development Commission, 2017. See also: http://report.businesscommission.org.

30. John Elkington, "Saving the Planet from Ecological Disaster Is a $12 Trillion Opportunity," *Harvard Business Review*. See also: https://hbr.org/2017/05/ saving-the-planet-from-ecological-disaster-is-a-12-trillion-opportunity.

31. Michael Liebreich, "The Secret of Eternal Growth," Initiative for Free Trade, October 29, 2018. See also: http://ifreetrade.org/article/ the_secret_of_eternal_growth_the_physics_behind_pro_growth_environmentalism.

32. https://www.kateraworth.com

33. https://marianamazzucato.com

34. Mariana Mazzucato, *Mission-Oriented Research and Innovation in the European Union*, Publications Office of the European Union, 2018.

35. *Novartis in Society*, 2018, https://www.novartis.com/sites/www.novartis.com/files/novartis-in-society-report-2018.pdf.

36. Tim West, "Sir Ronald launches an 'Impact Revolution'," *Pioneers Post*, October 15, 2018. See also: https://www.pioneerspost.com/news-views/20181015/ sir-ronald-launches-impact-revolution.

37. Chris Flood, "World Bank arm launches 'impact investment' standards," *Financial Times*, April 15, 2019.

38. https://www.clientearth.org/what-we-do/?utm_expid=131429874-4. svY3aZu0TaK2EzJKuf0OPQ.0&utm_referrer=https%3A%2F%2Fwww.clientearth. org%2Fwhat-we-do%2F

39. See, for example, the inaugural episode of the *Mothers of Invention* podcast with Mary Robinson and Maeve Higgins, which focuses on live examples of legal action being taken to address the climate issue. https://www.mothersofinvention.online/allrise.

40. Brian Kahn, "Exxon predicted 2019's ominous CO2 milestone in 1982," *Earther*, May 19, 2019. See also: https://earther.gizmodo.com/ exxon-predicted-2019-s-ominous-co2-milestone-in-1982-1834748763.

41. Chelsea Harvey, "CO2 Levels Just Hit another Record—Here's Why It Matters," *Scientific American*, May 16, 2019. See also: https://www.scientificamerican.com/article/ co2-levels-just-hit-another-record-heres-why-it-matters/.

42. Ucilia Wang, "New York Attorney General Files Suit against Exxon for Climate Fraud," *Climate Liability News*, October 24, 2018. See also: https://www.climateliabilitynews. org/2018/10/24/new-york-attorney-general-exxon-climate-fraud/.

43. Nick Cunningham, "Global fossil fuel subsidies hit $5.2 trillion," *OilPrice.com*, May 12, 2019.

44. Alex Steffen, "Predatory delay and the rights of future generations," *Medium*, April 30, 2016. See also: https://medium.com/@AlexSteffen/ predatory-delay-and-the-rights-of-future-generations-69b06094a16.

45. Myles McCormick, "Bayer to invest €5bn in alternative weedkillers," *Financial Times*, June 14, 2019. See also https://www.ft.com/content/e3b985ea-8e73-11e9-a1c1-51bf8f989972.

46. Leslie Hook, "Energy groups to be sued over climate change," *Financial Times*, June 10, 2019.

47. Steffen, "Predatory Delay."

48. The dam was a joint venture between Vale and BHP Billiton.

49. Lena Lee, "Carlos Ghosn: From Private Jet to 108 Days in Jail to His Rearrest," Bloomberg, March 6, 2019. See also: https://www.bloomberg.com/news/articles/2019-03-06/ from-private-jet-to-108-days-in-jail-carlos-ghosn-timeline.

50. https://su.org

51. https://leadersquest.org

52. http://lexicon.ft.com/

53. "Stranded Assets," Carbon Tracker, August 23, 2017. See: https://www.carbontracker.org/ terms/stranded-assets/.

54. "Stranded Assets."

CHAPTER 2

1. See the "Gradually, Then Suddenly" section of this chapter.

2. I have been very much influenced by *Exponential Organizations: Why New Organizations Are Ten Times Better, Faster, and Cheaper Than Yours (And What to Do About It)* by Salim Ismail, with Michael S. Malone and Yuri van Geest. New York: Diversion Books, 2014.

3. https://futurism.com/arnold-schwarzenegger-climate-change/

4. Bethany McClean, "How Elon Musk Fooled Investors, Bilked Taxpayers, and Gambled Tesla to Save SolarCity," *Vanity Fair*, August 25, 2019. See also: https://www.vanityfair.com/ news/2019/08/how-elon-musk-gambled-tesla-to-save-solarcity.

5. Tim O'Reilly, "Gradually, Then Suddenly," *O'Reilly Next: Economy Newsletter*, republished in *Exponential View*, January 11, 2018.

6. A large continent, with fifty-four countries and vast economic, political, and cultural diversity, so we should be careful of generalizing.

7. John C. Camillus, "Strategy as a Wicked Problem," *Harvard Business Review*, May 2008 issue. See also: https://hbr.org/2008/05/strategy-as-a-wicked-problem.

8. *Wicked Problems*, https://www.wickedproblems.com/1_wicked_problems.php.

9. The ten characteristics have been edited for simplicity.

10. World Economic Forum, "India Is Most at Risk from Climate Change," March 21, 2018. See also: https://www.weforum.org/agenda/2018/03/india-most-vulnerable-country-to-climate-change.

11. http://citeseerx.ist.psu.edu/viewdoc/download?doi=10.1.1.464.5287&rep=rep1&type=pdf

12. "Welcome to the Anthropocene," *The Economist*, May 26, 2011. See also: https://www.economist.com/leaders/2011/05/26/welcome-to-the-anthropocene.

CHAPTER 3

1. John Elkington, "Why Wall Street Needs a WCKD Ticker," *GreenBiz*, May 21, 2018.

2. https://plasticoceans.org/who-we-are/

3. Susan Freinkel, *Plastic: A Toxic Love Story*. Boston: Houghton Mifflin Harcourt, 2011.

4. Susan Freinkel, *Plastic*.

5. https://www.plasticsmakeitpossible.com/about-plastics/types-of-plastics/professor-plastics-how-many-types-of-plastics-are-there/

6. University of Georgia, "More than 8.3 billion tons of plastics made: Most has now been discarded," *ScienceDaily*, July 19, 2017. See also: www.sciencedaily.com/releases/2017/07/170719140939.htm.

7. "The known unknowns of plastic pollution," *The Economist*, March 3, 2018. See also: https://www.economist.com/international/2018/03/03/the-known-unknowns-of-plastic-pollution.

8. "WHO launches health review after microplastics found in 90 percent of bottled water," *The Guardian*, 15 March 2018. See also: https://www.theguardian.com/environment/2018/mar/15/microplastics-found-in-more-than-90-of-bottled-water-study-says.

9. https://www.newplasticseconomy.org

10. Rob Dunn, "Science Reveals Why Calorie Counts Are All Wrong," *Scientific American*, September 1, 2013. See also: https://www.scientificamerican.com/article/science-reveals-why-calorie-counts-are-all-wrong/.

11. "The Modern Diet Is Bad and Getting Worse: Study," *Newsweek* via *Reuters*, February 23, 2015. See also: http://www.newsweek.com/modern-diet-bad-and-getting-worse-study-308794.

12. "The Modern Diet Is Bad and Getting Worse."

13. http://www.who.int/mediacentre/factsheets/fs311/en/

14. http://www.who.int/topics/obesity/en/

15. http://www.who.int/mediacentre/factsheets/fs311/en/

16. https://www.ncbi.nlm.nih.gov/pmc/articles/PMC2879283/

17. Declaration of interest: The author has worked with Novo Nordisk in various ways since 1989.

18. "Cost of Global Diabetes Epidemic Soars to $850 Billion Per Year," *Fortune* via *Reuters*, November 14, 2017. See also: http://fortune.com/2017/11/13/diabetes-epidemic-cost-850-billion/.

19. https://en.wikipedia.org/wiki/Choice_editing

20. *The History of Antibiotics*, Microbiology Society, 2018. See also: https://microbiologysociety.org/education-outreach/antibiotics-unearthed/antibiotics-and-antibiotic-resistance/the-history-of-antibiotics.html.

21. A conversation with Dame Sally Davies, Council on Foreign Relations, September 23, 2016. See also: https://www.cfr.org/event/conversation-dame-sally-davies.

22. "Antibiotic Resistance," World Health Organisation fact sheet, updated November 2017. See also: http://www.who.int/mediacentre/factsheets/antibiotic-resistance/en/.

23. "Conversation with Dame Sally Davies."

24. "Antibiotic Resistance."

25. http://www.sciencemuseum.org.uk/superbugs

26. https://en.wikipedia.org/wiki/Hippocratic_Oath

27. Mohsin Hamid, *Exit West*. New York: Penguin Random House 2018. See also: https://www. penguinrandomhouse.com/books/549017/exit-west-by-mohsin-hamid/9780735212206/.

28. Louis Klee, "Unthinking Modernity: On the Great Derangement," *Overland* (blog), May 18, 2018. See also: https://overland.org.au/2018/05/ unthinking-modernity-on-the-great-derangement/.

29. Amitav Ghosh, *The Great Derangement: Climate Change and the Unthinkable*. Chicago: The University of Chicago Press, 2016. See also: https://www.press.uchicago.edu/ucp/books/book/ chicago/G/bo22265507.html.

30. Klee, "Unthinking Modernity."

31. Ghosh, *The Great Derangement*.

32. Omar El Akkad, *American War*. New York: Penguin Random House, 2018. See also: https://www.penguinrandomhouse.com/books/543957/ american-war-by-omar-el-akkad/9781101973134/.

33. Hugh Lewis, "Trouble in Orbit: the Growing Problem of Space Junk," *BBC News*, August 5, 2015. See also: http://www.bbc.com/news/science-environment-33782943.

34. Ruth Milne, "Antibiotic Resistance in Bacteria from Space," *Microbiology*, February 14, 2018. See also: https://naturemicrobiologycommunity.nature.com/users/59876-ruth-milne/ posts/30275-antibiotic-resistance-in-bacteria-from-space.

35. http://www.marketplace.org/topics/tech/junk-space-could-have-impact-earth

36. NASA, "Space Debris and Human Spacecraft," September 27, 2013, updated August 7, 2017. See also: https://www.nasa.gov/mission_pages/station/news/orbital_debris.html.

37. Dave Mosher and Andy Kiersz, "These Are the Countries on Earth with the Most Junk in Space," *Business Insider*, October 20, 2017. See also: http://www.businessinsider.com/ space-debris-garbage-statistics-country-list-2017-10.

38. Mosher and Kiersz, "These Are the Countries on Earth."

39. "Frequently Asked Questions: Orbital Debris," NASA. See also: https://www.nasa.gov/news/ debris_faq.html.

40. Sarah Scoles, "The Space Junk Problem Is About to Get a Whole Lot Gnarlier," *Wired*, July 31, 2017. See also: https://www.wired.com/story/ the-space-junk-problem-is-about-to-get-a-whole-lot-gnarlier/.

41. "Observations of Increasing Carbon Dioxide Concentration in Earth's Thermosphere," *Nature Geoscience*, 5, 2012, pages 868–871.

CHAPTER 4

1. The Kuhn Cycle: Thomas Kuhn's brilliant model of how scientific fields progress, *Thwink*. See also: http://www.thwink.org/sustain/glossary/KuhnCycle.htm.

2. Sean O'Neill, "Oxfam Staff Still Offering Aid for Sex, Report Claims," *The Times*, June 29, 2019.

3. Andrew Lynch, "How Are the Mighty Fallen," *The Sunday Times*, December 30, 2018.

4. "Under the Hood: How the Market Leaders Have Changed in the Digital Era," *Financial Times*, August 25, 2018.

5. Rana Foroohar, "Disruption Threatens the 'Superstars' Too," *Financial Times*, October 22, 2018.

6. Mark Hertsgaard and Mark Dowie, Mobiles, "Cancer and Inconvenient Truths," *The Observer*, July 15, 2018.

7. Sing Jung-a, "Samsung Finally Apologises to Workers Laid Low by Disease," *Financial Times*, November 24–25, 2018.

8. Sing Jung-a, "Samsung Finally Apologises."

9. Hiroko Tabuchi, "A Trump County Confronts the Administration amid a Rash of Child Cancers," *The New York Times*, January 2, 2019.

10. Pilita Clark and Leslie Hook, "Tetra Pak Plans Fightback in War on Plastic

Straws," *Financial Times*, May 25, 2018. See also: https://www.ft.com/content/ee6b50d8-5f6a-11e8-9334-2218e7146b04.

11. Essential reading on this issue: Naomi Oreskes and Erik M. Conway, *Merchants of Doubt: How a Handful of Scientists Obscured the Truth on Issues from Tobacco Smoke to Global Warming*. London: Bloomsbury Press, 2010.

12. Ben Webster, "Green energy predicted to wipe trillions from global economy," *The Times*, June 5, 2018.

13. "Corporate Social Responsibility: Friedman's View," https://bfi.uchicago.edu/news/feature-story/corporate-social-responsibilty-friedmans-view.

14. Leslie Hook and Anjli Raval, and Ed Crooks, "Pope Francis Urges Oil and Gas Groups to Tackle Climate Change," *Financial Times*, June 11, 2018.

15. Ed Crooks, "CofE leads call for Exxon to set emission cuts targets," *Financial Times*, December 17, 2018.

16. Andrew Ross Sorkin, "BlackRock's Message: Contribute to Society, or Risk Losing Our Support," *The New York Times*, January 16, 2018.

17. McKinsey Global Institute, "Sustainability's Deepening Imprint," https://www.mckinsey.com/business-functions/sustainability-and-resource-productivity/our-insights/sustainabilitys-deepening-imprint.

18. Lauren Helper, "Volkswagen and the Dark Side of Corporate Sustainability," *GreenBiz*, September 24, 2015. See also: https://www.greenbiz.com/article/volkswagen-and-dark-side-corporate-sustainability.

19. Ursula Weidenfeld, "Something Rotten at the Heart of German Industry," *Financial Times*, February 1, 2018.

20. Caitlin Morrison, "Carillion collapse: Who Was Behind the 'Recklessness, Hubris and Greed' That Led to the Demise of the Government Contractor?," *The Independent*, May 16, 2018. See also: https://www.independent.co.uk/news/business/analysis-and-features/carillion-collapse-latest-who-responsible-richard-adam-howson-philip-green-mp-report-a8353921.html.

21. Carillion plc, *Our Sustainability Approach*. Extracted from https://www.carillionplc.com/about-us/sustainability/, taken down shortly after the collapse became public knowledge.

22. Hannah Kuchler, "Facebook Still in Dock After 'Tsunami of Crises'," *Financial Times*, January 2, 2019.

23. Max Fisher, "Inside Facebook's Secret Rulebook for Global Political Speech," *The New York Times*, December 27, 2018.

24. Rana Foroohar, "Activist Chiefs Fill the Vacuum Left by Government," *Financial Times*, January 24, 2018.

25. Foroohar, "Activist Chiefs Fill the Vacuum."

26. "How 100% Renewable Electricity Is Fast Becoming the New Normal—CDP," RE100, January 22, 2018. See also: http://there100.org/news/14270139.

27. Ed Crooks, "Facebook sets 2020 deadline to cover 100% of electricity use via green energy," *Financial Times*, August 29, 2018.

28. Tom Hancock, "China's Recyclers Left Idle by Waste Import Ban," *Financial Times*, January 16, 2018.

29. Jamie Smyth, "Beijing Recycling Ban Leaves Australia Awash," *Financial Times*, December 31, 2018.

30. Ploy Ten Kate and Chang-Ran Kim, "Thai Floods Batter Global Electronics, Auto Supply Chains," *Reuters*, October 28, 2011.

31. "Kongjian Yu Featured in WEF Article," Terreform, August 28, 2019. See also: https://www.terreform.info/news/2019/8/28/kongjian-yu-featured-in-wef-article.

32. This was The Environment Foundation, which later became The Foundation for Democracy & Sustainability. One of the achievements of The Environment Foundation came from its decision to fight a legal battle with the UK Charity Commission, which refused to allow The Foundation to adopt sustainable development as a commercial objective, arguing that it was,

in fact, commercial. After a three-year battle, with the help of the late Stephen Lloyd of lawyers Bates Wells & Braithwaite, we won—and sustainable development became a charitable objective.

33. Ralph Atkins and Oliver Ralph, "Swiss Re Chief Warns That Market for Catastrophe Bonds Is Coming Under Increasing Strain," *Financial Times*, December 28, 2018.

34. Leslie Hook and Kerin Hope, "Scorched Earth," *Financial Times*, July 28–29, 2018.

35. David Faber, "California Utility PG&E Faces At Least $30 Billion Fire Liability, Sources Say," *CNBC*, January 7, 2019.

36. Peter Eavis, "Who Wins and Who Loses from PG&E Bankruptcy," *The New York Times*, January 29, 2019. See also: https://www.nytimes.com/2019/01/29/business/dealbook/pge-bankruptcy-winners-losers.html.

37. Accessed from: https://www.rockefellerfoundation.org/our-work/initiatives/100-resilient-cities/, January 8, 2019.

38. Eilie Anzilotti, "Why Did the Rockefeller Foundation Just Unceremoniously End Its Successful Resilience Program?," *Fast Company*, April 2, 2019.

39. Roger L. Martin, "The High Price of Efficiency," *Harvard Business Review*, January-February 2019. See also: https://hbr.org/2019/01/rethinking-efficiency.

40. Innovation Group/Sonar for JWT, *The New Sustainability: Regeneration*, September 2018. See also: https://www.jwtintelligence.com/trend-reports/the-new-sustainability-regeneration.

41. See, for example, https://www.cradletocradle.com.

42. A notable exception is Daniel Christian Wahl, for example in his book *Designing Regenerative Cultures*. Aberdour, Scotland: Triarchy Press, 2016.

43. https://www.drawdown.or.

44. Interest declared: I was part of the advisory network and listed as such in the book, but feel I did very little.

45. Involving design based on natural principles, see https://biomimicry.org/janine-benyus/.

46. Interest declared: I served on Biomimicry 3.8's advisory board for a number of years.

47. Merlyn Mathew, "Factory as a Forest: Reimagining Facilities as Ecosystems," *Interface* (blog), August 24, 2018. See also: https://blog.interface.com/factory-forest-reimagining-facilities-ecosystems/.

48. Background extracted from http://capitalinstitute.org/director/john-fullerton/.

49. John Fullerton, "Capitals in Context: Regenerative economies for a regenerative civilization," ICAEW, March 2016. See also: http://capitalinstitute.org/wp-content/uploads/2014/08/TECDIG148622-Capitals-in-context.pdf.

CHAPTER 5

1. Interest declared: I have been a strategic advisor to the Future-Fit Foundation for many years, https://futurefitbusiness.org/team_members/.

2. Anjli Raval, "BP Lobbied Against US Methane Rules Despite Green Public Stance," *Financial Times*, March 12, 2019.

3. Tier 1 suppliers supply the main company under consideration, while Tier 2 suppliers supply Tier 1 suppliers, Tier 3 suppliers supply Tier 2, and so on through the supply chain. So, Tier 4 suppliers are typically some way outside the direct and even indirect control of the main company.

4. See *The Breakthrough Challenge: 10 Ways To Connect Today's Profits With Tomorrow's Bottom Line*, John Elkington and Jochen Zeitz. San Fransisco: Jossey Bass/John Wiley & Sons, Inc., 2014.

5. Full disclosure: The author is a member of the Future-Fit Foundation Advisory Board.

6. All quotations taken from http://futurefitbusiness.org.

7. Accessed from https://thenaturalstep.org, January 12, 2019.

8. Based on "What Is Break-even Point?" Corporate Finance Institute. See also: https://corporatefinanceinstitute.com/resources/knowledge/finance/break-even-point-bep/.

9. Full disclosure: The author has worked with Novo Nordisk in many ways since 1989.

10. This kicked off with *The Green Consumer Guide*, published in 1988, and continued with a series of other books and reports.

11. "The Best-Performing CEOs in the World," *Harvard Business Review*, November 2015 issue. See also: https://hbr.org/2015/11/the-best-performing-ceos-in-the-world.

12. Lars Fruergaard Jørgensen, "Finding Strength Though Change," Novo Nordisk Annual Report 2018.

13. Geoff Kendall, personal communication, June 5, 2019.

14. Full disclosure: The author was involved for nine years on an Advisory Board for DJSI, from its launch.

15. Global Reporting Initiative, the leading sustainability reporting platform, where I was on the board for several years.

CHAPTER 6

1. I am indebted for this part of the definition to Patrick Thomas, then-CEO of Covestro.

2. Jane Wakefield, "Google's ethics board shut down," *BBC News*, April 5, 2019.

3. Amanda Lentino, "This Chinese Facial Recognition Start-up Can Identify a Person In Seconds," *CNBC*, May 16, 2019. See also: https://www.cnbc.com/2019/05/16/this-chinese-facial-recognition-start-up-can-id-a-person-in-seconds.html.

4. Emily Dreyfuss, "Jack Dorsey Is Captain of the *Twitannic* at TED 2019," *Wired*, April 21, 2019. See also: wired.com/story/ted-2019-jack-dorsey-captain-twittanic.

5. Dreyfuss, "Jack Dorsey Is Captain of the *Twitannic*."

6. Carole Cadwalladr, "Social Media Is a Threat to Democracy," *TEDBlog*, April 16, 2019. See also: https://blog.ted.com/social-media-is-a-threat-to-our-democracy-carole-cadwalladr-speaks-at-ted2019/.

7. John Elkington, "Saving the Planet from an Ecological Disaster Is a $12 Trillion Opportunity," *Harvard Business Review*, May 4, 2017. See also: https://hbr.org/2017/05/saving-the-planet-from-ecological-disaster-is-a-12-trillion-opportunity.

8. https://www.weforum.org/agenda/2016/01/the-fourth-industrial-revolution-what-it-means-and-how-to-respond/

9. https://www.weforum.org/centre-for-the-fourth-industrial-revolution/areas-of-focus

10. Associated Press, "Major Saudi Arabia Oil Facilities Hit by Houthi Drone Strikes," *The Guardian*, September 14, 2019. See also: https://www.theguardian.com/world/2019/sep/14/major-saudi-arabia-oil-facilities-hit-by-drone-strikes.

11. "Bitcoin Mining Ban Considered by China's Economic Planner," *BBC News*, April 9, 2019. See also: https://www.bbc.co.uk/news/technology-47867031.

12. "Synthetic Biology: A Whole New World," *The Economist Technology Quarterly*, April 6, 2019.

13. https://en.wikipedia.org/wiki/CRISPR

14. Jennifer Kahn, "Preparing to Unleash Crispr on an Unprepared World," *Wired*, March 19, 2019.

15. Clive Cookson, "Scientists Model 'Gene Drive' for Carrier Insect," *Financial Times*, April 29, 2019.

16. Olaf J. Groth, Mark J. Nitzberg, and Stuart J. Russell, "AI Algorithms Need FDA-style Drug Trials," *Wired*, August 16, 2019.

17. Karen Hao, "Training a Single AI Model Can Emit As Much Carbon As Five Cars In Their Lifetimes," *TechnologyReview*, June 6, 2019.

18. John Elkington, "The Elkington Report: Should Governments Make Emerging Technologies a Priority?," *GreenBiz*, March 23, 2015. See also: https://www.greenbiz.com/article/governments-make-emerging-technologies-priority.

19. "Carl Sagan: 'Science Is More Than a Body of Knowledge. It's a Way of Thinking,'

Carl Sagan's Last Interview—1996," Speakola. See also: https://speakola.com/ideas/carl-sagan-science-last-interview-1996.

20. https://transformativetechnologies.org/about-us/

21. http://50breakthroughs.org/aboutthestudy/

22. Sam Brown, "An Agile Approach to Designing for the Consequences of Technology," *Medium*, February 13, 2019. See also: https://medium.com/doteveryone/an-agile-approach-to-designing-for-the-consequences-of-technology -18a229de763b.

23. For this and following quotes see https://su.org/about/global-grand-challenges/.

24. https://exponentialroadmap.org

25. Mariana Mazzucato, *The Entrepreneurial State*. New York: Penguin Random House, 2018. See also: https://marianamazzucato.com/entrepreneurial-state/.

CHAPTER 7

1. https://ecohustler.com/culture/phil-kingston-the-82-year-old-rebel-arrested-11-times-for-climate-activism/

2. See Apple "Think Different" ad quotation, page 11.

3. "Obituary: ENDS Report founder David Layton," *ENDS Report*, October 28, 2009. See also: https://www.endsreport.com/article/1569430.

4. Thomas S. Kuhn, *The Structure of Scientific Revolutions*. Chicago: University of Chicago Press, 1962. See also: https://en.wikipedia.org/wiki/The_Structure_of_Scientific_Revolutions.

5. Lori Silverman, *Wake Me Up When The Data Is Over*. San Fransisco: Jossey Bass, 2008. See also: https://www.wiley.com/en-gb/Wake+Me+Up+When+the+Data+Is+Over:+How+Organizations+Use+Stories+ to+Drive+Results-p-9780470483305.

6. Our world in data, https://ourworldindata.org/internet.

7. Roberto Calasso, *The Unnamable Present*. London: Allen Lane, 2019.

8. Rachel Carson, *Silent Spring*. New York: Houghton Mifflin, 1962. See also: https://en.wikipedia.org/wiki/Silent_Spring.

9. Theo Leggett, "What Went Wrong Inside Boeing's Cockpit?," *BBC News*, May 17, 2019. See also: https://www.bbc.co.uk/news/resources/idt-sh/boeing_two_deadly_crashes.

10. Henry Grabar, "The Crash of the Boeing 737 Max Is a Warning to Drivers, Too," *Slate*, March 12, 2019. See also: https://slate.com/technology/2019/03/boeing-737-max-crashes-automation-self-driving-cars-surprise.html.

11. John Gapper, "Boeing's Hubris Blinded It to a Lurking Danger," *Financial Times*, April 11, 2019.

12. Jared Diamond, *Collapse: How Societies Choose to Fail or Succeed*. New York: Viking Press, 2005. See also: https://en.wikipedia.org/wiki/Collapse:_How_Societies_Choose_to_Fail_or_Succeed.

13. Jared Diamond, *Upheaval: How Nations Cope With Crisis And Change*. London: Allen Lane, 2019.

14. For this and following quote see Irwin Stelzer, "Why We Need to Rescue Capitalism," *The Sunday Times*, May 26, 2019.

15. Will Hutton, "The Boeing Scandal Is an Indictment of Trump's Corporate America," *The Observer*, April 7, 2019.

16. David Gelles and Natalie Kitroeff, "Boeing Believed a 737 Warning Light Was Standard. It Wasn't," *The New York Times*, May 5, 2019.

17. https://www.amfori.org

18. https://chiefreinventionofficer.com/about.

19. Green Swan Day 2019 was held at the WWT Wetlands & Wildfowl Centre in Barnes, London, UK. A documentary based on the event can be found here: https://www.youtube.com/watch?v=TXBzC14aH4M&feature=youtu.be.

20. https://su.org/about/global-grand-challenges/

21. *Green Swans: Sketching a Manifesto for Tomorrow's Capitalism*, Volans and Atlas of the Future, September 2019. See also: https://www.youtube.com/watch?v=TXBzC14aH4M&feature=yo utu.be.

22. http://livingplanetindex.org/projects?main_page_project=AboutTheIndex&home_flag=.

23. Quoted in Tim Harford, "How Economics Can Raise Its Game," *Financial Times*, June 29, 2019.

24. Sadly, she was ill on Green Swan Day, so couldn't make it, but more information on her work can be found here: http://www.carlotaperez.org. She is also mentioned in Chapter 8.

25. https://www.nobelprize.org/prizes/economic-sciences/2009/ostrom/facts/

26. Joseph Stiglitz, "The Climate Crisis Is Our Third World War. It Needs A Bold Response," *The Guardian*, June 4, 2019. See also: https://www.theguardian.com/commentisfree/2019/jun/04/climate-change-world-war-iii-green-new-deal.

27. https://www.kateraworth.com/doughnut/#

28. https://www.ucl.ac.uk/bartlett/public-purpose/people/mariana-mazzucato

29. Marjorie Kelly, *The Divine Right of Capital: Dethroning the Corporate Aristocracy*. San Fransisco: Berret-Koehler Publishers, Inc., 2001.

30. Paul Collier, *The Future of Capitalism: Facing the New Anxieties*. London: Allen Lane, 2018.

31. Steve Waygood, personal communication, April 21, 2018.

32. Steve Waygood, personal communication, January 28, 2019.

33. Robert G. Eccles and Svetlana Klimenko, "The Investor Revolution," *Harvard Business Review*, May-June 2019 issue. See also: https://hbr.org/2019/05/the-investor-revolution.

34. Richard Henderson, "Europe Leads $31tn Charge Into Sustainable Investing," *Financial Times*, June 1, 2019.

35. https://www.carbontracker.org

36. http://www.lse.ac.uk/GranthamInstitute/profile/nick-robins/

37. Roman Krznaric, "Why We Need to Reinvent Democracy for the Long-term," *BBC*, March 19, 2019.

38. Jieying Zheng, personal communication, June 26, 2019.

39. Steve Waygood, personal communication, April 21, 2018.

40. https://apolitical.co

41. https://www.bbc.co.uk/news/av/48404351/why-is-norway-the-land-of-electric-cars

42. Torben Iverson and David Soskice, *Democracy and Prosperity: Reinventing Capitalism Through a Turbulent Century*. Princeton, NJ: Princeton University Press, 2019.

43. https://press.princeton.edu/titles/14194.html

44. Tim Bradshaw, Shannon Bond, and Richard Waters, "Design for a New Generation," *Financial Times*, June 29, 2019.

45. Peter Campbell, "BMW Electric Margin to Rival Combustion by 2025," *Financial Times*, June 27, 2019.

46. Peter Campbell, "VW Plans to Roll Out 70 Fully Electric Models," *Financial Times*, March 13, 2019.

47. Ed Crooks and Anjli Raval, "Shell Aiming to Be Biggest Electricity Group As World Plugs Into Green Energy," *Financial Times*, March 14, 2019.

48. Eric Reguli, "A Tale of Transformation: the Danish Company that Went from Black to Green Energy," *Corporate Knights*, April 16, 2019.

49. Oliver Balch, "Umicore: from Smelter to Urban Miner," *Raconteur*, April 9, 2019. See also: https://www.raconteur.net/business-innovation/umicore-business-transformation.

50. Guy Chazan and Patrick McGee, "German 'Carland' Braced for Electric Shock," *Financial Times*, June 13, 2019.

51. Carl Meyer, "Bank of Canada Warns 'Fire Sales' of Carbon-intensive Assets Could 'Destabilize' Financial System," *National Observer*, May 16, 2019.

52. Tim Smit, personal communication, August 17, 2019.

53. John Elkington, "Climate Change Is an Overwhelming Problem. Here Are 4 Things Executives Can Do Today," *Harvard Business Review*, January 5, 2018. See also: https://hbr.org/2018/01/climate-change-is-an-overwhelming-problem-here-are-4-things-executives-can-do-today.

54. https://www.genfound.org/media/1436/pdf-genfoundwp2017-final.pdf

55. *Green Swans: Sketching a Manifesto for Tomorrow's Capitalism*, Volans and Atlas of the Future, September 2019. See also: https://www.youtube.com/watch?v=TXBzC14aH4M&feature=youtu.be.

CHAPTER 8

1. https://en.wiktionary.org/wiki/global_weirding

2. Ben Hoyle, "Clean-air Shelters to Open in Smoky Seattle," *The Times*, July 9, 2019.

3. Jude Webber, "Vast Clump of Seaweed Heads for Mexico," *Financial Times*, July 4, 2019.

4. Clive Cookson, "High Levels of Tiny Plastic Specks Found in Snowflakes," *Financial Times*, August 15, 2019.

5. Ipsos, "Majority Worldwide Say Their Society Is Broken," September 13, 2019. See also: https://www.ipsos.com/ipsos-mori/en-uk/global-study-nativist-populist-broken-society-britain.

6. Dominic Hofstetter, "The Perils of Imagined Permanence," *Medium*, March 28, 2019.

7. Peter Diamandis, "Musk vs. Bezos: The Great Migration Into Space," *LinkedIn*, May 19, 2019. See also: https://www.linkedin.com/pulse/musk-vs-bezos-great-migration-space-peter-h-diamandis.

8. Matt Simon, "The Sea Is Consuming Jakarta, and Its People Aren't Insured," *Wired*, downloaded July 19, 2019. See also: https://www.wired.com/story/jakarta-insurance/.

9. Jonathan Watts, "Indonesia Announces Site of Capital City to Replace Sinking Jakarta," *The Guardian*, August 26, 2019. See also: https://www.theguardian.com/world/2019/aug/26/indonesia-new-capital-city-borneo-forests-jakarta.

10. They say there is no new thing under the sun. Late in the process of writing this book a colleague, Ed Gillespie, sent me a link to a prior use of the term "Green Swan," in the field of national security, by Charlie Dunlap of Duke University. See also: https://sites.duke.edu/lawfire/2018/01/02/national-security-green-swans-for-2018/. The thinking is the same, in that Green Swans have an unexpectedly *positive* effect, though the scope here is considerably wider.

11. Rick Gladstone, "The Globe Is Graying Fast, U.N. Says in New Forecast," *The New York Times*, June 17, 2019. See also: https://www.nytimes.com/2019/06/17/world/americas/un-population-aging-forecast.html.

12. Tobias Buck, "Eastern Germany in Grip of Population Collapse," *Financial Times*, June 10, 2019.

13. Robin Harding, "Japan's Rate of Population Decline Speeds Up," *Financial Times*, April 13, 2019.

14. Darrell Bricker and John Ibbitson, *Empty Planet: The Shock of Global Population Decline*, Robinson/Little Brown Group, London, 2019.

15. John Loeffler, "How Algorithms Run the World We Live In," *Interest Engineering*, April 29, 2019. See also: https://interestingengineering.com/how-algorithms-run-the-world-we-live-in.

16. "Will Matteo Salvini Wreck the Euro?" *The Economist*, July 11, 2019. See also: https://www.economist.com/europe/2019/07/11/will-matteo-salvini-wreck-the-euro.

17. Jamie Susskind, *Future Politics: Living Together in a World Transformed by Tech*. Oxford: Oxford University Press, 2018. See also: https://www.un.org/sustainabledevelopment/sustainable-development-goals/.

18. http://livingplanetindex.org/home/index 19

19. Kara Swisher, "If You've Built a Chaos Factory, You Can't Dodge Responsibility for the Chaos," *The New York Times*, June 19, 2019.

20. https://www.un.org/sustainabledevelopment/sustainable-development-goals/

21. "Times letters: Business and the climate change rebellion," The Times, April 22, 2019. See also: https://www.thetimes.co.uk/article/

times-letters-business-and-the-climate-change-rebellion-x2tfq0rsj. To see the signatories for free, see here: https://jeremyleggett.net/2019/04/22/letter-to-the-times-by-business-leaders-supportive-of-extinction-rebellion-of-which-i-am-proud-to-be-one/.

22. For me, at least, other one-person Green Swans would include Rachel Carson (author of books like *Silent Spring*), Wangari Maathai (the first African woman to win the Nobel Peace Prize), James Lovelock (proponent of Gaia Theory), James Hansen (long-time climate scientist and activist), and the late Tessa Tennant, a long-time colleague and friend who pioneered sustainable investment.

23. Emma Brockes listens in to Alexandria Ocasio-Cortez and Greta Thunberg, "Show Up. Stand Up. Act," *Guardian Weekend*, June 29, 2019.

24. Somini Sengupta and Alexander Villegas, "Tiny Costa Rica Has a Green New Deal. It Matters for the Whole Planet," *The New York Times*, March 12, 2019.

25. Molly Taft, "Inside the Growing Climate Rebellion at Amazon," *Fast Company*, June 11, 2019.

26. "Open Letter to Jeff Bezos and the Amazon Board of Directors," Amazon Employees for Climate Justice, *Medium*, April 10, 2019.

27. Cory Doctorow, "Many of the Key Googler Uprising Organizers Have Quit, Citing Retaliation from Senior Management," July 16, 2019. See also: https://boingboing.net/2019/07/16/good-luck-meredith.html.

28. "Take Action to Stop Amazonia Burning" (editorial), *Nature*, September 10, 2019. See https://www.nature.com/articles/d41586-019-02615-3.

29. Javier C. Hernandez, "Journalists in Xi era: 'We're almost extinct'," *The New York Times*, July 15, 2019.

30. https://ocasio2018.com

31. Greta Thunberg's 2019 Davos speech to CEOs, https://www.fridaysforfuture.org/greta-speeches#greta_speech_jan25_2019.

32. Ali Smith, "They See Us As a Threat Because We Are Having an Impact," *The Observer*, July 21, 2019.

33. Duncan Austin, *Greenwish: The New Challenge Facing Sustainable Business*, May 16, 2019. Confidential at the time, now shared here: https://capitalinstitute.org/blog/greenwish/.

34. Jim Collins, *Good To Great: Why Some Companies Make The Leap . . . And Others Don't*. New York: HarperCollins Publishers, 2001. See also: https://www.harpercollins.com/9780066620992/good-to-great/.

35. https://bigthink.com/personal-growth/stockdale-paradox-confronting-reality-vital-success?rebelltitem=1#rebelltitem

36. Libby Bernick, "Can Sustainable Companies Get a Lower Cost of Capital?," *GreenBiz*, March 4, 2019. See also: https://www.greenbiz.com/article/can-sustainable-companies-get-lower-cost-capital.

37. https://www.wbcsd.org/Overview/About-us/Vision2050

38. Julian Hill-Landolt, personal communication, June 17, 2019.

39. I had first read his writing in *New Scientist* in 1975 when I was also writing for the magazine.

40. https://en.wikipedia.org/wiki/Electron_capture_detector

41. Based on the sort of timings laid out in *The Human Planet*.

42. James Lovelock, *Novacene: The Coming Age of Hyperintelligence*. London: Penguin Random House, 2019. See also: https://www.penguin.co.uk/books/313/313880/novacene/9780241399361.html.

43. Tom Knowles, "AI solves Rubik's Cube Quicker Than You Can Click Your Fingers," *The Times*, July 18, 2019.

44. https://en.wikipedia.org/wiki/Whole_Earth_Catalog

45. https://reviverestore.org

46. https://reviverestore.org/horseshoe-crab/

47. Ryan Phelan, personal communication, July 31, 2019.

48. https://www.hakaimagazine.com/news/synthetic-crab-blood-is-good-for-the-birds/

49. https://reviverestore.org/projects/woolly-mammoth/

50. John Thornhill, "The Return of the Luddites," *Financial Times*, July 13-14, 2019.

51. John Elkington, "Saving the Planet from Ecological Disaster Is a $12 Trillion Opportunity," *Harvard Business Review*, May 4, 2017. See also: https://hbr.org/2017/05/saving-the-planet-from-ecological-disaster-is-a-12-trillion-opportunity.

52. https://www.un.org/sustainabledevelopment/sustainable-development-goals/

53. Business Commission & Sustainable Development, *Better Business, Better World*, January 2017. See also: http://report.businesscommission.org/.

54. Interest declared: I have long been a member of Hazel Henderson's advisory board.

55. Ethical Markets, "Private green investing tops $10 trillion," media release, May 29, 2019.

56. Christopher Zara, "Investors Feast on Beyond Meat as Stock Skyrockets in NASDAQ Debut," *Fast Company*, February 5, 2019.

57. Emiko Terazono, "Vegan Backer Angles to Hook Fish Lovers with Plant-based Alternatives," *Financial Times*, August 19, 2019.

58. *Breakthrough Business Models: Exponentially More Social, Lean, Integrated and Circular*, Volans for the Business & Sustainable Development Commission, September 2016. See also: http://volans.com/wp-content/uploads/2016/09/Volans_Breakthrough-Business-Models_Report_Sep2016.pdf.

59. John Elkington, *The Chrysalis Economy: How Citizen CEOs and Corporations Can Fuse Values And Value Creation*. Oxford: Capstone Publishing/John Wiley & Sons Co., 2001.

60. See http://www.earth-policy.org/#. Les Brown, who I visited several times in Washington, D.C. at both the Worldwatch Institute and then the Earth Policy Institute, had a huge impact on my thinking over the decades.

61. Carlota Perez, "Why Everybody—Including Business—Should Support the Green New Deal," BTTR (Beyond The Tech Revolution), March 17, 2019. See also: http://beyondthetechrevolution.com/blog/why-everybody-including-business-should-support-the-green-new-deal/.

62. See, for example, Chris Hughes, "It's Time to Break Up Facebook," *The New York Times*, May 9, 2019. See also: https://www.nytimes.com/2019/05/09/opinion/sunday/chris-hughes-facebook-zuckerberg.html.

63. http://breakthrough.unglobalcompact.org

64. Lisa Kay Solomon, "How the Most Successful Leaders Will Thrive in an Exponential World," SingularityHub, January 11, 2017. See also: https://singularityhub.com/2017/01/11/how-the-most-successful-leaders-will-thrive-in-an-exponential-world/.

65. "Is Insectageddon Imminent?" *The Economist*, March 21, 2019. See also: https://www.economist.com/leaders/2019/03/21/is-insectageddon-imminent.

66. https://www.netflix.com/gb/title/80117542

67. "The Future of City Innovation," *Bloomberg Cities*, March 19, 2019.

68. See https://www.santafe.edu/people/profile/geoffrey-west. The best source for his thinking on cities is *Scale: The Universal Laws of Life, Growth, and Death in Organisms, Cities, and Companies*. New York: Penguin Random House, 2018. See also: https://www.penguinrandomhouse.com/books/314049/scale-by-geoffrey-west/9780143110903/.

69. Geoffrey West, "Scaling: The Surprising Mathematics of Life and Civilization," *Medium*, October 31, 2014. See also: https://medium.com/sfi-30-foundations-frontiers/scaling-the-surprising-mathematics-of-life-and-civilization-49ee18640a8.

70. https://x.company/press

71. Derek Thompson, "Google X and the Science of Radical Creativity," *The Atlantic*, November 2017. See also: https://www.theatlantic.com/magazine/archive/2017/11/x-google-moonshot-factory/540648/.

72. "Rethinking Food and Agriculture, 2020-2030: The Second Domestication of Plants and Animals, the Disruption of the Cow and the Collapse of Industrial Livestock Farming," RethinkX.

73. https://conservationxlabs.com

74. http://power.nridigital.com/power_technology_jun19/
the_big_exit_why_capital_is_deserting_coal

75. Anjli Raval, "Green Energy Switch Risks Leaving Oil Tanker Owners High and Dry,"
Financial Times, July 17, 2019.

76. https://www.carbontracker.org/reports/carbon-bubble/

77. Simon Edelsten, "The Investment Case for Cockroaches," *Financial Times*, July 20, 2019.

78. https://unepinquiry.org/publication/roadmap-for-a-sustainable-financial-system/

79. Mark Anderson, "A (Very) Close Look at Carbon Capture and Storage," *IEEE
Spectrum*, July 16, 2019. See also: https://spectrum.ieee.org/energywise/energy/
environment/a-very-close-look-at-carbon-capture-and-storage.

80. https://www.nationalgeographic.com/environment/2019/04/
alberta-canadas-tar-sands-is-growing-but-indigenous-people-fight-back/

81. Azeem Azhar, "Capitalism Without Capital," *Exponential View*, July 5, 2019. See also: https://
www.exponentialview.co/p/capitalism-without-capital.

82. Andrew Ellson, "High-flyers Must Save the Planet, Says Jet Boss," *The Times*, July 20 2019.

83. https://www.cisl.cam.ac.uk/about/news/
cisl-hosts-economic-transformation-discussions-250-senior-leaders-30th-anniversary

84. Peter Diamandis, "Elon's Neuralink & Brain-Machine Symbiosis," Peter Diamandis's blog,
July 21, 2019. See also: https://www.diamandis.com/subscribe.

85. https://chiefreinventionofficer.com/titanic-syndrome/

86. https://chiefreinventionofficer.com/about/

87. *Green Swans: Sketching a Manifesto for Tomorrow's Capitalism*, Volans and Atlas of the Future,
September 2019. See also: https://volans.com/greenswans-video.

ACKNOWLEDGMENTS

1. http://johnelkington.com/about/personal/others/

2. http://breakthrough.unglobalcompact.or.

3. https://capitalinstitute.org

4. Salim Ismail, with Michael S. Malone and Yuri van Geest, *Exponential Organizations: Why new
organizations are ten times better, faster, and cheaper than yours (and what to do about it)*. New
York: Diversion Books, 2014.

ANNEX

1. Eillie Anzilotti, "Cities Should Think about Trees as Public Health Infrastructure,"
Fast Company, February 10, 2017. See also: https://www.fastcompany.com/40474204/
cities-should-think-about-trees-as-public-health-infrastructure.

2. Anzilotti, "Cities Should Think about Trees."

3. Stefano Boeri Architetti, "Vertical Forest," https://www.stefanoboeriarchitetti.net/en/project/
vertical-forest/.

4. Joy Lo Dico, "Breathing Life into the City," *Financial Times Weekend*, August 10, 2019.

5. http://www.nationalparkcity.london

6. https://fs.blog/2014/04/antifragile-a-definition/

7. https://en.wikipedia.org/wiki/Political_activities_of_the_Koch_brothers

8. *The Great Hack*, Netflix, https://www.netflix.com/gb/title/80117542.

9. "Is Insectageddon Imminent?" *The Economist*, March 21, 2019. See also: https://www.
economist.com/leaders/2019/03/21/is-insectageddon-imminent.

INDEX

Note: Page numbers in *italics* indicate a figure.

A

Abbott, Jennifer, 26
abundance, world of, and technology, 37, 170
Acciona, 34
action guides, Future-Fit Foundation, 160–161
activist chief executives, 131, 132
activists/activism, 189–190, 227–228
Advanced Technology External Advisory
    Council, Google, 168
aeroponics, 171
Age of Consequences. *See* Anthropocene epoch
aging, as worldwide trend, 2–3, 222–223
agriculture, future of, 240–241
aircraft, unmanned, 178–179
Akerlof, George, 203–204
Akkad, Omar El, 110
Alberta oil sands industry, 244
algorithms, versus leadership, 223–230
Allianz, 69
Alphabet, 125, 131
Amazon, 52, 125, 131, 227
American War (Akkad), 110
Americas, European colonization of, 29, 43
Amfori, 197–198
Anderson, Ray, 142
Anderson, Ted, 168–169
Antarctic ozone hole, 196
Anthropocene epoch, 7, 27–29, 86–89,
    230–234
antibiotics, 102–108, 111
anti-satellite testing, 113
Apolitical, 211
Apple, 11–12, 24, 125, 131, 213–214
Apple, Martin, 174
Arbib, Jamie, 241
artificial intelligence (AI), 176–177, 231
assets, stranded, 71–73, 243
The Atlantic (magazine), 240
Atlas of the Future, 9–10, 248
atmosphere, space junk reentering, 114, 115
atmospheric carbon dioxide levels, 65
Attenborough, David, 43

Atwood, Margaret, 110
Auld, Graeme, 84–85
Austin, Duncan, 228
auto industry, 76–77, 78, 135–136, 214, 215
autonomous mobility, 178
Aviva, 210

B

B Corporations, 50, 239
B Lab, 50
bacteria, antibiotic-resistant, 104–107, 111
bad exponentials
    Anthropocene epoch, 86–89
    "gradually, then suddenly" transitions, 78–80
    overview, 76–78
    super wicked problems, 84–86
    wicked problems, 80–84
Bakan, Joel, 26
Barnes Wetland Centre, 200
Bayer, 68, 119
BBC, 194
Becker, Gary, 203
Bendell, Jem, 5
Benioff, Marc, 15, 131
Benyus, Janine, 142
Berdish, Dave, 76
Bernstein, Steven, 84–85
Better Business, Better World (report), 232–233
Beyond Meat, 233
Bezos, Jeff, 52, 155, 220, 227
billiard balls, 93
biology, synthetic, 180, 217–218
Biomimicry 3.8, 142
Biotechnology Bulletin (newsletter), 173
Bitcoin, 180
The Black Swan (Taleb), 2, 21, 254
Black Swans, 2, 166, 220–221. *See also* change
    process stages; technology; wicked
    problems
    defined, 7, 21–22
    historical, 41–42